Including Students with Severe and Multiple Disabilities in Typical Classrooms

Practical Strategies for Teachers

By June E. Downing, Ph.D.

Department of Special Education
California State University, Northridge

with invited contributors

·P·A·U·L·H·
BROOKES
PUBLISHING Co

Baltimore • London • Toronto • Sydney

Paul H. Brookes Publishing Co.
Post Office Box 10624
Baltimore, Maryland 21285-0624

Typeset by PRO-IMAGE Corporation, York, Pennsylvania.
Manufactured in the United States of America by
The Maple Press Company, York, Pennsylvania.

Library of Congress Cataloging-in-Publication Data

Downing, June, 1950–
   Including students with severe and multiple disabilities in
typical classrooms : practical strategies for teachers / by June E.
Downing with invited contributors.
      p.   cm.
   "Invited contributors, Fred P. Orelove, Joanne Eichinger, Mary Ann
Demchak"—CIP galley.
   Includes bibliographical references and index.
   ISBN 1-55766-239-8
   1. Mainstreaming in education—United States.   2. Handicapped
children—Education—United States.   I. Title.
LC4031.D69   1996
371.9'046'0973–dc20   96-6331
                                                                   CIP

British Library Cataloguing-in-Publication data are available from the British
Library.

Including Students with
Severe and Multiple Disabilities
in Typical Classrooms

Contents

About the Author

June E. Downing, Ph.D., Assistant Professor, Department of Special Education, California State University, Northridge, 18111 Nordhoff St., Northridge, CA 91330-8265.

Dr. Downing assists in the preparation of teachers to meet the needs of students having moderate to severe and multiple disabilities. In this capacity, she teaches courses, advises students, and supervises teachers in their practicum experiences. Dr. Downing has invested considerable time in providing inservice trainings to teachers, administrators, parents, and support staff around the country. She has been interested in the education of students having severe and multiple disabilities since 1974 and has served in the capacity of paraprofessional, teacher, work experience coordinator, consultant, and teacher trainer. Areas of current research include investigating related topics such as educating all students together, enhancing the sociocommunicative skills of students with severe disabilities, adapting for the unique needs of individual students, developing paraprofessional skills, and preparing teachers for inclusive education.

Also Contributing to This Volume

MaryAnn Demchak, Ph.D., Associate Professor, Department of Curriculum and Instruction, University of Nevada, Reno, NV 89557.

Dr. Demchak teaches graduate and undergraduate courses in special education. In addition, as the project director of the Nevada Dual Sensory Impairment Project, Dr. Demchak provides technical assistance to families and service providers of children who are deaf-blind. Her current research interests include inclusion of students with severe disabilities in typical classrooms, positive support for behavior problems, and collaborative teaming.

Joanne Eichinger, Ph.D., Associate Professor, Department of Curriculum and Instruction, State University of New York at Oswego, Oswego, NY 13126.

Dr. Eichinger teaches graduate courses to students working toward a master's degree in education. Prior to obtaining her doctorate at Syracuse University, Dr. Eichinger taught students with disabilities for 8 years. She also worked as the project coordinator and then director of the Northeast Region of The Association for Persons with Severe Handicaps technical assistance project, serving students with dual sensory impairments. Her research interests include changing attitudes toward persons with disabilities and efficacy of promising practices in inclusive elementary education classes.

Foreword

A revolution was brewing in the 1980s around how and where learners with disabilities should be educated. Indeed, these were not mere pedagogical questions; many people began to wonder whether individuals with disabilities, particularly those whose disabilities were considered severe, were valued enough to deserve equal consideration in their schooling. The revolution began to surface with the publication of three books in 1989: *Beyond Separate Education: Quality Education for All* (Lipsky & Gartner), *Educating All Students in the Mainstream of Regular Education* (Stainback, Stainback, & Forest), and *Integration Strategies for Students with Handicaps* (Gaylord-Ross). It is interesting, but should not be surprising, that not one of the chapter titles in any of these books used the word "inclusion." The concept indeed predated the language.

Since 1989, the field of severe disabilities has witnessed a proliferation of books, articles, curriculum guides, and other materials on inclusive education. Merely documenting them would take more space than this foreword can allow. In the midst of this explosion of books, then, comes June Downing's new work, with a deceptively simple title: *Including Students with Severe and Multiple Disabilities in Typical Classrooms: Practical Strategies for Teachers*. A potential reader—particularly one who is well-read in the inclusion literature—might be wondering whether to skip over this book, thinking that everything has already been said. That would be a bad mistake.

Downing has done something remarkable. Along with her capable contributors, Joanne Eichinger and MaryAnn Demchak, she has created a book that builds on our substantial knowledge base, but that offers fresh insights and surprises. The real secret to the book's success is suggested by its subtitle: *Practical Strategies for Teachers*. Readers looking for practical ideas will not be disappointed. Every chapter is generously studded with examples that are completely drawn and have the ring of authenticity to them. The students sound like real students, and the situations feel genuine. As I read the book, I found myself anxious to incorporate many of the examples into my own graduate course.

I do not want to leave the impression, however, that this book is aimed at the university level. Indeed, the writing is so clear and straightforward, so free of jargon, that members of instructional teams, administrators, and parents should be able to pick this book up and learn a great deal.

Apart from its practicality, there are other reasons that this book deserves a special spot on our shelves. Foremost among these reasons is the extent to which the examples emphasize learners with sensory impairments. While the inclusion literature has not ignored these students, it is fair to say that they are not very well represented. This is particularly true of the various commercial curriculum guides. Downing's book bridges this gap. Anyone working with a student who has a vision or hearing impairment, or both, should consider this book an essential addition to his or her library.

The examples, however, should inspire and benefit *all* readers. This is true in part because the examples are so vivid, allowing the reader to see clearly how they could work for any learner with a severe disability. But the applicability of examples beyond their ostensibly narrow description also works, because Downing has taken pains to stress the *process* of adapting curriculum and instruction to fit the needs and strengths of the individual. Downing and Eichinger state this clearly at the end of Chapter 1: "The underlying assumption is that *all* children can learn once we identify their special strengths and support them in their effort to achieve desired outcomes." And the remainder of the book does, indeed, incorporate those key elements we know to undergird effective instruction: teamwork, respect for others' ideas and experiences, cooperative learning, recognition of individual differences, and so forth.

In addition to its practicality and special treatment of learners with sensory impairments, two other features of this book stand out. First, Downing does not back down from the tough issues. She deals with designing and adapting curriculum not only in the traditional parts of elementary school (reading, writing, etc.), but also in such subjects as science and social studies, where she offers several (typically) excellent examples. Where some authors have shied away from the more challenging middle school and high school years, Downing jumps in with both feet, providing suggestions for adapting classes as diverse as woodshop and life enrichment. Further evidence of the book's can-do approach can be found in Chapter 9, which raises and provides responses to commonly voiced concerns in providing inclusive education. This chapter should serve to mollify those readers who, after reading the first eight chapters, still may be thinking, "Yeah, but what about . . . ?"

The last feature of this book I need to mention is that it is unfailingly positive and hopeful. I believe this hopefulness derives from several sources. First, Downing and her contributors lay a wonderful and solid foundation in the early chapters. The book thoughtfully makes the case that inclusive education is simply *good* education, not different education. Second, the accretion of example upon example gently leads the reader to conclude that anything is possible. Finally, Downing practices what she preaches: The book is respectful of children, families, and school personnel. The reader gains the sense that the author not only likes and respects learners, but would like nothing more than to help every person embrace these ideas and implement them, because students deserve nothing less.

The quiet revolution of the 1980s has evolved into the vocal realities of the 1990s and beyond. I think anyone with a serious interest in furthering the goals of inclusive education will find this book an invaluable companion.

Fred P. Orelove, Ph.D.
Virginia Institute for Developmental Disabilities
Virginia Commonwealth University
Richmond, Virginia

REFERENCES

Gaylord-Ross, R. (Ed.). (1989). *Integration strategies for students with handicaps.* Baltimore: Paul H. Brookes Publishing Co.

Lipsky, D.K., & Gartner, A. (Eds.). (1989). *Beyond separate education: Quality education for all.* Baltimore: Paul H. Brookes Publishing Co.

Stainback, S., Stainback, W., & Forest, M. (Eds.). (1989). *Educating all students in the mainstream of regular education.* Baltimore: Paul H. Brookes Publishing Co.

Preface

This book was developed as a direct result of teachers, paraprofessionals, parents, related service providers, and administrators asking in regard to students with severe and multiple disabilities: "So they're in the general education classroom; now what?" The desire to deliver quality services to children and youth with severe and multiple disabilities and the obvious frustration that results when this does not happen have served as major catalysts to put practical ideas down on paper. This volume offers a glimpse at some of the techniques and strategies used by teachers in providing students with severe and multiple disabilities education in truly inclusive environments.

The numerous examples included in this book are derived from specific research studies and direct observations by the authors of many classrooms across the country. The individual students described here exhibit a broad range of abilities in extremely diverse educational settings—urban, rural, well-supported, and inadequately supported schools. Despite differences, the students featured in this volume are learning. In addition, their teachers (in both general and special education), classmates, parents, teaching assistants, and a range of support individuals also are learning. As everyone learns, issues that were once difficult become easier to understand and new growth is possible.

Chapter 1 sets forth the rationale for this book, identifies its target population (students with severe sensory and multiple impairments) and clarifies what this book offers to educators, support staff, administrators, and parents.

A basic premise of this volume is that students are educated together, regardless of disability/ability. We thus felt it wise to devote part of our discussion to what is happening in general education classrooms. Chapter 2 presents a brief overview of educational practices that are considered effective teaching strategies for children without disabilities. The benefits of these practices are highlighted.

Although subsequent chapters focus on students in specific age groups, Chapter 3 examines general assessment and intervention practices across the age range. This chapter serves as a foundation for more specific age-related information provided later in the book.

Chapters 4, 5, and 6 describe various methods and adaptations to include, respectively, preschool, elementary-, and secondary-age children with severe and multiple disabilities within the general education classroom. Many examples of lessons and adaptations to enable the participation of students with different abilities are presented.

Including everyone in the general education system requires the effective use of all the people who attend and work in schools. Chapters 7 and 8 discuss, respectively, the important involvement of peers and adults alike and their combined efforts to support everyone in a worthwhile learning process.

Chapter 9, the final chapter, uses a question-and-answer format to address commonly asked questions that occur when teachers struggle to meet the diverse needs of all learners. Accompanying each question are responses that, we hope, will stimulate creative problem solving across a range of challenges posed by students with special needs.

Simply placing students together physically is not the goal of inclusive education. All children have a right to an education—to learn in the least restrictive environment possible. Although some children, especially those with severe and multiple disabilities, may have unique ways of learning, separating them from others who learn in a different way is unnecessary and could prevent them from achieving their full potential. We believe that children learn from other children and that, by doing so, everyone benefits. We also believe that teachers have the creativity, commitment, and love of teaching to make this happen. This book is written for those children and their teachers.

Acknowledgments

This book could not have been written without the support from a number of people—my own circle of friends. My co-authors on several of the chapters of this book, Drs. Joanne Eichinger and MaryAnn Demchak, are both colleagues and friends. Their willingness to help out when I needed them has made this book very special to me. Fred Orelove's contribution of the Foreword was another gift. He gave it willingly, despite being terribly busy. I will be forever grateful for his friendship. Another good friend, Fran Maiuri, from Alaska, obtained many of the wonderful pictures of students shown throughout the book. She eagerly shared photographs from her project in Anchorage. I owe her a lot for her love and support.

Cecilia Esguerra-Gunn, once playing the role of my secretary, did an outstanding job in the preparation of this manuscript. Nothing was too difficult for her to tackle, and I will be forever in her debt. I also need to thank everyone at Paul H. Brookes Publishing Company for their incredible support during the development of this book. Finally, this book is written with the support of all the students, their teachers, and parents who have taught me so much. This is their book.

This book is dedicated to all the students, their parents and family members, friends, teachers, teaching assistants, support staff, and administrators who have shown by their words and actions how important it is for everyone to belong.

A special dedication is made to three very special teachers from Tucson, Arizona, whose tragic and untimely deaths cut short their ability to positively influence the lives of students. We need more teachers like them. I miss them very much.

Elaine Prosnitz
Maureen Boyko
George Varghese

—J.E.D.

To my husband, Carl, for his love and support.

—M.A.D.

To my parents, the late Dorothy and Arthur Eichinger:
Thank you for always being there for me.

—J.E.

Including Students with Severe and Multiple Disabilities in Typical Classrooms

Chapter 1

EDUCATING STUDENTS WITH DIVERSE STRENGTHS AND NEEDS TOGETHER

Rationale and Assumptions

June E. Downing and Joanne Eichinger

The children and young adults with varying strengths and needs who are the focus of this book have been assigned many labels by the educational system. They have been labeled *multihandicapped, multihandicapped blind, multihandicapped deaf, dual sensory impaired* or *deaf-blind,* and *severe-profound/multihandicapped.* Yet such terms do not convey who these children are as people, how they learn, what they want to learn, what they need to learn, and what they prefer not to learn. It is therefore best to avoid using labels if possible and to address each child as a unique learner, with specific strengths as well as limitations (as is true of anyone). However, to provide some direction for readers in applying the information contained in this and the following chapters, some general characteristics of our target student population are described here.

The children and young adults targeted in this book—those with severe sensory and multiple impairments—are extremely diverse in their ages, abilities, interests, and experiences. What may be common to them all is difficulty learning through either the visual or auditory mode or both auditory and visual modes. These students also may find it hard to understand spoken or written language or to remain seated while performing desk work. These students tend to learn better when they are actively involved in the learning process and provided with tactile cues, pictures, objects, parts of objects, and clear models of behavior in addition to verbal information. They need to be allowed time to examine objects of interest and given many opportunities to perform meaningful tasks. Routines and repetition help to support understanding (Maxson, Tedder, Marmion, & Lamb, 1993).

When visual and auditory information is unclear or not readily accessible, the impact on learning can be severe. Most teachers teach using these two sensory modes, and so the student who does not have clear access to this information will not experience the same rich learning environment as other children. The problem is compounded when the student has limited movement as well or has limited experiences or opportunities to practice skills.

Another characteristic typical of many students with severe and multiple disabilities is the problem they experience in making and maintaining friendships. The difficulty with communication can cause even basic social interactions to be quite limited (Romer & Haring, 1994). These individuals may have little idea of how friendships are made, what social skills are needed, or how to act in public. Some of these young people may have retreated inside themselves, engaging in unique behaviors because of their inability to obtain necessary levels of stimulation.

HISTORICAL OVERVIEW

Prior to the passage of the Education for All Handicapped Children Act of 1975 (PL 94-142), students with severe sensory and multiple impairments were often denied access to public educational services because it was assumed they were unable to learn (Donder & York, 1984). Once education was mandated, the majority of these students were educated in segregated environments, including state developmental centers and segregated schools (Biklen, 1985; Donder & York, 1984). During the 1980s, there was a movement toward closing state institutions entirely or dramatically reducing their populations (Bruininks & Lakin, 1985). As a result of various court cases, there was a parallel shift in the delivery of services in schools. Many of the segregated schools were closed or reduced in size, and their students were gradually transferred to self-contained classes on general school campuses (Meyer & Kishi, 1985). With this move came an emphasis on social integration programs such as Special Friends (Voeltz, 1980, 1982), whereby students from general education classes would spend time interacting socially with students with severe and multiple disabilities in special education classrooms.

Only 20 years after the federal mandate, national organizations (The Association for Persons with Severe Handicaps, cited in Hardman, 1994; The Association for Retarded Citizens, 1992; the National Association of State Boards of Education, 1992), parents (Obierti, 1993; Vargo & Vargo, 1993), and some educators (Stainback & Stainback, 1990, 1992) are advocating full placement of learners with disabilities in general education classes. Thus, since the 1970s dramatic changes have occurred and continue to be proposed in the delivery of services for students with severe and multiple disabilities.

IMPORTANCE OF SYSTEMIC CHANGE

Despite the significant changes just noted, recent U.S. Department of Education data reveal that during the 1990–1991 school year, for students ages 3–21, only 6.7% of students labeled as having multiple disabilities and 10.9% of students labeled deaf-blind had a general education class as their primary placement (Snyder & Hoffman, 1994). Furthermore, these same census data reflect that one half of students labeled deaf-blind and one third of students labeled as having multiple disabilities are being served in very restrictive settings including public or private separate schools, public or private residential programs, and homebound or hospital instructional environments. These data seem to indicate that, although inclusion is being widely discussed in educational circles (e.g., see *Educational Leadership,* December 1994/January 1995), students who have multiple disabilities, including deaf-blindness, may be considered unlikely candidates for such placement.

Some isolated efforts are being made to include individual children with severe disabilities within particular schools or school systems (Bishop & Jubala, 1994; Ford & Fredericks, 1994; Vaughn, 1994). Whereas this approach may be successful for the student, it seems analogous to deals made with teachers in the 1980s to partially include students with severe disabilities in general education classes. The students themselves thrived, but teachers often experienced burnout in the absence of administrative backing.

Schools, therefore, need to address full inclusion in a more planned and systematic fashion. Full inclusion of learners with severe and multiple disabilities is more inclined to be successful and sustained if approached from a systemic perspective (Villa, Thousand, Stainback, & Stainback, 1992). This involves a shared-values philosophy that is articulated in the school mission statement (Schattman & Benay, 1992) and operationalized in the policies and behaviors of the professionals involved. One example of a district that embraced the full inclusion of its students with severe disabilities is Johnson City Central School District. Salisbury, Palombaro, and Hollowood (1993) documented the systems change process that occurred in an inclusive elementary school in that district over a 30-month period. Their study revealed that the change to an inclusive school occurred slowly, systematically, and within a collaborative process of decision making involving administration and staff.

Ideally, for inclusion to occur, a school district, university training program, and state education department all share the same philosophy and work collaboratively toward that goal. Since that is rarely the case, however, the next best scenario is for a particular school to develop a cohesive mission statement, along with an action plan for how inclusion will be conducted and what supports will be provided to teachers and students. This ongoing planning effort should involve all of the key players in this service delivery shift (e.g., teachers, teaching assistants, administrators, parents). One key support that has been identified as critical to full inclusion is a block of time for collaborative planning (Jorgensen, 1994; Logan et al. 1994–95). This aspect, in particular, would be very difficult to achieve without planning and support from the administrative level.

The emphasis of this book, however, is not on strategies for systemic change. An underlying premise of this book is that schools and school districts are committed to educating all students together and have made an effort to support this philosophy using a variety of general inclusive strategies (e.g., development of an inclusive mission statement, schoolwide staff training). Accepting this premise allows us to focus on specific teaching strategies and unique curricular adaptations across the age range (preschool through high school) that support effective educational programming for students with severe and multiple disabilities. Several authors address the systems change process in the professional literature (Calculator & Jorgensen, 1994; Salisbury et al., 1993). Additional resources for creating systems change are also found in Appendix A at the end of this book.

WHY EDUCATE THESE STUDENTS IN TYPICAL CLASSROOMS?

Students labeled as having severe sensory and multiple disabilities may appear to have such challenging impairments that their educational limitations are perceived as far exceeding their abilities. Their needs may appear to be so basic (e.g., simple communication skills, appropriate manipulation of objects, enhanced gross motor skills) that teaching these students in typical classrooms that are highly academic seems improbable or, at the least, impractical. Yet these are the very students that can benefit considerably from the learning opportunities that typically occur in general education classrooms. With limited information available to these students from the two major sensory modes—vision and hearing—these students need the almost constant stimulation, the numerous opportunities to interact, and the readily available instructional models from peers that occur in typical classrooms.

Special educators, no matter how highly motivated or skilled, cannot provide the necessary ongoing stimulation in self-contained classrooms. The battle against the relatively long periods of time during which students must wait for adult attention in such classrooms has been well documented (Houghton, Bronicki & Guess, 1987; Richards & Sternberg, 1992). In addition, interaction between students who possess the same multiple and challenging disabilities is minimal, if it occurs at all (Romer & Haring, 1994; Rowland, 1990). These individuals require very responsive communicative partners to reinforce their attempts to interact. Educating students together who have the same difficulty in communication provides neither the necessary responsive partners nor the typical communicative role models that are essential for enhancing social interactions. For instance, when the special educator is assisting one student, the other students in the room are unable to help each other or even socialize with one another in any sort of fulfilling way. In a typical classroom, when adults cannot attend to a given student, the time can be filled with peer interactions for general social reasons or for more specific learning purposes. General education classrooms offer the stimulation, challenge, and learning opportunities that are extremely difficult to replicate in a self-contained classroom. Yet mere physical presence in typical classrooms is not sufficient to ensure the development of communicative, social, or friendship skills (Biklen, 1985). These students need to be an integral part of the classroom and accepted as full-time members who contribute in a positive way to the overall dynamics of the learning environment. Ford and Fredericks (1994), for example, have documented the success of the inclusion process for a fourth grader with deaf-blindness. This book contains numerous other examples of the benefits *for all students* of including students with multiple impairments in the general educational setting.

DESIRED OUTCOMES FOR STUDENTS

Regardless of whether a student has a severe multiple disability or not, our future goals for all students upon graduation are similar. In general, we hope that students will be productive, contributing members of society who follow rules of social conduct and get along effectively with others. We also hope that students will lead happy, rewarding lives. In interviews with parents about their dreams and hopes for their children with multiple disabilities and deaf-blindness, Giangreco, Cloninger, and Iverson (1993) found that parents' valued outcomes included a safe, stable home, access to a variety of places to engage in worthwhile activities, meaningful relationships, personal choice and control, and being safe and healthy. Such valued outcomes are certainly not limited to children with severe disabilities. Recognizing the shared common goals for all students clarifies the rationale for educating students together and greatly diminishes the need for separate education.

OUTCOMES OF INCLUSIVE EDUCATIONAL PRACTICES

In recent years, numerous individuals have examined the outcomes of inclusive educational practices from various perspectives (parents, general education teachers, special education teachers, and students). This research has generated information relative to the benefits not only to students with severe disabilities but to their peers without disabilities as well.

Benefits to Students with Severe Disabilities

Teacher Perspectives   Much of the literature documenting positive outcomes for students with severe disabilities in inclusive classrooms comes from research involving teachers. Giangreco, Dennis, Cloninger, Edelman, and Schattman (1993) interviewed 19 general education teachers who had at least one student with a severe disability in their class. They reported that students with severe disabilities were more aware and responsive and had increased skill acquisition when educated in general classrooms than in self-contained settings.

York, Vandercook, Macdonald, Heise-Neff, and Caughey (1992) used questionnaires to survey general and special education teachers and middle-school students. Four of the seven general education teachers surveyed said that students with disabilities were part of the class and were accepted. The special educators surveyed noted that students with severe disabilities who were educated in general classrooms were included more in the school community and experienced growth in terms of skill acquisition.

Downing, Eichinger, and Williams (1996) interviewed nine general education teachers and nine special education teachers relative to perceived benefits of inclusion for students with severe disabilities. Results indicated that teachers regarded the rich learning environment of the typical classroom as beneficial to the student with severe disabilities in developing appropriate social and behavioral skills as well as friendships.

Finally, Janzen, Wilgosh, and McDonald (1995) interviewed five general educators and one resource room teacher and found that these teachers reported that students with moderate and severe disabilities developed a sense of belonging to the group and were aware of their classmates as demonstrated by smiles, hugs, eye contact, and reaching toward them. These teachers also felt that these students had progressed in physical skill development, had increased appropriate behaviors, and had decreased inappropriate behaviors.

Student Perspectives   York et al. (1992) also surveyed students about their perceptions of the integration of students with severe disabilities. Overall, the middle-school students noted positive changes in the students with severe disabilities since the inception of integration. The perceptions of the middle-school students were that students with disabilities had changed socially (e.g., were more talkative, fun, cooperative, happy), had more friends, and had reduced levels of inappropriate behaviors (e.g., hugging).

Multiple Perspectives Peck et al. (1994) followed 35 students with mild to severe disabilities, from preschool to middle-school age, who were in inclusive settings over a 2-year time frame. They used multiple measures to collect data, including parent and teacher interviews, surveys, videotape recordings, and narrative records of the teachers and students in classroom and other school settings. They reported three major outcomes for the students with disabilities. First, the students achieved membership and a sense of belonging. Second, there were numerous opportunities to develop meaningful social relationships. Third, the authors noted developmental changes, including increased social and communication skills, improved academic skills for the older students, and improved preacademic skills for the preschoolers.

Parent Perspectives Parent perspectives also have been examined. Davern (1994) conducted semistructured in-depth interviews with 21 parents representing 15 families who had children with disabilities ranging from mild to severe. All the children were being educated in inclusive settings. Davern reported that parents cited increased social involvement outside of school and communication and behavioral gains as benefits of inclusion. In another study, interviews with 13 parents of children with severe disabilities educated in general education settings indicated that the children had acquired academic, communication, social, and behavioral skills, as well as developed friendships and a sense of belonging (Ryndak, Downing, Jacqueline, & Morrison, 1995). Similarly, one parent reported academic, social, and emotional growth experienced by her son who has Down syndrome, as a result of being in a kindergarten class (Elias, Francisco-Medvin, Schefer, & Tenn, 1986).

Student Outcomes Hunt, Farron-Davis, Beckstead, Curtis, and Goetz (1994) compared outcomes for students with severe disabilities in general education classes with outcomes for students with disabilities in special education classes. The areas examined were quality of the individualized education program (IEP), curricular content of the IEP, engaged time, integrated activities, affective demeanor, and social interactions. The authors found that the IEP objectives for students in full-inclusion settings included more instruction of basic skills and more participation with peers who do not have disabilities than for students in self-contained classes. The overall quality of the IEP objectives was considered higher for the students in the full-inclusion settings. Students in the full-inclusion settings had more academic activities and fewer recreation and leisure activities than did students in the self-contained settings. When the authors observed the actual behaviors of students, the students in the general education classes were alone less and were more often actively engaged in the activities of the day than were students in self-contained classes. They were also more involved in academic skill activities and less involved in critical skill activities than students in special education classes. Regarding social interactions, students in general education classes initiated more interactions, and these interactions were more social and less task-related. Similar findings were noted by Hunt and Farron-Davis (1992), who followed students with severe disabilities from their self-contained classes to fully included settings. When these students were in general education settings, the overall quality of their IEPs was higher, and their IEPs included more integrated activities than when they were in self-contained settings.

Other researchers have documented actual child-change behaviors of students with severe disabilities in inclusive settings. Hunt, Staub, Alwell, and Goetz (1994) described the results of a study involving three students with severe, multiple disabilities who were fully included in three second-grade classes. They demonstrated communication and motor skill acquisition for all three students during a mathematics unit, in which each lesson was structured using cooperative learning groups. Specifically, by the end of the second intervention phase, the students were consistently and independently passing out materials, acknowledging other group members (via eye contact and smiling), and asking for a turn (via hitting a switch to activate a prerecorded message). The researchers also documented that the students continued to demonstrate those skills in follow-up sessions with different students in newly configured cooperative groups.

Hanline (1993) assessed social interactions between preschoolers labeled as "profoundly disabled" and their peers without disabilities in a full-inclusion program. She noted that in play-based contexts, the students with disabilities interacted with their peers during the majority of the observation sessions. Furthermore, the interactions of the students with disabilities were similar in length to those of the preschoolers without disabilities.

Extending beyond social interactions, Staub, Schwartz, Gallucci, and Peck (1994) examined four friendships between elementary students with severe disabilities and their classmates without disabilities. All of these relationships developed from nontutorial activities and contexts.

Numerous benefits for students with severe disabilities exist to support their full inclusion in typical classrooms. These include benefits as perceived by others (parents, teachers, and students) as well as actually observed behaviors of the students themselves.

Benefits to Students without Disabilities

Teacher and Parent Perspectives   As was the case when describing benefits to students with severe disabilities, much of what we know about benefits to students without disabilities in inclusive settings has been reported by teachers and parents. Peck, Carlson, and Helmstetter (1992) examined the perceptions of 125 parents of typical children and 95 teachers involved with children with mild to severe disabilities included in general education classrooms at the preschool or kindergarten level. They reported that overall parent perceptions were very favorable, with five positive outcomes emerging. These were that 1) the children without disabilities became more accepting of individual differences, 2) they were more aware of other children's needs, 3) they were more comfortable with people with disabilities, 4) they were more helpful in general to other children, and 5) they were less prejudiced about people who are different. Similarly, teacher responses were positive overall, with the first three positive outcomes noted as well.

In interviews involving teachers who had at least one student with a severe disability in their class, acceptance, improved social and emotional development, and flexibility emerged as benefits for the students without disabilities (Gian-greco, Dennis, Cloninger, Edelman, & Schattman, 1993). Similarly, the majority of the general education teachers interviewed by York et al. (1992) stated that students without disabilities benefited by becoming more accepting, more un-derstanding, and more aware of the similarities they shared with students with disabilities. Downing et al. (1996) found that teachers (both special and general education) felt that students without disabilities acquired appreciation for and demonstrated acceptance of students with severe and multiple disabilities. Teach-ers also reported that students without disabilities acquired leadership skills and enhanced their self-esteem.

Student Perspectives   Helmstetter, Peck, and Giangreco (1994) surveyed 166 high school students to determine outcomes of interactions with students with severe disabilities. The respondents interacted with the students with mod-erate or severe disabilities through attendance in general education classes, Spe-cial Friends programs (Voeltz, 1980, 1982), or tutorial programs. The authors reported seven positive outcomes: increased responsiveness to others' needs, val-uing relationships with persons with disabilities, personal development, more tolerance for others, increased appreciation for human diversity, development of personal values, and positive changes in peer status.

One benefit to students without disabilities as a result of inclusion is op-portunities for friendship. Using a case study approach, Staub et al. (1994) dis-cussed the nature of friendships between four elementary students without disabilities and four classmates with severe disabilities. The authors described these relationships as rich and varied.

Impact on Learning   Although concerns have been expressed regarding the impact of inclusion on learners without disabilities—specifically, that inclu-sion will negatively affect their learning (Shanker, 1994–95)—the literature does not seem to bear this out. When asked to respond to the statement that having children with disabilities in the class resulted in children without disabilities receiving less teacher attention, both teachers and parents disagreed with the statement (Peck et al., 1992). In a study examining the effects of cooperatively structured groups, students without disabilities provided cues, prompts, and re-inforcement to a student with severe disabilities in their cooperative group. The researchers examined the achievement levels of the students without disabilities who provided the assistance to students with severe disabilities. They found that the students providing assistance made gains in achievement of mathematics skills comparable to those made by students without disabilities who were part of control groups in which there were no students with severe disabilities (both groups of students without disabilities were at similar math levels to begin with) (Hunt, Staub, Alwell, & Goetz, 1994).

POTENTIAL BARRIERS TO SUCCESSFUL INCLUSION

Perhaps the greatest barrier to the successful inclusion of children with severe sensory and multiple impairments in typical learning environments is the fear of what *might* happen or what might *have to* happen. Since few students with these disabilities are fully included in general education classes, information per-taining to their successful learning and to the necessary supports that promote this success are not readily available or known to most teaching teams. These children tend to be judged on how they perform in self-contained classrooms and on developmental scales (Baumgart et al., 1982; Linehan, Brady, & Hwang, 1991). This instructional context obscures the ability to perceive them as capable learners in need of typical interactions and educational situations. Not knowing what is possible and how supports can be used to promote all students' learning can create an unwillingness to change. A change in attitude is the basic step that must occur before educating all students together can be successful. With a change of attitude from "You can't do it and so you can't be a part of it" to "You can't do it now and so I must find a way to help you be a part of it," the movement toward inclusive education can be realized. The focus must shift from a deficit orientation to an ability orientation, realizing that additional support may be necessary and is acceptable. Inclusive education builds on the principle of interdependence among learners and the realization that students will excel in some skills but not others. The heterogeneity of learners in typical classrooms allows the give and take necessary for students to learn from each other.

Due to the relatively recent trend of including children with multiple and sensory impairments in education settings, there may be a shortage of trained personnel to promote this type of learning situation (Luiselli, Luiselli, DeCaluwe, & Jacobs, 1995). Until personnel preparation programs can shift their training strategies to an inclusive approach, schools and school districts must engage in intensive in-service training of their staffs. Although certain staff members may have considerable experience working with the target population, the skills required for inclusive programming are substantially different and will require additional training for most people. Skills needed to use traditional assessments, implement developmental curricula, and remediate deficit skills will be considerably less important than collaborative teaming skills, peer in-servicing, facilitating peer interactions, and adapting the typical curricular materials for diverse learners (Edelson-Smith, Prater, & Sileo, 1993). Nationally funded programs that have focused on this issue are available to provide the in-service training that may be needed. These resources are cited in Appendix B at the end of this book.

OVERVIEW OF SUCCESSFUL STRATEGIES FOR INCLUSIVE EDUCATION

Perhaps the most critical strategy for creating successful learning experiences for all children, regardless of disability, in general education settings, is teamwork. Much has been written about the need for effective team collaboration in the educational planning of students with severe and multiple disabilities (Downing & Bailey, 1990; Giangreco, Cloninger, & Iverson, 1993; Meyer & Eichinger, 1994; Rainforth, York, & Macdonald, 1992; Romer & Byrne, 1995; Utley, 1993). The need for creative problem solving and innovative delivery of services requires cooperative and ongoing interactions among trained professionals, teaching assistants, and family members. Setting realistic goals for the whole child demands a commitment from all team members to contribute their expertise in such a way that the child does not become fragmented into various specialty areas. Respect for others' ideas, experiences, and skills, regardless of degree or certification, is essential if the child's best interests are to guide the process.

The recognition that all children learn differently and at different rates and are motivated to learn different things assists the process of inclusive education.

Not all children in a classroom obtain the same level of knowledge or understanding in the course of a school year. What is critical, however, is that *all* students have access to the information, whether or not similar goals are reached. When individuals, regardless of age, are confronted with a new learning task, not all of the individuals will master the material; some will attain only a partial level of understanding. Nevertheless, individuals should not be denied access to information for which mastery is doubtful. Motivation to learn, the individual's perception of the need to learn the material, plus natural ability to learn will combine to play major roles in the level of skill mastery. The concept of partial participation (Ferguson & Baumgart, 1991) supports the idea that participation in various learning activities will be realized differently by different students. Whereas active participation in the learning process is a goal for all students, the level of participation will vary depending on such factors as abilities, interest, and past experiences. Realizing that all individuals will acquire different levels of skill and understanding of material/activities may help teachers to welcome diverse learners in the classroom. For instance, whereas Joe, who is a fifth grader without disabilities, masters the multiplication tables from 0 to 10, Jeff, who is a fifth grader with severe intellectual, visual, and behavioral problems, learns to match numbers to a large calculator in preparation for shopping excursions. The skills of both students were learned during the same mathematics class in fifth grade. The mastery level was significantly different, with both boys attaining the skills needed for their present and future lives.

Cooperative learning has been one positive strategy in support of the inclusion of students with quite different learning abilities (Putnam, 1993). Cooperative learning typically allows for greater interactions among students, movement from one learning group to another, and greater acceptance of individual learning styles (Slavin, 1990; Stevens, Slavin, & Madden, 1991). For the child with multiple impairments including a sensory loss, the action focus of this type of learning can provide the stimulation needed to maintain interest in and attention to the task. In addition, the enhanced focus on hands-on, active involvement of students in learning is particularly beneficial to students who require more information than a strict lecture format can provide. Students with impaired sensory input will learn more effectively if given the opportunity to explore, touch, interact, and perform. Of course, this type of instruction also has obvious benefits for students without disabilities. Outcomes such as higher achievement, increased use of higher-level reasoning strategies, more positive relationships with students with disabilities, and higher levels of self-esteem have been documented in the literature (Johnson, Johnson, & Maruyama, 1983; Johnson, Maruyama, Johnson, Nelson, & Skon, 1981).

Finally, the creativity of teaching staff (teachers, teaching assistants, support staff) and other students will make it possible to see beyond imposed barriers and develop ways of including all students. The emphasis on critical thinking skills and creative problem solving for today's students applies equally well to today's teachers. The presence of a child with severe sensory and multiple disabilities in the typical classroom provides a challenging opportunity to apply such skills. Personnel preparation programs will do well to develop creative thinking skills, problem-solving skills, and team collaboration on the part of future teachers.

PURPOSE OF THIS BOOK

This book's primary purpose is to provide educators, support staff, parents, and other family members with strategies they can use successfully to include children with severe sensory and multiple impairments in the typical learning environment of public schools on a full-time basis. Practical suggestions are given for children of different ages and abilities, to serve as catalysts for effecting the changes needed for individual children. Specific examples—many from the authors' actual experience—are included to aid in implementing the suggested ideas. To assist teachers who are specifically teaching children with sensory impairment in addition to other challenges, all examples target these children. However, the authors strongly feel that the information and examples provided in this book hold considerable value and applicability to a wide range of students with moderate to profound disabilities without a sensory impairment. Students without sensory impairment will likely need fewer or less extensive curricular modifications.

Although each child must be treated as a unique individual and, therefore, every situation will be different, the intent of this book is to stimulate the critical thinking and problem solving that are crucial to any team effort to include those children who may learn differently than the typical child. The underlying assumption is that *all* children can learn once we identify their special strengths and support them in their effort to achieve desired outcomes.

REFERENCES

Association for Retarded Citizens of the United States, The. (1992). *Report card to the nation on inclusion in education of students with mental retardation.* Arlington, TX: Author.

Baumgart, D., Brown, L., Pumpian, I., Nisbet, J., Ford, A., Sweet, M., Messina, R., & Schroeder, J. (1982). Principle of partial participation and individualized adaptations in educational programs for severely handicapped students. *Journal of The Association for Persons with Severe Handicaps, 7,* 17–27.

Biklen, D. (1985). *Achieving the complete school: Strategies for effective mainstreaming.* New York: Teachers College Press.

Bishop, K., & Jubala, K. (1994). By June, given shared experiences, integrated classes, and equal opportunities, Jaime will have a friend. *Teaching Exceptional Children, 27*(1), 36–40.

Bruininks, R.H., & Lakin, K.C. (Eds.). (1985). *Living and learning in the least restrictive environment.* Baltimore: Paul H. Brookes Publishing Co.

Calculator, S.N., & Jorgensen, C.M. (1994). *Including students with severe disabilities in schools: Fostering communication, interaction, and participation.* San Diego: Singular Publishing Group.

Davern, L. (1994). Parents' perspectives on relationships with professionals in inclusive educational settings. *Dissertation Abstracts International,* 9522518.

Donder, D., & York, R. (1984). Integration of students with severe handicaps. In N. Certo, N. Haring, & R. York (Eds.), *Public school integration of severely handicapped students* (pp. 1–14). Baltimore: Paul H. Brookes Publishing Co.

Downing, J., & Bailey, B. (1990). Sharing the responsibility: Using a transdisciplinary team approach to enhance the learning of students with severe disabilities. *Journal of Educational and Psychological Consultation, 1,* 259–277.

Downing, J., Eichinger, J., & Williams, L. (1996). Inclusive education for students with severe disabilities: Comparative views of principals and educators at different levels of implementation. *Remedial and Special Education.* Manuscript submitted for publication.

Edelson-Smith, P., Prater, M.A., & Sileo, T. (1993). The impact of current issues in teacher education on the preparation of special educators. *Issues in Special Education and Rehabilitation, 8*(1), 7–16.

Education for All Handicapped Children Act of 1975, PL 94-142. (August 23, 1975). Title 20, U.S.C. 1401 et seq: *U.S. Statutes at Large, 89,* 773–796.

Elias, L., Francisco-Medvin, R., Schefer, B., & Tenn, E. (1986). Jason goes to kindergarten. *Exceptional Parent, 16*(5), 12–13.

Ferguson, D.L., & Baumgart, D. (1991). Partial participation revisited. *Journal of The Association for Persons with Severe Handicaps, 16,* 218–227.

Ford, J., & Fredericks, B. (1994). Inclusion for children who are deaf-blind. *Network, 4*(1), 25–29.

Giangreco, M.F., Cloninger, C., & Iverson, V. (1993). *Choosing Options and Accommodations for Children: A guide to planning inclusive education.* Baltimore: Paul H. Brookes Publishing Co.

Giangreco, M., Dennis, R., Cloninger, C., Edelman, S., & Schattman, R. (1993). I've counted Jon: Transformational experiences of teachers educating students with disabilities. *Exceptional Children, 59,* 359–372.

Hanline, M.F. (1993). Inclusion of preschoolers with profound disabilities: An analysis of children's interactions. *Journal of The Association of Persons with Severe Handicaps, 18,* 28–35.

Hardman, M.L. (1994). *Inclusion: Issues of educating students with disabilities in regular education settings.* Boston: Allyn & Bacon.

Helmstetter, E., Peck, C.A., & Giangreco, M. (1994). Outcomes of interactions with peers with moderate or severe disabilities: A statewide survey of high school students. *Journal of The Association for Persons with Severe Handicaps, 19,* 263–276.

Houghton, J., Bronicki, G.J., & Guess, D. (1987). Opportunities to express preferences and make choices among students with severe disabilities in classroom settings. *Journal of The Association for Persons with Severe Handicaps, 12,* 18–27.

Hunt, P., & Farron-Davis, F. (1992). A preliminary investigation of IEP quality and content associated with placement in general education versus special education classes. *Journal of The Association for Persons with Severe Handicaps, 17,* 247–253.

Hunt, P., Farron-Davis, F., Beckstead, S., Curtis, D., & Goetz, L. (1994). Evaluating the effects of placement of students with severe disabilities in general education versus special education classes. *Journal of The Association for Persons with Severe Handicaps, 19,* 200–214.

Hunt, P., Staub, D., Alwell, M., & Goetz, L. (1994). Achievement by all students within the context of cooperative learning groups. *Journal of The Association for Persons with Severe Handicaps, 19,* 290–301.

Janzen, L., Wilgosh, L., & McDonald, L. (1995). Experiences of classroom teachers integrating students with moderate and severe disabilities. *Developmental Disabilities Bulletin, 23*(1), 40–57.

Johnson, D.W., Johnson, R., & Maruyama, G. (1983). Interdependence and interpersonal attraction among heterogeneous and homogeneous individuals: A theoretical formulation of a meta-analysis of the research. *Review of Educational Research, 53,* 51–54.

Johnson, D.W., Maruyama, G., Johnson, R., Nelson, D., & Skon, L. (1981). The effects of cooperative, competitive, and individualistic goal structures on achievement: A meta-analysis. *Psychological Bulletin, 89,* 47–62.

Jorgensen, C.M. (1994). Essential questions—inclusive answers. *Educational Leadership, 52*(4), 52–55.

Linehan, S., Brady, M., & Hwang, C. (1991). Ecological vs. developmental assessment: Influences on instructional expectations. *Journal of The Association for Persons with Severe Handicaps, 16,* 146–153.

Logan, K.R., Diaz, E., Piperno, M., Rankin, D., MacFarland, A.D., & Bargamian, K. (1994–95). How inclusion built a community of learners. *Educational Leadership, 52*(4), 42–44.

Luiselli, T.E., Luiselli, J.K., DeCaluwe, S.M., & Jacobs, L.A. (1995). Inclusive education of young children with deaf-blindness: A technical assistance model. *Journal of Visual Impairments and Blindness, 89,* 249–256.

Maxson, B.J. Tedder, N.E., Marmion, S., & Lamb, A.M. (1993). The education of youth who are deaf-blind: Learning tasks and teaching methods. *Journal of Visual Impairments and Blindness, 87,* 259–262.

Meyer, L., & Eichinger, J. (1994). *Program quality indicators (PQI): A checklist of most promising practices in educational programs for students with disabilities.* (Available from The Association for Persons with Severe Disabilities, 29 W. Susquehanna Ave., Suite 210, Baltimore, MD 21204.)

Meyer, L.H., & Kishi, G.S. (1985). School integration strategies. In K.C. Lakin & R.H. Bruininks (Eds.), *Strategies for achieving community integration of developmentally disabled citizens* (pp. 231–252). Baltimore: Paul H. Brookes Publishing Co.

National Association of State Boards of Education. (1992, October). *Winners all: A call for inclusive schools.* Alexandria, VA: Author.

Obierti, C. (1993). A parent's perspective. *Exceptional Parent. 23*(7), 18–21.

Peck, C.A., Billingsley, F., Staub, D., Gallucci, C., Schwartz, I.S., & White, O. (1994, December). *Analysis of outcomes and contexts in inclusive school environments.* Paper presented at the meeting of The Association for Persons with Severe Handicaps, Atlanta.

Peck, C.A., Carlson, P., & Helmstetter, E. (1992). Parent and teacher perceptions of outcomes for typically developing children enrolled in integrated early childhood programs: A statewide survey. *Journal of Early Intervention, 16*(1), 53–63.

Putnam, J.W. (Ed.). (1993). *Cooperative learning and strategies for inclusion: Celebrating diversity in the classroom.* Baltimore: Paul H. Brookes Publishing Co.

Rainforth, B., York, J., & Macdonald, C. (1992). *Collaborative teams for students with severe disabilities: Integrating therapy and educational services.* Baltimore: Paul H. Brookes Publishing Co.

Richards, S.B., & Sternberg, L. (1992). A preliminary analysis of environmental variables affecting the observed biobehavioral states of individuals with profound handicaps. *Journal of Intellectual Disability Research, 36*(4), 403–414.

Romer, L.T., & Byrne, A.R. (1995). Collaborative teaming to support participation in inclusive education settings. In N.G. Haring & L.T. Romer (Eds.), *Welcoming students who are deaf-blind into typical classrooms: Facilitating school participation, learning, and friendships* (pp. 143–169). Baltimore: Paul H. Brookes Publishing Co.

Romer, L.T., & Haring, N.G. (1994). The social participation of students with deaf-blindness in educational settings. *Education and Training in Mental Retardation and Developmental Disabilities, 29,* 134–144.

Rowland, C. (1990). Communication in the classroom for children with dual sensory impairments: Studies of teacher and child behavior. *Augmentative and Alternative Communication, 6,* 262–274.

Ryndak, D.L., Downing, J.E., Jacqueline, L.R., & Morrison, A.P. (1995). Parents' perceptions after inclusion of their child with moderate or severe disabilities in general education settings. *Journal of The Association for Persons with Severe Handicaps, 20,* 147–157.

Salisbury, C., Palombaro, M., & Hollowood, T. (1993). On the nature and change of an inclusive elementary school. *Journal of The Association for Persons with Severe Handicaps, 18,* 75–84.

Schattman, R., & Benay, J. (1992). Inclusive practices transform special education in the 1990s. *School Administrator, 49*(2), 8–12.

Shanker, A. (1994–95). Full inclusion is neither free nor appropriate. *Educational Leadership, 52*(4), 18–21.

Slavin, R. (1990). *Cooperative learning: Theory, research, and practice.* Englewood Cliffs, NJ: Prentice Hall.

Snyder, T.D., & Hoffman, C.M. (1994). *Digest of education statistics.* Pub. No. NCES 94-115. Washington, DC: U.S. Department of Education, Office of Educational Research and Improvement.

Stainback, W., & Stainback, S. (Eds.). (1990). *Support networks for inclusive schools: Interdependent integrated education.* Baltimore: Paul H. Brookes Publishing Co.

Stainback, S., & Stainback, W. (1992). *Curriculum considerations in inclusive classrooms: Facilitating learning for all students.* Baltimore: Paul H. Brookes Publishing Co.

Staub, D., Schwartz, I.S., Gallucci, C., & Peck, C. (1994). Four portraits of friendship at an inclusive school. *Journal of The Association for Persons with Severe Handicaps, 19,* 314–325.

Stevens, R., Slavin, R., & Madden, N. (1991). Cooperative integrated reading and composition (CIRC): Effective cooperative learning in reading and language arts. *Cooperative Learning, 11*(4), 6–18.

Utley, B. (1993). Facilitating and measuring the team process within inclusive educational settings. *Clinics in Communication Disorders, 3*(2), 71–85.

Vargo, J., & Vargo, R. (1993). Inclusive education: Right for us. *Inclusion Times for Children and Youth with Disabilities, 1*(2), 3. (Newsletter published by National Professional Resources, Port Chesler, NY.)

Vaughn, T.B. (1994). Brad was autistic. *Learning, 23*(3), 58.

Villa, R.A., Thousand; J.S., Stainback, W., & Stainback, S. (Eds.). (1992). *Restructuring for caring and effective education: An administrative guide to creating heterogeneous schools.* Baltimore: Paul H. Brookes Publishing Co.

Voeltz, L. (1980). Children's attitudes toward handicapped peers. *American Journal on Mental Deficiency, 84,* 455–464.

Voeltz, L. (1982). Effects of structured interactions with severely handicapped peers on children's attitudes. *American Journal on Mental Deficiency, 86,* 180–190.

York, J., Vandercook, T., Macdonald, C., Heise-Neff, C., & Caughey, E. (1992). Feedback about integrating middle-school students with severe disabilities in general education classes. *Exceptional Children, 58,* 244–258.

Chapter 2

INSTRUCTION IN THE GENERAL EDUCATION ENVIRONMENT

Joanne Eichinger and June E. Downing

The first part of this chapter highlights the changes that have occurred in approaches in general and special education since 1980. Parallels in these changes are then discussed. This analysis is followed by a discussion of "promising practices" in general education for the inclusion of learners with severe and multiple disabilities. Each of these discussions has four components: first, the empirical or theoretical base related to that practice, including data for learners with disabilities, if these data exist; second, the elements of that practice; third, the rationale for utilizing the practice with students with severe and multiple disabilities; and, fourth, practical strategies for using the practice with this population of students.

RECENT CHANGES IN GENERAL EDUCATION

Since 1980, numerous changes have occurred in general education in response to the call for restructuring. Overall, there has been an increasing emphasis on a more holistic approach to education. This is a result of the constructivist movement, which emphasizes that learning is individualized, social, and occurs in context. Students construct and build upon their own knowledge via interactions with their environments (Reid, Kurkijian, & Carruthers, 1994). Thus, the teacher serves as a facilitator or mediator of learning, as opposed to a disseminator of knowledge. The work of Vygotsky (1978) has been influential in this shift in thinking and practice. The constructivist approach runs counter to a strict behaviorist/reductionist approach to teaching and learning, which tends to stress the remediation of deficit skills. Poplin and Stone (1992) provided an excellent description of the differences between these two learning theories, and Brooks and Brooks (1993) compared characteristics in traditional classrooms with those in constructivist classrooms. The constructivist approach lends itself to inclusion, because it emphasizes that learning is a social process, thus stressing peer-to-peer learning and support. It is also compatible with individual student goals and outcomes, because acquisition of knowledge is based on students' abilities and interests. In speaking of constructivism, Jackson, Reid, and Bunsen (1993) assert that it

> provides a framework for accepting all students as equal members of a community of learners rather than as differentially positioned achievers on a hierarchical skill sequence. This acceptance contrasts markedly with one of the legacies of past interpretations of the reductionist perspective: requiring individuals to "earn" membership in the school community through the acquisition of externally defined "functional" or "appropriate" skills (pp. 292–293).

The whole-language approach to language arts instruction is one instructional philosophy that embraces the constructivist model (Goodman, 1986). This integrated language arts approach uses the child's own experiential base for learning oral and written communication and, as such, is very child centered. Reading is taught within a natural context (e.g., reading "big books," reflective journals) as opposed to drill and practice workbooks. Specific reading skills, such as phonics instruction, are also taught within a natural and meaningful context. For example, a teacher may select a particular big book, based on the phonics and rhyming words that can be highlighted. Routman (1992) suggests that teachers engage students in inquiry to discover the sounds and rules, as opposed to telling students the letters and the sounds. He asserts that the ultimate goal is for the student to use the skill purposefully and independently in other contexts. This direct application enables the learner to use this new information as a strategy in other contexts.

Cooperative learning (Johnson & Johnson, 1987) has also gained widespread acceptance as a promising practice in general education since the 1970s. Used at all grade levels, although perhaps more frequently in elementary classes, cooperative learning operates under the principle that learning is social. A departure from traditional lecture and workbook approaches, in which students work independently, the cooperative learning model involves students actively assisting each other in the learning process.

Thematic teaching units, another approach that harmonizes with the holistic trend, have become more prominent in general education classrooms (see Kovalik & Olsen, 1992). Thematic teaching units ensure that content is integrated across several curricular areas, highlighting the natural linkages for students. There is more repetition of content and therefore more opportunity for learning, since related concepts may be developed in more than one curricular area.

Another concept that is consistent with the holistic model and has influenced educational practices in some schools is the theory of multiple intelligences (Gardner, 1983). According to this theory, individuals possess and demonstrate intelligence in various ways (e.g., spatially, interpersonally). When this theory is applied in practice, the curricular content moves beyond linguistic and logical mathematical areas to incorporate other facets such as the visual arts and interpersonal relationships. By using this approach, students from diverse backgrounds can draw upon their strengths for further educational development.

In the area of assessment, there has been a gradual shift away from standardized testing and toward more authentic and performance-based evaluation. Assessment is conducted on an ongoing basis, as an integral part of the instructional process. These more holistic approaches to assessment are consistent with constructivist beliefs about teaching and learning (Shavelson, Baxter, & Pine, 1992). One example is portfolio assessment, in which samples of the child's work are kept throughout the year to document progress (Bunce-Crim, 1992). The emergence of technology, particularly in multimedia, supports the use of portfolio assessment by capturing students' written work and creative work (e.g., videotape performances) on CD-ROM (Santulli, 1994).

RECENT CHANGES IN EDUCATIONAL APPROACHES FOR STUDENTS WITH SEVERE DISABILITIES

Similarly, the last 15 years have witnessed a dramatic shift in the recommended approach for educating learners with severe disabilities. Until the late 1970s, a developmental curricular approach dominated instructional procedures for this population of students. This approach was characterized by a belief that in each curricular area (e.g., cognitive, motor), a hierarchical sequence of skills existed, and that students needed to acquire prerequisite skills before moving on to higher-level skills. Assessments based on developmental checklists yielded developmental ages, which were used to determine instructional activities, materials, and performance criteria.

In the late 1970s, a functional curricular model was proposed (Brown et al., 1979). This model stated that students with severe disabilities should be taught the skills they will need to be as independent as possible in school, home, community, and work settings. Instead of teaching individual motor skills, socialization skills, communication skills, and so forth, at a designated time (often out-of-context) and according to a prescribed hierarchy, these skills would be embedded in skill routines that would be taught at naturally occurring times (e.g., communication skills would be taught to students at recess). This shift toward contextually based instruction appears to parallel the shift toward more holistic concepts that came to dominate general education practices.

In addition, the shift from a multidisciplinary-related service delivery model to a transdisciplinary model or an integrated therapy model (a variation of the transdisciplinary model) for students with severe disabilities furthermore parallels the shift in service delivery in general education. Within a transdisciplinary model, the child is viewed holistically by all team members (Campbell, 1987; Downing & Bailey, 1990). Each of the related service providers (e.g., occupational therapist, orientation and mobility specialist, physical therapist) assesses the student and makes recommendations that can be implemented by a number of people, one of whom choreographs the instructional program (typically the teacher). These recommendations involve skills to be taught in natural contexts, rather than in isolation. For example, a physical therapist might recommend that a kindergarten student learn to transfer from his wheelchair to a standing position, then use a wheeled walker to go 10 feet from the play center to the snack table with minimal assistance. The therapist would teach the teaching staff how to have the student do this. Once they were trained, the therapist would provide ongoing consultation to monitor the student's progress, ensure that the training was being implemented correctly and targeted at other appropriate times (e.g., on the way to physical education or lunch), and answer any questions the staff might have. Assessment of performance would occur on an ongoing basis using the natural routines and contexts for instruction. This model also values the parent as a key team member. Thus, this related service delivery model (York, Rainforth, & Giangreco, 1990), along with current assessment approaches that utilize parent input for program planning (Giangreco, Cloninger, & Iverson, 1993), ensures that the student's program is inherently child-centered. In the integrated therapy approach, the delivery of therapy in a synthesized fashion within functional activities and in natural contexts ensures that the activity and the therapy are directly related to functional outcomes.

ANALYSIS OF CURRICULAR CHANGES FOR STUDENTS WITH AND WITHOUT DISABILITIES

Several parallels exist between the evolution of curricular program implementation for learners with severe disabilities and for students without disabilities. Both fields have embraced a more holistic approach to education that is child-centered, with teaching taking place in natural and social contexts. As a result, activities planned for students tend to be more meaningful. Other approaches to assessment, such as portfolio assessment, which stresses more authentic evaluation, are being used in conjunction with standardized assessment.

However, several of the instructional approaches that have formed the cornerstone of education for learners with severe disabilities rely on a behavioral model (e.g., shaping using reinforcement of successive approximations). As stated earlier, strict adherence to behaviorism can run counter to a holistic constructivist approach, since behavioral interventions support the identification of and instruction in discrete learning steps. Many behavioral approaches also rely on the use of highly individual and direct instruction. Moreover, past educational practices for students with severe disabilities were developed for use in self-contained classes or segregated schools, since these were the predominant settings for learners with severe disabilities in the 1970s and 1980s. With the move toward inclusive practices, persons involved in special education are rethinking practices that would be suitable in general education settings. This evolution in the field is likely to continue for some time.

Billingsley and Kelley (1994) investigated the perceptions of 53 professionals in education for students with severe disabilities involving the appropriate or inappropriate use of certain instructional approaches. These individuals responded to 51 instructional approaches and noted whether they felt each was a sound practice and whether it was appropriate in general education academic and nonacademic settings. Many of the items in this study considered unsound or inappropriate by the professionals are based on behavioral approaches or approaches that rely on one-to-one instruction. Thus, it appears that professionals in the area of severe disabilities are recognizing the need to modify or delete some practices that were considered state-of-the art approaches for students in self-contained classes and replace them with more "normalized curricular practices."

Billingsley and Kelley (1994) recognized that different findings might have emerged had general education teachers been surveyed. This point highlights a key issue in the quest for meaningful curricular content for learners with severe disabilities in general education classrooms. It is important that general education teachers feel comfortable with the techniques and procedures used with these students. Because general educators are often the individuals implementing these techniques, it is important to determine what they feel are effective strategies.

Some research has already begun to emerge in this area. Giangreco, Dennis, Cloninger, Edelman, and Schattman (1993) reported that "teachers frequently favored the use of typical activities, materials, and approaches over special ones" (p. 367). Downing, Eichinger, and Williams (1996) found that of 18 general and special educators interviewed, 11 (61%) felt that some form of adaptations were important to use with students having severe disabilities in inclusive settings. Half of the respondents mentioned the need for multimodal instruction, and 7 felt that one-to-one instruction was important. Five of the teachers stated that the same teaching strategies work for all students.

Due to the relative novelty of full inclusion for students with severe and multiple disabilities, a database of empirically validated "best practices" for these learners in general education classes has not yet emerged. A holistic constructivist-oriented approach may be optimal overall, but with some students or some learning outcomes (e.g., those involving more motor components, such as eating routines), a more behavioral approach may be more appropriate. Salisbury, Gallucci, Palombaro, and Peck (1995) conducted a qualitative study to assess strategies used by general educators to promote social relationships among students with and without severe disabilities in regular classrooms. The five major strategies that emerged were 1) active facilitation of social interactions, 2) empowering students, 3) building a sense of classroom community, 4) modeling acceptance, and 5) developing school organizational supports. As researchers and practitioners continue to examine the outcomes for students with severe disabilities in general education settings, more dialogue should occur around this topic.

PROMISING PRACTICES FOR STUDENTS WITH SEVERE DISABILITIES IN GENERAL EDUCATION SETTINGS

This section addresses educational approaches used in typical learning environments that appear to be "promising practices" for learners with severe and multiple disabilities. Teaching strategies (e.g., cooperative learning), constructivist approaches to instruction (e.g., whole-language instruction), and placement strategies (e.g., multi-age groupings) are discussed. All of these approaches appear to accommodate diversity among learners. Because teachers can influence changes made in school buildings through site-based management, they can be advocates for changes such as multi-age groupings in their building. However, given the practical nature of this book, multi-age groupings are discussed in only a cursory fashion, because a decision to incorporate them would fall under the administrative domain.

Because of the still-infrequent cases of full inclusion for learners with severe and multiple disabilities in general education classes, few efficacy studies have been conducted to determine teaching strategies that are successful with these learners. Thus, the strategies cited here are offered as "promising practices" for two reasons. First, for some of these techniques (e.g., cooperative learning), data indicate that the technique was successful for learners with severe and multiple disabilities in general education classes and other contexts. Second, for other strategies (e.g., thematic teaching units), learning characteristics of students with severe and multiple disabilities suggest the need for such an approach.

Cooperative Learning

Empirical Database   Much of the literature on use of cooperative learning with students with disabilities involves students with mild disabilities who were mainstreamed after the passage of PL 94-142, the Education for All Handicapped Children Act of 1975. Several studies found that cooperative learning promoted more helping between students with and without disabilities than did individualistic or competitive learning (Armstrong, Johnson, & Balow, 1981; Cooper, Johnson, Johnson, & Wilderson, 1980; Johnson & Johnson, 1982).

Other researchers examined the effects of goal structure on the social interactions between students without disabilities and students labeled as having moderate mental retardation, with similar results. For instance, a cooperatively structured learning approach used during a recreational bowling activity was associated with more positive social interactions than an individualistic situation (Johnson, Rynders, Johnson, Schmidt, & Haider, 1979; Rynders, Johnson, Johnson, & Schmidt, 1980).

Putnam, Rynders, Johnson, and Johnson (1989) expanded this research base by studying the effects of cooperative skill instruction on the social interactions between students without disabilities and students with moderate and severe disabilities in a science class. They found that students with disabilities who had been explicitly instructed in cooperative behaviors had higher levels of eye contact and vocalizations with students without disabilities. In two other studies involving students with severe multiple disabilities, the cooperative method was found to be more effective, at least initially, than a nonstructured (laissez-faire) condition (Cole, 1986; Cole, Meyer, Vandercook, & McQuarter, 1986).

Eichinger (1990) compared social interactions between students with severe multiple disabilities and fourth and fifth graders without disabilities as a function of goal-structured activities. Students without disabilities who were involved in cooperatively structured activities vocalized more with students with severe disabilities during free play generalization sessions than students without disabilities who were involved in individualistically structured activities. Students with severe disabilities who were in the cooperative learning mode had more positive facial affect, engaged in higher levels of cooperative play, and had fewer intervals in which no vocalizations occurred between them and students without disabilities than did students in the individualistic condition.

As described in Chapter 1, Hunt, Staub, Alwell, and Goetz (1994) documented the success of cooperative learning in terms of communication and motor skill acquisition for three students with severe multiple disabilities who were being educated in three second-grade classes. All of the teachers interviewed as part of a qualitative study on inclusive education indicated that they used cooperative learning as one strategy to promote social relationships among students with and without disabilities in elementary school classes (Salisbury et al., 1995).

Thus, although none of these studies compared the use of cooperative learning with other types of goal structures in general education classrooms, three studies (Hunt et al., 1994; Putnam et al., 1989; Salisbury et al., 1995) demonstrated the efficacy of this practice for students with severe disabilities in general education classes. Along with the evidence supporting cooperative learning with students with severe disabilities in other instructional contexts, this suggests that cooperative learning would be an effective instructional practice.

Elements of Cooperative Learning Johnson, Johnson, Holubec, and Roy (1984) described four components of cooperative learning: positive interdependence; individual accountability, interpersonal and small-group skill development and group processing, and face-to-face interactions.

Positive interdependence refers to the cooperative goal structure built into each lesson. Students work together to attain a common goal (e.g., a group product). Often students share materials (e.g., jigsaw approach) to promote positive interdependence (Johnson & Johnson, 1987).

Individual accountability means that every student must contribute to the final product or outcome. Students are typically assigned various roles within cooperative groups (e.g., praiser, checker, encourager, materials manager).

Regarding *interpersonal and small-group skill development* a social skill objective is taught and evaluated within each lesson. The same social skill objective may be pursued over a long time period. For example, in a kindergarten class, sharing might be the targeted social skill. Processing is done at the end of the lesson by asking the students how they performed relative to the social skill objective and then by offering constructive feedback to the students.

In addition to monitoring social skill acquisition, academic skill acquisition is monitored. The teacher's role is to observe and provide feedback to the students. Observation sheets can be used to aggregate feedback relative to academic or social skill performance.

Students in cooperative groups have numerous opportunities for *face-to-face interactions*. These verbal exchanges occur within the interdependent structure that is created. Teachers should ensure that cooperative groups are formed heterogeneously, with students mixed by culture, ethnicity, gender, and ability. Typically, groups stay intact for approximately 4–6 weeks so that the desired interaction skills can be acquired.

Why Cooperative Learning Is Appropriate Cooperative learning allows students to be actively involved in their own learning. For the child with severe and multiple impairments including a sensory loss, this approach can provide the stimulation needed to maintain interest and attention to the task. In addition, the hands-on involvement of students in the learning process is particularly beneficial to students who require more information than that embodied in a traditional lecture format. Students with impaired sensory input learn more effectively if given the opportunity to explore, touch, interact, and perform. The assignment of a specific role within the cooperative group ensures that each student is an active participant, although perhaps with assistance provided.

The interpersonal objectives built into every cooperatively structured lesson are highly recommended for students with severe and multiple disabilities, who often need to develop more adaptive social skills. Students are thus provided numerous opportunities to work on basic social skills (e.g., taking turns, sharing materials) as well as more sophisticated social skills (e.g., initiating conversations).

How Cooperative Learning Can Be Used   Putnam (1993) provided a detailed exploration of cooperative learning practices in inclusive settings. Case study examples of how the approach can be used in general education classes that include students with severe and multiple disabilities follow. First, however, as a general suggestion, when planning cooperative learning lessons, teachers should attend to cultural and language issues. For example, if a child has limited English proficiency, that child should be in a group with a student who speaks the child's native language as well as English and can act as a mediator for the child. Harry et al. (1995) provide an excellent discussion of cultural and language issues pertaining to the inclusion of learners with severe disabilities in general education classes. Individual case examples of cooperative learning are included next.

Michaela, age 6, loves to be with people, is interested in books, and has good auditory discrimination skills. She also has severe spastic quadriplegia, a moderate vision impairment, and a mild hearing loss. She is a member of a half-day kindergarten class. After reading various books on different animals as well as a visit to the local petting zoo, her class breaks into groups of five. Each group is instructed to work together to create a wall mural to hang in the hall outside the classroom. One large sheet of paper and one set of markers is given to the group. Since all of the kindergarten students are working on the floor, Michaela is positioned prone over a small wedge at the edge of the paper. Physical assistance is provided to her as needed to help her draw or to pass supplies to a peer. The social skill of sharing is targeted for instruction. Michaela performs the role of praiser by hitting a switch to activate a tape recorder with prerecorded messages on it (e.g., "That looks really pretty. You are all working really hard. Good for us!").

Antwan, age 8, is in third grade. Antwan is eager to learn and is quite strong willed. Antwan is blind and is just learning to use some speech. His science class is working on a unit on the solar system. As part of this unit, students work in groups for different activities. Each group is assigned a planet and is instructed to write a one- to two-page report on the planet as well as to make a papier mâché replica of the planet. Antwan performs the role of materials manager. He makes sure that all the resource texts and other materials are taken out at the beginning of the work session and are put away afterwards. After listening to a videotape on the solar system, Antwan contributes information for the written report by responding to yes/no questions put to him by his peers. He also works with his group members on the papier mâché planet.

Juan, age 10, is a member of a fifth-grade class that uses whole-language instruction as the basis for reading instruction. Juan has strong preferences, likes to tease, and is curious. He has a hearing impairment, developmental delays, and a physical impairment. It is decided that Juan's class will write a short play for the rest of the school and for the parents. The teacher assigns students to work in cooperative learning groups. Each group is responsible for one aspect of the production, including: making invitations; making scenery; making costumes; planning a menu and making food for parents the day of the play; and taking roles as actors and actresses in the play. Juan works with three peers to make the invitations. He works with Kyle on typing on the computer, printing out, and then delivering invitations to 10 classes in the building, using a bag attached to his wheeled walker. The group works on the social skill of listening to other people's ideas and providing feedback to come to consensus on the design of the invitations. Juan gives feedback by shaking his head yes or no when asked if he likes specific aspects of the design.

Paula, age 14, is in eighth grade. She is very sociable, loves to laugh, and has several friends. Paula has a severe hearing impairment, substantial cognitive delay, and some emotional challenges. She is taking a class in home economics, which meets twice a week. During cooking activities, her teacher assigns students to groups of five. Each group is responsible for making enough food for the group, including preparation and cleanup. A pictorial recipe is used. Paula is assigned the role of checking to see that everyone completes their job; in addition, she will set the table.

Carmen, age 17, attends physical education class with her high school classmates. Carmen has strong opinions on most topics, wants to be included in everything, and is sensitive to others' feelings. She also has a mild hearing impairment, is very myopic (nearsighted), has severe physical impairments, and uses facial expressions, objects, and some pictures for her expressive communication. Instead of a competitive game, the physical education teacher organizes groups of six students. One activity involves rotating the basketball among the six students to see how many baskets they can make from a designated spot within 5 minutes. Then they play again to try to beat their combined scores. The social skill they are working on is providing encouragement and support. All students are encouraged to provide praise (e.g., group cheers). Carmen uses her prone stander and throws the ball to a teammate of her choice, who then takes a shot at the basket. Using a switch to activate a voice output communication aid (VOCA), she also cheers on her team.

Thematic Teaching Units

Empirical or Theoretical Base Thematic teaching relates to a body of knowledge called brain-based learning, which contends that the disciplines relate to each other and share common information that can be recognized and organized by the brain (Caine & Caine, 1991).

On the basis of brain research conducted by numerous individuals, Kovalik and Olsen (1992) enumerated eight components that they feel are directly connected to improved performance for children and adults. These are: absence of threat (trust), meaningful content, choices, adequate time, enriched environment, collaboration, immediate feedback, and mastery. The "integrated thematic instruction model" was developed to represent what is known about brain research, curriculum development, and teaching strategies in which curriculum and instruction correspond to the way children naturally learn.

Other writers have examined how thematic instruction can be used. Jacobs, Hannah, Manfredonia, Percivalle, and Gilbert (1989) and Jacobs (1991) have provided excellent discussions of interdisciplinary curriculum, and include examples of interdisciplinary units for a kindergarten through sixth-grade class and for a high school class. Perkins (1989) discussed ways in which teachers can conceptualize appropriate themes for students. Additional information on thematic units has been provided by Foster, Konar, Williamson, and Brumbaugh (1991).

Elements of Thematic Teaching Units Thematic teaching units expand upon a previously used teaching strategy called unit teaching, in which a series of lessons is centered around a particular theme in one content area (e.g., science). Thematic teaching also centers around a specified theme (e.g., "the world of work"), but lessons are taught in a number of different content areas that relate to the theme. Language and reading activities related to the theme transcend the various content area lessons.

Lapp and Flood (1992) recommended that teachers follow three steps when planning a thematic teaching unit. First, decide what the theme will be. Student input may be provided at this step to ensure that the content is of interest to them. Second, decide what content area skills will be taught and what reading and language activities and materials will be used. Third, develop the specific content and steps for each of the lessons.

Why Thematic Teaching Units Are Appropriate Thematic teaching units allow greater continuity in programming around a particular topic. Thus, natural connections can intentionally be ensured for all students. This is extremely important for students with severe disabilities, because they have difficulty generalizing to other settings or persons (Coon, Vogelsberg, & Williams, 1981; Horner, Bellamy, & Colvin, 1984).

Also, lessons taught within thematic teaching units tend to be very project based (Wolk, 1994). As a result, students are actively engaged in the learning process. Art activities (e.g., dioramas), reading/language arts activities (e.g., writing and acting out a play), and social studies activities (e.g., simulating a city government within a classroom) all promote student participation.

How Thematic Teaching Can Be Used A high school thematic teaching unit could focus on the theme of "social responsibility." The teaching team decides that the students will be given a framework in which to work, but that students will decide the particular social issue they wish to pursue in various classes. The germination of the unit begins in government class, where students generate a list of social problems that exist in our world. Using a brainstorming approach, they generate possible solutions to four current problems in society (crime, drugs, social injustice, homelessness). As a class they decide they would like to focus on homelessness.

At this point, the team meets to plan how this topic can be developed across the curriculum. In English class, students read and discuss the excerpt in the *Utne Reader*, "A Day in the Homeless Life," by Collette Russell (1990). Students then decide which of two activities they wish to pursue. The first option is to research the extent of the problem in their own and surrounding communities and provide a brief written and oral report on the topic. This would be followed by writing letters to local and state officials highlighting the problem and the need to remedy it. The second option is to research the organization Habitat for Humanity and prepare a written and oral report on the work of this organization worldwide. Students are encouraged to work in small groups (two to four students) on the selected activity.

In physical education, students have designed a fundraising program called "Hoops for Homes." Students ask for pledges for the number of hoops they make over a 1-month period. One week of class time is devoted to this mini basketball unit. Students also are given the opportunity to make hoops after school when the gym is not in use. All of the money is donated to Habitat for Humanity.

In art class, students are asked to choose a medium to create an artistic representation of homelessness. Some students use pencil line drawings, while others use chalk, paint, or three-dimensional paper representations. One student, with his parents' assistance, obtains participants' permission and does a photographic essay on homelessness.

In government class, students conduct a 2-week food and clothing drive. This involves generating notices of the drive on the computer and distributing them to other classes. The collected food and clothing are then sorted and taken to a local shelter.

José is a friendly teenager who enjoys sports and most recreational activities. José, who has Down syndrome, a mild to moderate hearing loss, and a moderate vision loss, participates in the homeless project in English class by listening to the story read to him by a partner. He works in a group of three to research homelessness in his community and compose two letters to various officials. He offers one idea for how the problem can be addressed. After the letter has been handwritten by other students, he types it onto the computer. Once the letter is completed and addressed, he assumes responsibility for putting it into the envelope, sealing it, putting a stamp in the proper corner, and getting it to the outgoing mailbox in the school's main office.

In gym class, José participates in the "Hoops for Homes" program and collects his pledges. He assists with collecting and counting the pledge money each day (first sorting it into easily recognizable denominations). In art, he cuts pictures out of magazines to depict what homelessness means to him. In government class, he works with five other students to sort the food and clothing and deliver it to a homeless shelter.

Whole-Language Instruction

Empirical or Theoretical Base   Considerable information has been written on using whole-language approaches in general education settings (e.g., Church, 1994; Goodman, 1986; Whitmore & Goodman, 1992). Much of the literature supporting this approach for students with disabilities centers on students with mild disabilities (Dudley-Marling, 1994; Palincsar, Klenk, Anderman, Parecki, & Wilson, 1991). However, Tefft-Cousin, Weekly, and Gerard (1993) documented the success of this approach with two students, one of whom has Down syndrome and the other who has mental retardation. Benefits of whole-language instruction for students who are deaf also have been investigated (Conway, 1985). The emphasis of whole-language instruction on language experiences of the child, rather than strict sound/symbol association, eases the difficulty of reading and writing for children with hearing impairments.

Elements of Whole-Language Instruction   The whole-language approach to language arts instruction represents a philosophical approach rather than a teaching strategy. In this integrated approach, reading, writing, spelling, speaking, and listening are taught simultaneously. Literacy is acquired via naturalistic, functional reading and writing situations. The teacher acts as a facilitator of learning in this student-centered approach, drawing on the student's own experiential background and understanding, and thus building on the student's strengths as opposed to deficits. Oral language is used as the basis for acquiring written expression. Teachers create a print-rich environment (e.g., label things in the classroom, have numerous books and magazines available for students to read by themselves or with a partner, and have various written material on walls and blackboards). Also, they provide stimulating language experiences. Reading to students is recommended at all age levels, and books on tape are readily available in the classroom and library. For young children, predictable books are used to stimulate a child's receptive and expressive language capabilities.

Instruction takes place within meaningful contexts. For example, young children might write letters to classmates or pen pals using invented spelling. Older students might carry on a dialog with teachers or peers via written communication in journals. There is a strong emphasis on developing comprehension of text.

The whole-language approach departs from the use of traditional reading groups. In addition to whole-class instruction, children work with others or on their own. The teacher meets with the students regularly to provide direct instruction (e.g., to work on writing a conclusion to a story). Sometimes direct instruction occurs with small groups of children who need the same concept explained. (This is done on an as-needed basis, as the teacher analyzes the children's work.) Dudley-Marling (1994) provided numerous examples of how whole-language instruction was conducted in a third-grade setting and how students who were struggling with literacy were provided the necessary support and assistance.

Assessment is done by using portfolios or anecdotal recordings taken during actual language situations (Lapp & Flood, 1992). A child's written language samples may be collected over a year's time and analyzed for growth and goal setting (Atwell, 1987).

Why Whole-Language Instruction Is Appropriate   Children with severe and multiple disabilities may profit from being in a classroom where a whole-language approach is used because of the individualized nature of this approach. Literacy is promoted through multiple sign systems (e.g., music, dance, art, sign language), in addition to reading and writing. This perspective naturally allows students with severe disabilities including sensory impairments to use and develop the nonsymbolic (e.g., facial expressions) or symbolic (e.g., picture symbols) means of communication that are most appropriate. Proponents of this approach reject the labeling of learners and assume that all students can participate in emergent literacy according to their interests (Smith-Burke, Deegan, & Jaggar, 1991). Because this approach is based on a constructivist view that learning is social, it affords the student with severe and multiple disabilities numerous opportunities to develop social interaction skills within the instructional framework (e.g., paired reading).

How Whole-Language Instruction Can Be Used   An example of how the whole-language approach can be used in a third-grade class was provided in the previous section on cooperative learning. In a fifth- and sixth-grade combination class, students read the story "Sarah, Plain and Tall" (MacLachlan, 1985). After the students read the story, the teacher encourages them to generate information about the story, which she places on a web or map on the board. The information is used by students to report on the story. In addition, students make dioramas depicting various aspects of Sarah's life and the period during which she lived. For example, Kathy, age 11, is curious, independent, and good with her hands.

She is totally blind, has moderate hearing loss, and uses a hearing aid. She listens to the story "Sarah, Plain and Tall," read by a partner. She is learning to raise her hand and provide information about the setting when the class is constructing the web. With the assistance of a paraprofessional, she writes a three-sentence paragraph about the story. She works with two other students to construct a diorama of Sarah's home. During recess, she plays with one girlfriend, using a slightly adapted version of hopscotch, a game that was also popular during Sarah's life.

During whole-language reading instruction, some time is spent working alone or in small groups, with the teacher circulating around the classroom to offer assistance as needed. This time provides an excellent opportunity for students with severe and multiple disabilities to receive some of their itinerant or related services. These services will naturally vary depending on the levels of sensory involvement and the intellectual capabilities of the student. For example, Diane who is 8, has average intelligence, and is totally blind, may be learning braille from the itinerant vision specialist.

Given the types of activities used in whole-language-oriented classrooms, it may be easier to address individual students' language goals. For instance, Tameka, age 12, is functionally deaf-blind, with spastic quadriplegia. She works with a speech and language therapist on increasing the use of nonsymbolic communication (gestures, body movements, etc.), initiating communication through vocalizations, and rejecting items in an appropriate way (currently she screams to communicate the function of rejecting). The speech-language therapist instructs the other adults and children in the room about the need to respond to Tameka's vocalized initiations so that she will continue to initiate communication. She also instructs them on how to interpret the nonsymbolic communication she already has in her repertoire and how to respond to it. For example, when Tameka raises her right arm, she means that she wants more of something. To achieve these goals, the speech-language therapist helps create situations in which opportunities to communicate are present. She shares specific strategies such as giving Tameka only limited time with something she really needs or wants (e.g., the soft rubber coin purse she is allowed to fiddle with to relieve tension), so that she will be motivated to request it again. During this time, she also may show others how to offer Tameka things she likes (her fan that attaches to her wheelchair) and things she does not like (art work) to teach her the refusal behavior of pushing it away to substitute for screaming. This is done by physically prompting her to "push away" the undesired item and then respecting that communication response.

During this time frame, students with severe and multiple disabilities might be working with a student without disabilities on related reading activities. For example, Jenna, age 9, might be sequencing and then reviewing her line-drawn picture schedule for the day with her friend, Tatiana.

Meaningful writing activities could be taught during this time using a variety of different modes (see Chapter 5 of this volume). Students could write lists of gifts desired for a birthday, Hannukah, or Christmas, or a list of friends and their birthdays. For older students, writing activities could range from developing a grocery list, to making a telephone tree of friends, to filling out a job application. Modifications to the classroom environment also can be made to accommodate learners with sensory impairments. For example, when labeling things in the classroom, the teacher can label them with a word in braille or print, a sign representation, and a line-drawing representation.

Multiple Intelligences

Elements of Multiple Intelligences
The theory of multiple intelligences holds that intelligence is not a single construct that can be quantified as an isolated unit of measure. Gardner's 1983 analysis questioned the validity of attempting to measure intelligence by removing a person from his or her environment to test performance on isolated tasks that have no relevance to everyday life. He contended that intelligence goes beyond what is typically measured by such tests (linguistic and logical problem-solving skills). Gardner reconceptualized intelligence as the ability to solve a problem or to create a product that would be considered useful in at least one cultural setting (Goldman & Gardner, 1989).

Gardner described seven categories of intelligences: logical-mathematical, linguistic, musical, bodily kinesthetic, spatial, interpersonal, and intrapersonal. Logical-mathematical intelligence is the ability to use numbers or logical reasoning well. Linguistic intelligence refers to the ability to use words effectively, either verbally or in writing. Musical intelligence is manifested in the ability to hear themes, to think in musical terms, to understand how themes are transformed, and to be able to follow the themes in a musical piece (Goldman & Gardner, 1989). Bodily kinesthetic intelligence refers to the ability to successfully manipulate one's body to express feelings or ideas or to use one's hands to create or transform something. Spatial intelligence is characterized by the capacity to view the world in a spatial framework and to transform elements spatially. Interpersonal intelligence refers to the capacity to understand others, including perceiving the moods and cues of others. Intrapersonal intelligence is the ability to self-reflect and understand oneself, and to use this knowledge to guide one's behavior.

Empirical or Theoretical Base
In recent years, schools have worked to implement practices that support the multiple intelligences theory of learning. Project Spectrum, for example, is a program that is designed to assess students' capabilities in all of the intelligences (Krechevsky, 1991). Others have described programmatic efforts to use the seven intelligences throughout the curriculum (Hoerr, 1992; Olson, 1988). Ellison (1992) described how students and parents are involved in setting goals for the coming school year. This individualized approach has helped parents appreciate the gifts their children bring to a learning situation.

An additional informative resource is Armstrong's 1994 book on the theory and practical application of the multiple intelligences theory, including a chapter on the application of this theory to students with special needs.

Why Multiple Intelligences Is Appropriate
By its nature, the theory of multiple intelligences is vital to the field of special education. It encourages educators to move away from a deficit-oriented, remediation model of service delivery to a student-centered, strength-oriented, and compensatory model of service delivery. The gifts and strengths of students who have been labeled as having severe and multiple disabilities often have been overlooked in favor of an overall IQ or mental age score. The assessment process used to obtain this score removes the student from any familiar or practical environment and de-

pends on strong communication skills. Such an evaluation process places this student at a distinct disadvantage and fails to identify strengths the student possesses (e.g., the ability to hide hearing aids within seconds despite constant observation). Armstrong (1994) enumerates seven differences between a deficit paradigm and a growth paradigm. A focus on deficits only serves to exclude individuals from many valued activities, further limiting their life experiences and opportunities for growth. A focus on abilities and ways to compensate for limitations (e.g., synthesized or digital speech to allow access to computer programs) highlights the unique gifts and talents that all students possess and allows individuals to learn together.

How Multiple Intelligences Can Be Used Students with severe and multiple disabilities, and especially those with additional sensory impairments, need teachers who can recognize their strengths in different areas and use these to enhance learning. The multiple intelligences theory can be used when developing an individualized education program (IEP) for a student with severe disabilities including sensory losses, by drawing upon the strengths of the child. For example, Mary, age 15, has profound hearing loss and moderate vision loss. Her teacher develops activities in which Mary is encouraged to use her residual vision to obtain information (e.g., pictorial schedule, photographs of activities). She is sociable, and the teacher encourages her to further develop those skills via extracurricular activities. Last year, she served as a student council representative.

In terms of classroom practices, the theory of multiple intelligences places much less emphasis on passive learning (e.g., lecture) and more emphasis on alternative ways of learning, including movement, manipulation of objects, music, and social interactions. Students are encouraged to develop their strengths and interests, with the teacher following their lead and taking advantage of incidental learning opportunities as they emerge. Teachers are less "directors of learning" or givers of knowledge and more facilitators of learning. For example, Brise is 12 and labeled deaf-blind (although she does have functional vision and hearing). She has a strong interest in life-and-death issues (e.g., she is fascinated by dead leaves, trees, plants, and animals). When allowed to pursue this interest, she goes to the library and looks through books and magazines for relevant pictures. She expresses her interest to both peers and adults using a few signs ("dead," "not grow," "black") and she uses gestures to gain another's attention to share her interest. When "forced" to spend significant time investigating other topics, Brise can become aggressive toward others and destructive of property. Knowing Brise's strengths and interests helps her teachers plan accordingly so that different skills such as comprehending information, expressing oneself, and comparing similarities and differences can be taught using the subject matter of Brise's choice. Topics that Brise has limited interest in are introduced to her, but the time spent on these topics fluctuates according to her needs. She is always provided with choices of topics so that she can maintain the highest possible interest in the learning process.

Multi-age Groupings

Empirical or Theoretical Base George (1992) described a successful project involving multi-age grouping within a middle school. Students were heterogeneously grouped in teams consisting of sixth, seventh, and eighth graders. Within each team, students were grouped for reading or mathematics based on achievement regardless of grade level. Noted benefits included more positive home–school connections, more positive peer relationships, and improved time on task.

Using a case study format, Hunter (1992) described the process undertaken in an elementary laboratory school to move from a traditional model to a nongraded school, using a team-teaching approach. One benefit documented for the older students in the class who were shy is that they bloomed as they modeled their skills for younger classmates. Hunter noted that after a few years, when a suggestion was made to return to a traditional, self-contained classroom, none of the teachers volunteered.

In reference to multi-age grouping, Murray (1993) noted:

> Students gain from the extended relationship with their teacher, staying with him or her for more than one year. They learn to work comfortably and effectively together. . . . New students to the classroom also settle in more quickly because they have older peers to show them the ropes. (p. 176)

Elements of Multi-age Groupings   Multi-age groupings are also referred to as nongraded instruction or combination classes. In this type of administrative structure, students are not homogeneously grouped by age, ability, or grade level. Rather, they are grouped with other children, within an age range of 2–4 years (Hunter, 1992). For example, a class might consist of students who would traditionally be in kindergarten, first, or second grade.

Because of the variance in ages, opportunities for incidental peer modeling and coaching are present. Planned peer tutoring can also be incorporated, as this practice has proven effective for learners with severe disabilities in self-contained classes (Almond, Rodgers, & Krug, 1979; Folio & Norman, 1981; Kohl, Moses, & Stettner-Eaton, 1983; McHale, Olley, Marcus, & Simeonsson, 1981). An important consideration in implementing a peer-tutoring program in a classroom is to ensure that every student has the chance to be a tutor at some point. For example, a student who has dual sensory impairment could tutor others in American Sign Language.

Why Multi-age Groupings Are Appropriate   Multi-age groupings naturally accommodate individual differences among children. According to Murray (1993), this placement arrangement is child centered, uses formative evaluation, and is more flexible in terms of the curriculum. It tends to utilize an active learning, experiential approach that is very useful for students with severe and multiple disabilities. Another benefit is that often students remain with the same peers/teacher for more than a year. Given the time it may take for a teacher to determine the strengths, learning capabilities, and interests of a student with severe and multiple disabilities, this type of placement arrangement may promote higher rates of learning. In addition, classmates have more time to get to know the student who has a severe and multiple disability and to develop friendships.

How Multi-age Groupings Can Be Used   As noted previously, the decision to move to multi-age groupings is not likely to be under the jurisdiction of a teacher. However, when inclusion first emerged, the team-teaching model, in which a general education class merged with a class of students with severe disabilities, began to proliferate. Sometimes this merger included students from combination classes (Tefft-Cousin, Weekly, & Gerard, 1993). Although this model includes the positive component of a team-teaching approach, an inherent problem is that students with severe or multiple disabilities are overrepresented in this type of class composition. Also, students with severe disabilities may not be attending their neighborhood school, which is of critical importance (Sailor, 1989). Therefore, we recommend that when nongraded instruction is used, students with severe and multiple disabilities should attend their neighborhood schools and be placed in classes after careful consideration of class makeup.

SUMMARY

This chapter has highlighted the changes that have occurred in general and special education over the last 15 years. A brief analysis of the parallels that exist between these changes was provided so that the similarities of these two systems can be seen. Based on these changes, promising educational practices for students with severe and multiple disabilities in general education settings were described. Although this chapter contains a few specific examples of the techniques and strategies presented here, numerous other examples are found in the succeeding chapters.

As special and general education become less disparate systems and, instead, collaborate to address the needs of all school-age children, the perceived need to isolate individual students based on limitations will become less common. Creating one unified educational system can foster the professional development of teachers and administrators alike through access to combined skills and knowledge. An enriched learning environment is then available for all students.

REFERENCES

Almond, P., Rogers, S., & Krug, D. (1979). Mainstreaming: A model for including elementary students in the severely handicapped classroom. *Teaching Exceptional Children, 11,* 135–139.

Armstrong, B., Johnson, D.W., & Balow, B. (1981). Effects of cooperative versus individualistic learning experiences on interpersonal attraction between learning disabled and normal progress elementary school students. *Contemporary Educational Psychology, 6,* 102–109.

Armstrong, T. (1994). *Multiple intelligences in the classroom.* Alexandria, VA: Association for Supervision and Curriculum Development.

Atwell, N. (1987). *In the middle: Writing, reading, and learning with adolescents.* Portsmouth, NH: Heinemann.

Billingsley, F., & Kelley, B. (1994). An examination of the acceptability of instructional practices for students with severe disabilities in general education settings. *Journal of The Association for Persons with Severe Handicaps, 19,* 75–83.

Brooks, J.G., & Brooks, M.G. (1993). *In search of understanding: The case for constructivist classrooms.* Alexandria, VA: Association for Supervision and Curriculum Development.

Brown, L., Branston, M., Hamre-Nietupski, S., Pumpian, I., Certo, N., & Gruenwald, L. (1979). A strategy for developing chronological age appropriate and functional curricular content for severely handicapped adolescents and young adults. *Journal of Special Education, 13*(1), 81–90.

Bunce-Crim, M. (1992). Writing evaluation: Tracking daily progress. *Instructor, 101*(7), 24–26.

Caine, R.N., & Caine, G. (1991). *Making connections: Teaching and the human brain.* Alexandria, VA: Association for Supervision and Curriculum Development.

Campbell, P.H. (1987). The integrated programming team: An approach for coordinating professionals of various disciplines in programs for students with severe and multiple handicaps. *Journal of The Association for Persons with Severe Handicaps, 12,* 107–116.

Church, S.M. (1994). Is whole language really warm and fuzzy? *Reading Teacher, 47,* 362–370.

Cole, D.A. (1986). Facilitating play in children's peer relationships: Are we having fun yet? *American Educational Research Journal, 23,* 201–215.

Cole, D.A., Meyer, L.H., Vandercook, T., & McQuarter, R.J. (1986). Interactions between peers with and without severe handicaps: The dynamics of teacher intervention. *American Journal of Mental Deficiency, 91,* 160–169.

Conway, D. (1985). Children (re)creating writing: A preliminary look at the purposes of free-choice writing of hearing-impaired kindergarteners. *Volta Review, 87,* 91–107.

Coon, M.E., Vogelsberg, R.T., & Williams, W. (1981). Effects of classroom public transportation instruction on generalization to the natural environment. *Journal of The Association for Persons with Severe Handicaps, 6,* 46–53.

Cooper, L., Johnson, D.W., Johnson, R., & Wilderson, F. (1980). Effects of cooperative, competitive, and individualistic experiences on interpersonal attraction among heterogeneous peers. *Journal of Social Psychology, 111,* 243–252.

Downing, J., & Bailey, B. (1990). Sharing the responsibility: Using a transdisciplinary team approach to enhance the learning of students with severe disabilities. *Journal of Educational and Psychological Consultation, 1,* 259–278.

Downing, J., Eichinger, J., & Williams, L. (1996). Inclusive education for students with severe disabilities: Comparative views of principals and educators at different levels of implementation. *Remedial and Special Education.* Manuscript submitted for publication.

Dudley-Marling, C. (1994). Struggling readers in the regular classroom: A personal reflection. *Reading Horizons, 34,* 465–487.

Education for All Handicapped Children of 1975, PL 94-142. (August 23, 1975). Title 20, U.S.C. 1400 et seq: *U.S. Statutes at Large, 89,* 773–796.

Eichinger, J. (1990). Goal structure effects on social interaction: Nondisabled and disabled elementary students. *Exceptional Children, 56,* 408–416.

Ellison, L. (1992). Using multiple intelligences to set goals. *Educational Leadership, 50*(2), 69–72.

Folio, M., & Norman, A. (1981). Toward more success in mainstreaming: A peer teacher approach to physical education. *Teaching Exceptional Children, 13*(3), 110–115.

Foster, A., Konar, S., Williamson, S., & Brumbaugh, A. (1991). Connect your curriculum. *Instructor, 101*(2), 24–32.

Gardner, H. (1983). *Frames of mind: The theory of multiple intelligences.* New York: Basic Books.

George, P. (1992). *How to untrack your school.* Alexandria, VA: Association for Supervision and Curriculum Development.

Giangreco, M., Cloninger, C.J., & Iverson, V.S. (1993). *Choosing options and accommodations for children: A guide for planning inclusive education.* Baltimore: Paul H. Brookes Publishing Co.

Giangreco, M., Dennis, R., Cloninger, C., Edelman, S., & Schattman, R. (1993). I've counted Jon: Transformational experiences of teachers educating students with disabilities. *Exceptional Children, 59,* 359–372.

Goldman, J., & Gardner, H. (1989). Multiple paths to educational effectiveness. In D.K. Lipsky & A. Gartner (Eds.), *Beyond separate education: Quality education for all* (pp. 121–139). Baltimore: Paul H. Brookes Publishing Co.

Goodman, K. (1986). *What's whole in whole language.* Portsmouth, NH: Heinemann.

Harry, B., Grenot-Scheyer, M., Smith-Lewis, M., Park, H., Xin, F., & Schwartz, I. (1995). Developing culturally inclusive services for individuals with severe disabilities. *Journal of The Association for Persons with Severe Handicaps, 20*(2), 99–109.

Hoerr, T.R. (1992). How our school applied multiple intelligences theory. *Educational Leadership, 50*(2), 67–68.

Horner, R.H., Bellamy, G.T., & Colvin, G.T. (1984). Responding in the presence of non-trained stimuli: Implications of generalization error patterns. *Journal of The Association for Persons with Severe Handicaps, 9,* 287–295.

Hunt, P., Staub, D., Alwell, M., & Goetz, L. (1994). Achievement by all students within the context of cooperative learning groups. *Journal of The Association for Persons with Severe Handicaps, 19,* 290–301.

Hunter, M. (1992). *How to change to a nongraded school.* Alexandria, VA: Association for Supervision and Curriculum Development.

Jackson, L., Reid, D.K., & Bunsen, T. (1993). Reader response, alternative dreams: A response to Felix Billingsley. *Journal of The Association for Persons with Severe Handicaps, 18*(4), 292–295.

Jacobs, H.H. (1991). The integrated curriculum. *Instructor, 101*(2), 22–23.

Jacobs, H.H., Hannah, J., Manfredonia, W., Percivalle, J., & Gilbert, J.C. (1989). Descriptions of two existing interdisciplinary programs. In H. Jacobs (Ed.), *Interdisciplinary curriculum: Design and implementation* (pp. 39–51). Alexandria, VA: Association for Curriculum and Development.

Johnson, D., & Johnson, R. (1987). *Learning together and alone: Cooperation, competition, and individualization.* Englewood Cliffs, NJ: Prentice Hall.

Johnson, D.W., & Johnson, R. (1982). Effects of cooperative and individualistic instruction of handicapped and nonhandicapped students. *Journal of Social Psychology, 118,* 257–268.

Johnson, D.W., Johnson, R.T., Holubec, E., & Roy, P. (1984). *Circles of learning: Cooperation in the classroom.* Alexandria, VA: Association for Supervision and Curriculum Development.

Johnson, R., Rynders, J., Johnson, D.W., Schmidt, B., & Haider, S. (1979). Producing positive interactions between handicapped and nonhandicapped teenagers through cooperative goal structuring: Implications for mainstreaming. *American Educational Research Journal, 16,* 161–167.

Kohl, F., Moses, L., & Stettner-Eaton, B. (1983). The results of teaching fifth and sixth graders to be instructional trainers with students who are severely handicapped. *Journal of The Association for Persons with Severe Handicaps, 8,* 32–39.

Kovalik, S., & Olsen, K.D. (1992). *Integrated thematic instruction: The model.* Village of Oak Creek, AZ: Susan Kovalik and Associates.

Krechevsky, M. (1991). Project Spectrum: An innovative assessment alternative. *Educational Leadership, 48*(5), 43–48.

Lapp, D., & Flood, J. (1992). *Teaching reading to every child.* New York: Macmillan Publishing Co.

MacLachlan, P. (1985). *Sarah, plain and tall.* New York: Harper & Row.

McHale, S.M., Olley, J.G., Marcus, L.M., & Simeonsson, R.J. (1981). Nonhandicapped peers as tutors for autistic children. *Exceptional Children, 48*(3), 263–265.

Murray, L.B. (1993). Putting it all together at the school level: A principal's perspective. In J.I. Goodlad & T.C. Lovitt (Eds.), *Integrating general and special education* (pp. 175–201). New York: Macmillan Publishing Co.

Olson, L. (1988). Children flourish here: Eight teachers and a theory changed a school world. *Education Week, 7*(1), 18–19.

Palincsar, A.M., Klenk, L., Anderman, E., Parecki, A., & Wilson, A. (1991). Exploring zones of proximal development for literacy acquisition with young children identified as learning disabled. *Exceptionality Education Canada, 1*(3), 105–125.

Perkins, D.N. (1989). Selecting fertile themes for integated learning. In H.H. Jacobs (Ed.), *Interdisciplinary curriculum: Design and implementation* (pp. 67–76). Alexandria, VA: Association for Supervision and Curriculum Development.

Poplin, M., & Stone, S. (1992). Paradigm shifts in instructional strategies: From reductionism to holistic/constructivism. In W. Stainback & S. Stainback (Eds.), *Controversial issues confronting special education: Divergent perspectives* (2nd ed., pp. 153–179). Boston: Allyn & Bacon.

Putnam, J. (Ed.). (1993). *Cooperative learning and strategies for inclusion: Celebrating diversity in the classroom.* Baltimore: Paul H. Brookes Publishing Co.

Putnam, J.W., Rynders, J.E., Johnson, R.T., & Johnson, D.W. (1989). Collaborative skill instruction for promoting positive interactions between mentally handicapped and nonhandicapped children. *Exceptional Children, 55,* 550–557.

Reid, K., Kurkijian, C., & Carruthers, S. (1994). Special education teachers interpret constructivist teaching. *Remedial and Special Education, 15,* 267–280.

Routman, R. (1992). Teach skills with a strategy. *Instructor, 101*(9), 34–37.

Russell, C.H. (1990, September/October). A day in the homeless life. *Utne Reader, 41,* 52–53.

Rynders, J.E., Johnson, R., Johnson, D.W., & Schmidt, B. (1980). Producing positive interaction among Down syndrome and nonhandicapped teenagers through cooperative goal structuring. *American Journal of Mental Deficiency, 85,* 268–283.

Sailor, W. (1989). The educational, social, and vocational integration of students with the most severe disabilities. In D.K. Lipsky & A. Gartner (Eds.), *Beyond separate education: Quality education for all* (pp. 53–74). Baltimore: Paul H. Brookes Publishing Co.

Salisbury, C.L., Gallucci, C., Palombaro, M.M., & Peck, C.A. (1995). Strategies that promote social relations among elementary students with and without severe disabilities in inclusive schools. *Exceptional Children, 62*(2), 125–137.

Santulli, P. (1994, September). *Methods of assessment in education today.* Paper presented at the "Central New York Consortium in Education: A Program for New Faculty," Syracuse.

Shavelson, R.J., Baxter, G., & Pine, J. (1992). Performance assessments, political rhetoric, and measurement reality. *Educational Researcher, 21*(4), 22–27.

Smith-Burke, M.T., Deegan, D., & Jaggar, A.M. (1991). Whole language: A viable alternative for special and remedial education. *Topics in Language Disorders, 11*(3), 58–68.

Tefft-Cousin, P., Weekly, T., & Gerard, J. (1993). The functional uses of language and literacy by students with severe language and learning problems. *Language Arts, 70,* 548–556.

Vygotsky, L.S. (1978). *Mind in society.* Cambridge, MA: Harvard University Press.

Whitmore, K.F., & Goodman, Y.M. (1992). Inside the whole language classroom. *School Administrator, 49*(5), 20–26.

Wolk, S. (1994). Project-based learning: Pursuits with a purpose. *Educational Leadership, 52*(3), 42–45.

York, J., Rainforth, B., & Giangreco, M. (1990). Transdisciplinary teamwork and integrated therapy: Clarifying the misconceptions. *Pediatric Physical Therapy, 2*(2), 73–79.

Chapter 3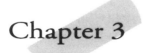

FIRST STEPS

Determining Individual Abilities and How Best to Support Students

June E. Downing and MaryAnn Demchak

This chapter examines key initial educational concerns of inclusive settings across the age range from preschool through high school. For inclusion to be a successful experience for the student with severe sensory and multiple impairments, careful attention must be paid to determining individual student strengths and needs, the type of support needed, the most appropriate people to provide the support, and the most appropriate manner in which to provide it. These topics are addressed as the first steps in an ongoing process for including students with severe sensory and multiple impairments in typical educational classrooms.

DETERMINING STUDENTS' STRENGTHS AND NEEDS

Too often, assessment procedures in the educational system target student deficits, especially when the student has severe sensory and multiple impairments. The focus tends to accentuate what the student cannot do, rather than what he or she *can* do. The emphasis is thus on remediating skill deficits without much regard for whether or not the skills are valued by the individual, family, friends, or community. In addition, many assessment procedures require the student to demonstrate skills out of the normal context in which they are used and at the whim of the assessor. If the student fails an item (i.e., the skill is not demonstrated), little if any consideration is given to the reason for the failure. It is not clear whether the student is actually unable to perform the desired skill, or lacks sufficient motivation at the time, or has no reason to perform the skill when requested. As a result, assessments that use developmental scales and anticipated behavior normed on typical child development tend to provide a very negative

35

picture of a student who has severe sensory and multiple impairments. What is more, the typical approach to assessment does not include any reference to the actual demands of the natural environment or to the preferences of the individual. Therefore, the assessment results provide very limited information regarding what the student actually *needs* to learn and *wants* to learn. Consequently, considerable time can be devoted to determining a student's developmental profile that may have little to do with helping him or her learn what needs to be learned. Students with severe sensory and multiple disabilities, not to mention their teachers and parents, may find this process frustrating and unrewarding.

An alternative assessment process—an ecological-functional assessment that is both observational and activity based—is recommended that does not expect the student with multiple impairments to perform tasks out of context. Rather, such an assessment takes into account the student's motivation and need to perform a given task (Downing, in press), thus enabling a more accurate picture of a student's interests and abilities, as well as areas requiring intervention (Downing & Perino, 1992; Linehan, Brady, & Huang, 1991). This type of assessment leads directly to intervention strategies that occur in natural contexts at natural times of the day and also helps the student acquire the skills needed to be as successful as possible within meaningful activities.

The first step in this assessment process is to identify what the individual can do, enjoys doing, and needs to do as determined by individual and family preferences and environmental demands. This information can be obtained formally by using a number of individual and parent interview formats (see Giangreco, Cloninger, & Iverson, 1993). Alternatively, the information can be collected informally by talking with the student and/or those closest to him or her about present and future aspirations and by observing the student in typical environments. In either case, it is important to remember that this type of assessment is dynamic and ongoing; the information will need to be checked, rechecked, and revised as individual abilities, needs, and desires change. Although this information can be reviewed any time the individual or other team member feels it would be helpful, it should be reviewed at least once a year.

The information obtained from this interaction with the student and family members helps to determine activities that the student likes to do (e.g., play in water) as well as activities that need to be performed (e.g., get dressed in the morning). It also identifies the environments in which these activities will most likely be performed (e.g., operating a computer in the computer lab). The importance of empowering the family and student to play a major role in this assessment process is well supported by the special education field (Giangreco et al., 1993; Turnbull & Turnbull, 1990). The family as a primary source of information to determine a student's strengths, needs, and future aspirations is critical to meaningful assessment and intervention (Schwartz, 1995). Family input helps to determine skills and activities that are important to the student. These activities then become critical areas of immediate intervention if the requisite skills are lacking. Also, general skill areas will emerge as either strengths or needs (e.g., Jill enjoys being with people, but needs a different way to express herself). These general skill areas (e.g., communication, social skills) are required in many activities across different environments. The ecological-functional assessment approach allows these types of skills to be assessed and subsequently targeted for intervention, in the actual settings and activities where needed, rather than assessing the skills in isolation, as they frequently are in a developmental approach.

The second major step in this assessment process is to delineate the typical skills required by the activity. Such a delineation is outlined in Table 3.1. Once these skills are documented (by watching a same-age individual perform the activity), the individual student's performance is evaluated to determine skills that are already in the student's repertoire and those that are lacking. Table 3.2 provides an example of this procedure for an eighth grader in science class. See Downing (in press) for a detailed description of the entire process and accompanying forms. By recording possible reasons why a skill is lacking during the performance (e.g., student cannot hear the teacher direct the class to line up at the door), considerable information can be obtained to aid in the development of the individualized education program (IEP) and the overall intervention process. The more activities that are assessed across different settings and situations, the more accurate and thorough is the understanding of the student's abilities and needs.

Careful documentation of how the student responds under natural conditions in age-appropriate settings (e.g., general education classrooms) provides valuable information on ways the student receives information and acts on it. Part of the ecological-functional assessment process involves determining the natural cues that exist to prompt or guide behavior for all students. Some of these cues are obvious and clearly related to the desired behavior (e.g., the teacher says to put materials away and line up for recess). Other cues are harder. to determine, yet have a definite impact on resulting behavior (e.g., feeling the need to use the restroom serves as a catalyst to raise one's hand and request permission to leave the classroom). Identifying the typical or expected behaviors of various activities and the natural cues that exist to prompt the behaviors helps to pinpoint where a student with severe sensory and multiple disabilities may have difficulty responding as desired. For example, a student who has very limited vision and a severe hearing impairment will not receive the verbal cues from the teacher to prepare for the next activity. This student may also miss the visual cues of classmates putting away their work and getting out needed material for the next activity. This student cannot be expected to follow cues not received. Since there may be no way to facilitate this student's reception of the natural cues in the classroom to perform, adaptations will need to be made to enhance the student's independence and to facilitate ongoing placement with his classmates. The adaptations do not need to be complex and may be as simple as having a classmate tactually and visually cue this student to check his tactile schedule of activities in order to understand the need to make the transition.

Table 3.1. Completing a functional-ecological assessment

Step 1:	Gather information regarding activities the person can do, enjoys doing, and needs to do. Determine priority activities and environments for intervention.
Step 2:	Watch a same-age peer to identify the typical skills required by the activity.
Step 3:	Observe the student to determine the skills that he or she can already do and those that are lacking.
Step 4:	Record possible reasons the student cannot perform a particular skill.
Step 5:	Develop the IEP using the above information.
Step 6:	Implement instruction using natural cues and appropriate adaptations.

Table 3.2.   Discrepancy analysis of science class

Student: Eighth grader (myopic, hearing impaired, moderate mental retardation, short attention span)

Activity: Science class—eighth grade

Peer inventory	Cues	Student performance	Discrepancy	Teach or adapt
1. Enter science class	Time to go to science class	+		
2. Find seat and sit down	Knowledge of seating assignments	—	Not motivated, can't hear well, doesn't understand	Peer cues him to sit down, uses body to guide
3. Listen to teacher for 15 minutes	Teacher giving instruction/ information	—	Not motivated, can't hear well, doesn't understand	Student does adapted work of organizing materials for the assignment; he receives praise for attending to task.
4. Get out materials	Teacher directions	—	Doesn't understand; little motivation	Teacher assistant (TA) directs attention to peers; praises any effort; starts to take out materials to cue him.
5. Perform assignment within allotted time (come up with list of rules that differentiate one species from another)	Assignment/ knowledge of teacher expectations	—	Has difficult time staying on task	Teacher uses colorful pictures of different species and pairs with a peer. He sorts pictures into *same* and *different* piles. TA uses timer and praises for 5 min. of on-task behavior. He takes a short break, then returns to task. Peer writes rules for him.
6. Put away materials	Teacher directions/ time	—	Doesn't hear teacher or understand; dislikes change	TA directs attention to his peers; shows him pictorial schedule of next class; praises any effort; starts to put materials away as a cue to him.
7. Get ready to go to next class	End of science class	—	Doesn't like next class	Teacher pairs him up with other students going to class. TA allows a water fountain break before class.

Note: Each of the steps in this activity can be analyzed further into smaller skills to facilitate learning and identify progress. An example of this further analysis can be found in Figure 3.2.

It is important to obtain as much information as possible regarding how a student performs during various activities and responds to the natural cues that exist for all students, in order to help clarify the most effective way that the student learns. Analyzing several activities and documenting the student's performance in these activities will help to determine areas in which adaptations in materials and instruction will be necessary. Information from this assessment can contribute significantly to the development of the IEP and to the manner in which IEP goals and objectives are met. In addition, cumulative information from this assessment procedure becomes part of a portfolio on the student, providing future teachers and other team members with an important tool to support the student's continued progress.

DEVELOPING THE IEP

The IEP should be developed by a team composed of family members as well as the various professionals and paraprofessionals who work with the student with severe sensory and multiple disabilities. Professionals from numerous disciplines could potentially be on the team: teacher(s), vision specialist, hearing specialist/audiologist, occupational and physical therapists, orientation and mobility specialist, communication specialist, adapted physical educator, and others. Paraprofessionals involved in the classroom are also crucial team members, who will frequently be involved in implementing instruction or overseeing various activities. Therefore, they should be active, contributing members.

As mentioned previously, it is imperative that family members be active participants on the educational team. It is insufficient to simply present the family with a completed IEP for their approval. Rather, family members can 1) provide information during the assessment process, 2) identify priorities, 3) help develop goals and objectives, 4) provide input regarding how and where instruction will occur, and 5) assist with carryover to the home. However, it is essential to remember that degree of family involvement will vary from family to family. Families should be provided with choices regarding the type and amount of involvement that they wish to have in the IEP process.

IEP goals and objectives are derived from the results of the assessment process (i.e., those skills needed to complete an activity that are apparently lacking for a specific student). IEP objectives will not target all missing skills, but only those considered most critical for more independent performance in the most meaningful activities and that have a high probability of being attained. A few quality objectives that target a number of critical skills within valued and frequently engaged-in activities are recommended over numerous objectives that target skills in isolation from any recognizable purpose. For example, an objective such as "Sally will make better use of her vision" would be replaced by what Sally needs to do with her vision to perform more efficiently (e.g., "During computer lab, Sally will follow the cursor and make appropriate choices from the software program in 18 of 20 opportunities"). IEP objectives do not target isolated skills written by individual specialists on the team (e.g., vision specialists, hearing specialists, occupational therapists). Instead, these team members, along with family members, pool their expertise to create one IEP that includes objectives that are activity-based and reflect the numerous skills required by the activity.

Table 3.3 provides samples of IEP goals and objectives for students having severe sensory and multiple impairments.

BLENDING INDIVIDUAL NEEDS WITH GENERAL EDUCATION CURRICULUM

Once individual strengths and needs have been identified and documented in the form of IEP goals and objectives, the next step is to implement the program. Because IEP goals and objectives usually target typical skills required to perform similarly to others of the same age, much of the ecological-functional assessment process naturally takes place within typical classrooms and other settings frequented by same-age students. Information obtained from such assessment has a direct relationship to the classroom situation. There is no need to interpret developmental scores to determine what they mean in terms of the daily curriculum in the classroom. (Other portions of this assessment will occur at home and in the community, but for the purposes of this book, the focus remains on classroom and school settings.)

In the course of the assessment process, it may emerge that the structure and dynamics of the classroom and the needs of the student appear to be at odds with one another. For instance, a classroom may be very noisy and unstructured,

Table 3.3. Examples of IEP goals and objectives for individual students with severe sensory and multiple disabilities

Goal	Objective
To develop friendships	When approached by a peer, Jeff will not react by hitting, but will take the arm offered him for sighted guidance and walk cooperatively with classmate from the playground back to class once a day for 3 weeks.
To improve independence in mobility	Following each class period, when asked by a peer using sign "WHERE NOW?" Karen will look at the picture schedule, point to the next activity, then proceed without stopping until she reaches the correct destination for each scheduled period for 5 consecutive days.
To develop social skills necessary for friendships	During third-grade music class, Robin will look at a peer when the peer says her name, extend her hand, and grasp the instrument or book given her by her peer in 9 out of 10 consecutive opportunities.
To enhance decision-making skills in daily activities	During lunch, Casey will look at each food item before indicating her choice to a peer by reaching for one item in 9 out of 10 opportunities.
To develop skills needed for interactive play	While shooting baskets with classmates, Jenny will look toward a peer who calls her name, extend her arms to try to catch the ball, and throw the ball at the basket or to another classmate in 10 consecutive attempts.
To develop basic social interaction skills	At the beginning of each new class period, when a peer or teacher greets Robert by name, Robert will turn toward the person in 9 out of 10 opportunities.
To acquire mathematics skills needed for community living	During seventh-grade pre-algebra class, Frank will successfully complete 8 of 10 word problems involving purchases (determining sufficient funds to purchase items) for 5 consecutive mathematics classes.
To enhance expressive communication skills	During creative writing period, Susan will spontaneously produce a two-word signed phrase describing a picture or photograph for 10 consecutive pictures that comprise her journal.

which tends to create problems for the student who responds better to quiet and structure. Physical considerations also may arise. A small classroom with limited access may be difficult for a student using a wheelchair or having medical equipment needs. Students who have limited or no vision may perform more efficiently under conditions where they can maneuver easily without fear of tripping or being hurt and where they can count on materials being in a specific place. Identifying the strengths and limitations of various classroom environments represents a critical component of the ecological process. Factors to consider include teacher style, organization, room layout, accessibility, noise level, lighting, acoustics, and other similar variables. In many schools, options for students allow a match between student strengths and needs and the characteristics of the classroom. There may be two or three classrooms and teachers at a specific grade level, one of which may represent a better match than the others. At the middle and high school levels, the variety of class options for students eases the difficulty of finding the best match between student needs and learning environments. However, even when no options exist (e.g., one fifth-grade class), certain modifications can be made to facilitate learning. For instance, the student may need to be seated close to the classroom teacher, have access to better lighting, and use an FM system to gain more auditory information. The team works together to creatively enhance the learning environment to meet the unique needs of a given student. Accommodations should not be overly extensive or interfere with the learning of the other students. In fact, accommodations often can enhance everyone's learning ability. For example, better lighting and contrast may make it easier for all students to view information on a chalkboard.

The important factor to remember when analyzing a typical classroom for a particular student is to avoid focusing mostly on deterrents (e.g., teacher doesn't like other adults in the room, is strict, likes quiet, has high expectations). Rather, the emphasis should be on what the teacher is doing that could be supportive (e.g., teacher encourages students to problem solve, has computers in the room and uses them frequently, has interactive materials and activities, and has high expectations). Concentrating on potentially negative aspects will only produce barriers and will thwart inclusive education. Focusing on strengths and skills allows for the development of building blocks for a firm inclusive foundation.

WORKING ON IEP OBJECTIVES IN TYPICAL CLASSROOMS

The IEP does not address all activities performed in a typical classroom on a daily basis; however, many skills targeted in IEP objectives are likely required throughout the day in a range of ongoing activities. The team needs to identify the various opportunities to practice targeted IEP skills across different functional activities. An activity/IEP objective analysis form developed by Fox and Williams (1991) is recommended for this purpose. An adaptation of this form is provided in Figure 3.1 for a student with severe sensory and multiple disabilities. Obviously, inclusion is not something that is done "after" IEP objectives have been worked on in another setting. Rather, full-time participation in typical activities and classrooms with classmates who do not have disabilities provides the necessary environment in which to meet these objectives. The importance of this full-time participation is particularly clear when the outcomes desired for

Activity/IEP Objective Matrix

Student   Jennifer
Grade   5th
School Year   1994-95
Teachers   Mrs. Hill (5th grade), Ms. Lott (Support)

Activities/Subjects → IEP Objectives ↓	Social Studies	Math	Reading	PE	Lunch
To recognize pictures for expressive communication purposes	— Use daily schedule to get out book — Match pictures related to social studies	— Determine story problem for peers by matching same pictures	— Answer questions by pointing to pictures	— Choose equipment, using photographs — Choose partner using school photographs	— Use pictures to request type of milk from cafeteria person — Point to pictures to converse with peers
To follow directions quickly	— Watch peers get out materials and follow their lead — Sequence pictorial cards in order — Put away materials and get ready for next subject	— Watch peers get out materials and follow their lead — Work on math skills as instructed — Change activity when directed	— Watch peers get out materials and follow their lead — Find appropriate page in book — Answer questions by pointing — Put away materials and get ready for next subject	— Line up for PE — Move to area on floor by PE teacher — Follow teacher and group	— Line up for lunch with class — Go to lunch room — Stay at table until dismissed
To interact with peers in positive way	— Sit with classmate — Do not destroy peer's work — Pass out materials	— Sit with classmate — Do not destroy peer's work — Pass out materials	— Sit with classmate — Choose book to read from peer — Respond to peer's questions	— Respond to peers when they initiate — Share equipment — Clap for them when they do well	— Respond to peers when they initiate — Initiate topics using schedule and magazine — Respond to peer's questions

To make decisions	— Decide who will read to her — Request help when needed — Pick appropriate pictures from 3 pictures based on question	— Decide which math activities to do — Decide which manipulatives to use: 1st, 2nd, 3rd	— Choose book to read — Choose peer to read with — Choose place to read	— Decide which 2 of 3 exercises to do and in what order	— Choose milk — Choose person to sit next to — Choose where to go when finished eating and with whom
To increase physical strength and endurance	— Sit at desk with good posture for 10 min. — Squeeze glue to get picture on paper	— Sit at desk with good posture for 10 min.	— Sit at desk with good posture for 10 min. — Hold book upright for peer to read.	— Add 1 more exercise at warmup — Exercise each week — Hold door open for class	— Open milk carton — Carry own tray to table
To work independently	— Stay on task without adult nearby for 10 min. — Raise hand to get help	— Stay on task without adult nearby for 10 min. — Raise hand to get help	— Stay on task without adult nearby for 10 min. — Raise hand to get help	— Stay on task without adult nearby for 10 min. — Start each exercise/activity on own — Raise hand to get help	— Stay on task without adult nearby for 10 min. — Obtain milk with peer support — Eat meal with no prompts

Figure 3.1. Adapted activity/IEP objectives form for student with severe sensory and multiple disabilities.

students include belonging to a social group and working collaboratively with peers (Schnorr, 1990).

This analysis of opportunities for learning (i.e., examining typical classroom activities) according to targeted IEP objectives for a given student can occur across the age range from preschool through high school. Once opportunities to target needed skills have been identified by the team, each activity will need to be carefully analyzed to determine the most effective way for learning to occur for a given student. The team will need to determine the most appropriate physical position for the student, the most effective way for the student to participate, and the most efficient means of providing needed support. Table 3.4 lists specific questions that need to be addressed by the team to ensure the successful inclusion of students with severe sensory and multiple impairments.

DETERMINING INDIVIDUAL LEARNING STYLES

Although students targeted in this book have at least one sensory limitation in addition to other multiple disabilities, each has a distinct and unique way of learning. Some children, for instance, will acquire considerable information via the auditory mode even though they have a moderate hearing loss, whereas others will not find this type of information helpful; in fact, it may even prove confusing. Some students will make considerable use of visual information, despite the fact that they have a severe visual impairment, whereas others will not be able to process any visual information because both eyes have been enucleated (surgically removed). For some students, encouraging tactile exploration of information will be very informative, whereas others, especially those with a physical impairment such as cerebral palsy that affects all limbs, may not find this information beneficial. Many students with multiple disabilities may need to actively engage in an activity in order to understand it. These students learn by doing, especially if the distance senses of vision and hearing do not provide the

Table 3.4.   Questions for educational team to ask to accommodate inclusive learning

1. What is the best position for the student?
   - Where are the other students? On the floor? At desks? Standing at tables?
   - What allows the student the greatest movement needed for the activity? The best vision? The best hearing?
   - Is the student physically isolated or right with the others?

2. Is the student able to obtain information from the teacher?
   - What is the learning style of the student?
   - Does the student learn in an auditory, visual, tactile and/or kinesthetic way? Is the necessary information available in the activity?
   - Can additional information be added to an activity to make it more understandable to a given student?

3. How can the student participate?
   - Can the student raise his or her hand to gain attention? Is another way possible (e.g., switch-activated voice output mode)?
   - Can the student respond verbally to questions? If not, can he or she be given choices of objects and/or pictures as responses?
   - Can the student engage in movement related to the activity? (e.g., act out a skit, pass items, get out and put away materials)?
   - How does participation in each activity support the student's IEP objectives?

4. Who can assist in the learning process?
   - Can other students help? Teachers? Support staff? Volunteers? Older students?

needed information. Still other students, owing to their severe physical impairments, may not be able to fully engage in an activity and will need other ways to learn.

There is no formula to determine the mode(s) that best help a given student to learn. Some students do better with a certain learning mode in one situation and need a different strategy for another situation. Often, the type of activity has a direct bearing on how best to teach a student. For example, learning to bring food to one's mouth to eat may be best taught by having the student *do* it. On the other hand, to learn how to get the teacher's attention, watching other students raise their hands may be the most powerful way to teach this behavior. Providing students with multiple ways of obtaining the necessary information (whether visual, auditory, kinesthetic, or tactile) and drawing their attention to the most important aspects of the lesson may be the most effective strategies. This approach not only has merit for students who are having difficulty obtaining information via one mode (usually the visual mode) but also could obviously benefit many students without disabilities. The focus of the intervention should be on ensuring that the student understands what is expected (through a variety of sources) and then assisting the student to use whatever information is available to learn the steps of the activity. When students remove their hearing aids or throw away their glasses, it may signal to teachers that the information obtained via these modes may not be helpful or that it may be overwhelming (e.g., the student who just begins wearing glasses to correct a severe vision impairment and who must learn to use vision). Alternative approaches to teaching can then be considered. The question to ask is whether the child needs to see or hear to perform as expected or whether the child can bypass these sensory modes and still learn. In other instances, the child may gradually learn to use the information obtained through hearing or vision. The emphasis is on helping the child to be most successful, not on conforming to a specified style of learning.

DIRECT INSTRUCTION

It is essential that all students—with and without disabilities—receive direct instruction and are taught in systematic ways. Instructors of typical students teach reading, writing, spelling, and mathematics systematically by breaking down targeted activities into steps and teaching in a sequential fashion. Similarly, a student with severe sensory and multiple disabilities must be taught in an organized fashion. Some students with severe impairments may not be learning the academics targeted for their peers. Other students with severe sensory and multiple impairments will be learning academics but may be taught in a different manner from that used with their typical peers owing to different learning styles. Regardless of the activities and targeted skills, all students need to be taught in a planned manner.

For example, students without disabilities are frequently taught using procedures that have the same theoretical basis as those used with students with disabilities. A student may be taught to spell the word *receive* through a process of gradually providing greater degrees of assistance. First, the student may simply be told to "remember the rule." If the student is still unable to spell the word, an additional prompt may be given to "remember *i* before *e*." If the student is still having difficulty, the final prompt may be given: "Remember the rule is *i* before *e* except after *c*." The student is systematically given greater assistance until the task is performed correctly. Similarly, students are provided with corrective feedback when errors are made, as well as with reinforcement for correct or improved responses.

Students with severe sensory and multiple disabilities are also taught through prompts, corrective feedback, and reinforcement. However, the prompts used may look a bit different from those used with students without disabilities because of the need to consider the student's disabilities and unique learning styles. Teaching procedures may be used to teach the student with severe impairments alternative skills from those targeted for other students. For example, a student learning to use a switch as a means of participating in an activity will initially need to be taught to activate the switch. The student might first be prompted to activate the switch by having someone tap the switch to draw the student's attention to it. If the student does not respond, a teacher or peer might tap the student's hand. If another prompt is needed, someone might provide minimal physical assistance to aid the student in turning on the switch. The prompts provide increasing degrees of assistance until the student is able to complete the targeted skill (similar to providing increasing assistance to spell *receive*). Simply including a student with severe sensory and multiple disabilities in a typical classroom does not mean that instruction of that student no longer needs to occur. If an activity is important enough to target in the IEP as an objective, it is important enough to teach systematically.

The effectiveness of systematically instructing students with severe and multiple impairments is well documented (Snell & Brown, 1993). All students learn skills, and subsequently maintain those skills, through an instructional paradigm that includes 1) procedures (e.g., response prompts) designed to make it more likely that a targeted behavior will occur (i.e., the student initially learns a behavior or attempts to more fluently perform the behavior) and 2) procedures that follow correct and incorrect responses (e.g., reinforcement and corrective feedback, respectively). These procedures are briefly described here. Resources that examine the procedures in greater detail are listed in Appendix C, at the end of this book.

Prompting Behaviors to Occur

Both students with and without disabilities can learn many skills through shaping procedures that are frequently used in conjunction with teaching prompts. Shaping initially involves accepting approximations of the targeted behavior that ultimately lead to the desired behavior. For example, with a young child who is learning to sign, the teacher may accept approximations of initial signs to teach the child that signing is valuable and meaningful. Eventually, the child will be expected to produce the signs accurately. Shaping procedures occur across classrooms, grade levels, and curricular activities. Teachers teach all students to read, write, complete art products, use computers, and numerous other activities by shaping behavior. For example, teachers will frequently accept "invented spellings" that approximate correct spellings from beginning writers prior to expecting those students to spell accurately. Sometimes this shaping procedure occurs quickly for students, and at other times the process is quite lengthy, with students requiring many opportunities to practice the skill. Frequently, shaping procedures are used in tandem with teaching prompts that are designed to increase the likelihood that the target behavior will occur.

All teachers typically use a variety of teaching prompts: verbal instructions, modeling or demonstrations, gestures, pictorial or other visual cues, and various degrees of physical assistance. Regardless of the prompt used, it is essential to remember that the prompt should be systematically faded, or removed, so that the student is cued by the natural cues in the setting (e.g., the student is cued by occurrences in the classroom to activate a switch, rather than by someone providing physical guidance). Demchak (1990) described several different prompting techniques that have been successfully employed with students having a wide range of disabilities: increasing assistance, decreasing assistance, graduated guidance, as well as progressive and constant time delay. Wolery, Ault, and Doyle (1992) provided concrete guidelines for using these and other procedures to teach various skills and activities. Table 3.5 briefly explains each prompting procedure. In addition to following the guidelines provided by Demchak (1990) and Wolery et al. (1992) regarding how prompts can be systematically removed, it is important that the student have sufficient time to respond after being given any prompt. Providing a delay before giving another prompt avoids overmanipulation and also allows the student time to determine what behavior is expected or needed so that he or she can initiate a response. Providing sufficient response time (i.e., several seconds) should be started early in the teaching process to increase the likelihood that the student will respond to natural cues rather than contrived prompts.

Variations of prompting procedures may be necessary for students who have difficulty receiving visual and/or auditory information or difficulty engaging in physical movements. Deciding which teaching prompts and cues to use with the student with severe sensory and multiple disabilities will depend on how the student best learns and the particular aspects of a given task (e.g., what skills are required). For example, learning to run a software program usually relies on vision, with the learner watching the teacher activate the machine, insert the disk,

Table 3.5.   Procedures for prompting students with severe disabilities

Increasing assistance	Consists of a hierarchy of prompts arranged in order from presumed least informative to most informative assistance for a given activity; also known as system of least prompts or least-to-most prompts
Decreasing assistance	Begins with the most informative prompt needed for the individual to respond in a given activity and moves through a specified hierarchy to less-informative levels of assistance; also known as most-to-least prompts
Graduated guidance	Degrees of physical assistance provided from most intrusive to least intrusive, with amount of assistance varying within a teaching instance as the student responds (i.e., teacher makes moment-to-moment decisions regarding amount of assistance) and if appropriate
Constant time delay	Initial teaching opportunities provided at a 0-second delay, with all subsequent teaching trials provided at a predetermined delay interval (e.g., 5 seconds)
Progressive time delay	Initial teaching opportunities provided at a 0-second delay, with the amount of time between the natural cue and the prompt gradually increased (e.g., increments of 2 seconds) to allow the student to respond

and push different keys. If the student does not have sufficient vision to learn the skills involved, then the teacher will have to adapt to a tactile mode with auditory cues. The student will feel for the disk-insert slot and may use small tactile markers (e.g., hardened glue dots on a sticky backing) to identify the important keys to push. Auditory cues (e.g., "first . . . , then . . . ") may help the student acquire the appropriate sequence of steps. Obviously, chronological age–appropriate software programs that provide auditory information/feedback will be critical for this student.

Modeling the desired response is one of the most commonly used ways to teach a new skill. Modeling can be done verbally, as when teaching a foreign language; visually, as when teaching a matching task or tumbling skill; and both visually and auditorily, as in teaching reading. The natural tendency to rely on vision is obvious, with teachers often giving cues such as "eyes on me," "watch me," or "do it like this." A severe visual impairment can put a student at a serious disadvantage in a classroom that relies heavily on students imitating modeled behavior. In addition, if the child also has a severe auditory impairment that prevents him or her from hearing the cue to watch the model, then the child may completely miss general interactions as well as specific instructional information.

Many children with a severe sensory and multiple disability can use their vision for learning; however, they may need the demonstration or relevant stimulus to be brought closer and made clearer/brighter. They may also need to have their attention specifically directed to the stimulus, and they will require sufficient time to assimilate the available information. This student can still benefit from this teaching technique. However, students who do not have sufficient vision to benefit from this approach will need to receive information in another way. A tactile model may need to be provided, so that the information can be received through touch. For instance, in physical education class, a student who is blind (or deaf-blind) and is being taught softball will need to use a batting tee as well as time to explore the tee tactually (feel the tee and the ball on it). This student should then be allowed to stand behind a batter who demonstrates the swing needed to hit the ball. The student needs to feel the bat and that the ball is no longer on the tee. The student's hands can be placed over the batter's hands to gain an understanding of the movement involved. To teach a new skill, considerable tactile modeling may be necessary (done on the sidelines with help from peers who are not currently batting). Once the student understands the expectation, just feeling the batting tee, being given the bat, and being appropriately placed to best make contact probably will suffice. A runner can then offer to be a sighted guide for this student around the bases.

Although students with severe and multiple disabilities are often physically manipulated through activities, greater control over the learning process and less resistance may develop if at an early age the child can be encouraged to put his or her hands on the instructor's and obtain information that way. This technique of modeling allows the student more control over the situation and may be particularly beneficial for students who display tactile defensiveness. It also encourages taking initiative in the learning process and actively making use of the sense of touch to compensate for the loss in visual and auditory input.

Other examples of tactile modeling involve giving the student a model to examine before expecting the behavior. For instance, if students are given an assignment to write a book, the student without visual or auditory access will need to feel a book with tactile illustrations in it. He or she will need to examine the number of pages, binding, and cover before being expected to relate the materials he or she has been given to the expected final product.

A multimodal approach to prompting is generally recommended for all students, so that individual learning styles can be addressed within the same lesson (Sobsey & Wolf-Schein, 1991). Recognizing the natural cues for any given activity can help teachers determine the most appropriate prompts to use (i.e., those that attract the student's attention to the natural cues, if at all possible). The previously discussed modifications to teaching prompts also provide considerable information as to the teacher's expectations for performance.

Students with access to limited sensory information as well as difficulty processing that information and/or acting on it typically require numerous opportunities to learn most skills. Breaking down steps into small skills as needed by the individual student, and consistently applying specific prompting strategies across the teaching staff, are recommended practices (Brown & Snell, 1993; Orelove & Sobsey, 1991). Figure 3.2 provides an example of a step in an activity

Student: _____

Activity: Science

Step 5 (of Table 3.2):   Perform assignment within allotted time

Task Analysis for Student	9/10	9/11	9/12	9/13	9/14	Teach/Adapt
• Takes picture given to him						Move picture across visual field to gain attention; hold in palm close to him; wait; praise any approximation.
• Scans materials to find picture that is similar to simple picture						Slowly model desired behavior at least three times; draw attention to pictures; wait; use flashlight to cue him to start scanning; praise attention to pictures.
• Correctly sorts similar pictures of animals						Reduce number of pictorial choices; keep choices very different so right match is obvious; give immediate feedback.
• Responds in an appropriate way to feedback (whether right or wrong); does not get angry and continues to work						Model correct match; physically guide him to make correct match; praise for staying on task, not just for doing it correctly; go to next item.
• Works for at least 5 min. without leaving task or becoming upset						Let him use timer — he sets; let him take break for 2 min. if he requests one using the request card; praise for staying on task.

Note: Could be any science activity — planets, plants, animals, archeology, and so on. Items/pictures would change with topic.

Figure 3.2.   Task analysis of one step in eighth-grade science activity for student with myopia, hearing impairment, mental retardation, and short attention span.

that has been broken down into smaller skills to better identify student strengths and needs and document progress in learning the step (the analyzed step is taken from the eighth-grade science activity featured in Table 3.2). In Figure 3.2, step 5 (performing the assignment within the allotted time) is analyzed specifically for the eighth grader who was myopic (nearsighted), had a hearing impairment, had moderate mental retardation, and had a short attention span. For each skill required to do this step, specific teaching prompts are provided and space is available to collect data on the student's performance. Clearly identifying the desired skills of this step in the activity as well as specific strategies to shape the behavior help all instructional staff be more consistent in their teaching approach. The overall goal in teaching new behavior is to have the student recognize when the behavior is needed or expected across natural environments, and to attempt the new behavior at that time. Once demonstrated (even if only partially), the behavior can be guided into a closer approximation and then reinforced so that it will be strengthened over time.

These prompting techniques are not only beneficial for students with disabilities, but hold merit for students without disabilities as well. Perhaps the most critical factor to remember about any instructional technique with any student is that it be provided in a manner that is positive, respectful to the learner, consistent across teachers and activities, and efficient.

Responding to Correct Behaviors: Reinforcement

The purpose of reinforcement is to strengthen desired or targeted behaviors by presenting a consequence contingent on the occurrence of the behavior. Ultimately, the only way that teachers know whether or not a particular reward is reinforcing is by its effect on behavior. If a consequence is a reinforcer, then the future probability of the targeted behavior increases (i.e., the behavior is strengthened). If the behavior does not increase, the consequence that the teacher chose to use was not actually a reinforcing one, even though the consequence may have been viewed as pleasant by the student.

Providing reinforcers to the student with severe sensory and multiple disabilities can be difficult, depending on how the student receives information. Usually teachers let students know when their efforts have been successful by giving a smile, nod, or verbal praise. Some students with sufficient vision or hearing can receive and respond positively to such feedback. Other students may require a pat on the back in addition, to understand that they have done as expected. If the student is self-motivated to engage in the activity, then the successful completion of the activity may provide sufficient feedback.

Considerable information exists on using reinforcement when teaching, especially when tasks are not inherently motivating (Haney & Falvey, 1989; Kennedy & Haring, 1993; Orelove & Sobsey, 1991). This information is not repeated here, with the exception of a few critical points concerning reinforcement.

Reinforcement is unique to the individual. Reinforcers are idiosyncratic in that what is effective for one person may be ineffective for another. Even primary reinforcers, such as food and drink, hold unequal value per individual. Discovering what reinforces a given student can require considerable investigative work involving the individual, family members, friends, and professionals on the team. This precise determination is especially necessary when the individual cannot communicate preferences or desires clearly and/or may have become comfortable interacting with a limited number of things to the exclusion of other possibilities. One child may be very motivated by looking at motorcycle pictures, whereas another child may do almost anything for a luggage tag. Assuming that all students are motivated by the same rewards would be a faulty premise. Furthermore, the rate at which reinforcement is required will vary from individual to individual and from activity to activity. That is, one student may require more frequent reinforcement than another student. The art of teaching requires that the student not receive too much or too little of the needed reinforcement to maintain successful performance.

Reinforcement is dynamic. The perceived value of reinforcers can change from moment to moment for the person receiving the reinforcer. Thus, what is effective today may be ineffective tomorrow. In some instances, what is initially effective early in a school day may no longer be effective later in the day. This dynamic nature of reinforcement can frustrate both parent and teacher who may be struggling to motivate a given child. However, this aspect of reinforcement is true for all of us. Our interests change and we can quickly become satiated with one consequence if it is readily available. In addition, other environmental factors (both internal and external) may play a major role in determining the strength of a given reinforcer. For example, the child may not feel well, causing any reinforcer to lose its effectiveness. In addition, other students in the classroom may have access to something new and interesting that distracts the child and reduces the power of the reinforcer.

Reinforcers must be thinned. The overall goal of education is to teach children to learn how to learn and to be motivated to learn. Therefore, it is essential that the teacher move from providing external, contrived reinforcers to natural reinforcers or self-reinforcement. The goal of self-motivation across different activities is a valuable aspiration for all children. However, self-motivation may not always be possible. Even though many adults may enjoy their careers, few would work for no pay. There may always be situations requiring that external reinforcement be present. The goal may be for the student to learn to work for deferred gratification rather than an immediate reward, so as not to interrupt efficiency of performance. Again, the teacher's skill is called upon to provide sufficient reinforcement to acquire and maintain the skill, but not so much reinforcement as to create dependency on immediate rewards and thus reduce proficiency. Carefully monitoring students' progress under different reinforcement conditions (e.g., type of reinforcer and frequency of reinforcement) and thinning as quickly as possible to natural reinforcers (e.g., natural teacher praise, feeling good about engaging in or completing the task) will help to determine the most effective procedure for each student.

Responding to Incorrect Behaviors: Corrective Feedback

When the student provides an incorrect response, corrective feedback is needed so that the behavior can be changed as targeted. Providing such feedback should be immediate so that the student can distinguish between desired and ineffective behavior. In addition, if the student has not produced the desired response, continuing the task incorrectly can further confuse him or her and interfere with efficient learning.

Teachers inform students of errors by verbally stating that they made a mistake, asking them to try again, pointing out where the mistake occurred, or providing the correct response. For some students with severe sensory and multiple impairments, corrective feedback can be very confusing. It may seem like another additional step in a sequence of steps that has already confused them. Care must be taken to quickly intercede to shape the desired response before inappropriate responses are learned. For example, Sharon is learning to affix her name on her tactile art work using braille labels of her name. She gets the sheet of braille labels of her name and removes one from the sticky backing. However, she tries to put her name on the tactile art work where it will not stick well, rather than on the paper holding the artwork. Her teacher prevents her from making this mistake by blocking the action and guiding Sharon's hands to the edge of the paper instead.

ADAPTATIONS

In addition to a variety of teaching strategies, adaptations play a major role in helping students acquire valuable skills. The chapters following provide multiple examples of adaptations used across the age span and in different situations. This section gives general information about adaptations that can be helpful for the student with severe sensory and multiple disabilities. Five categories of adaptations are presented: 1) adaptations for vision impairments, 2) adaptations for hearing impairments, 3) tactile adaptations, 4) adaptations for physical disabilities, and 5) adapted activities.

Adaptations for Vision Impairments

Specific adaptations for children with visual impairments are individualized according to the child's particular needs and visual condition. Adaptations can assist children with visual impairments to use any residual vision that they have more effectively and efficiently. (For detailed information on teaching children with visual impairments to use their vision, the reader is referred to Downing & Bailey, 1990, 1993.) Adaptations also accommodate the needs of the student with no vision by recognizing the potential need to move safely in a given environment, organize materials for easy recovery, and have sufficient room for tactile materials.

In general, it is important to remember that children with multiple and sensory impairments should be positioned appropriately prior to making visual demands. If children are not positioned appropriately, their energy is more likely to go toward maintaining upright posture, balance, and so forth, than toward using their vision efficiently (Levack, 1994). As with motor skills, it is recommended that a team member, or consultant to the educational team, have expertise in the vision area in order to make pertinent recommendations regarding specific adaptations for a particular child. Several resources exist for assisting teachers to make adaptations for students with visual impairments, as well as those with multiple disabilities, including: Bailey and Downing, 1994; Kelley, Davidson, & Sanspree, 1993; Levack, 1994. According to Levack (1994), adaptations can be made in the following areas: in color and contrast; in illumination; in space and illumination; in size and distance; with vision devices; in visual cues; in materials; in the immediate work space; and in the larger environment.

Frequently, several modifications can be combined to meet the needs of a particular student. Again, the adaptations are specific to the student's needs and to his or her particular impairment. In specifying adaptations it is important to be knowledgeable as to the type of visual impairment. For example, the recommendations following may be relevant for a preschooler with a cortical visual impairment. Cortical visual impairment refers to damage that has occurred to the visual cortex or visual pathways (i.e., there is difficulty processing visual information), rather than to the eye structure. Such impairment can result in fluctuating vision, inattentiveness to visual cues, preference of touch to vision in exploring objects, greater peripheral than central vision, and difficulty with visual clutter (e.g., with figure-ground discrimination or seeing objects placed close together) (Levack, 1994). Some adaptations that are specific to Seth, a child with such impairment, are as follows:

1. When Seth is in his wheelchair, he frequently uses a tray that attaches to the chair. However, it is possible to see through the tray, and it becomes difficult for Seth to discriminate visually what is on the tray versus what is underneath the tray. Therefore, the educational team covered the underside of the tray with black, nonglare paper to reduce visual clutter.

2. With cortical visual impairment, color vision is typically intact, and it was observed that Seth generally responds well to items that are bright, fluorescent colors. Thus, toys (e.g., balls, balloons, puppets, blocks), play dough and clay, paints, construction paper, and other materials that are brightly colored were used.

3. One of Seth's educational goals targets making a choice between two objects or items during free play, snack, or any other appropriate time. To enhance the likelihood that Seth can visually discriminate between the two choices, it was recommended that the items used for choice making be placed several inches apart from each other. Seth was then taught to look at first one choice and then the other (by moving first one then another to trigger the use of his peripheral vision) before selecting his preference.

4. Seth is also encouraged to touch each of the choices, as a supplement to using his vision to explore options.

5. At snacktime, Seth sits in a bolster chair at a table with other children. A blue nonslip placemat is used to provide a contrasting background on the table to assist Seth in using his vision to locate snack items as well as to keep them from sliding on the table.

6. Seth has more difficulty using his vision if he is tired, if there are numerous extraneous distractions (e.g., noise), or if he is positioned inappropriately. The team tries to keep this in mind before placing demands on Seth to perform visually.

7. Finally, Seth appears to be unusually sensitive to bright sunlight during outside play. Therefore, his family provided both sunglasses and a hat with a visor so that Seth could choose, on a daily basis, which he would wear for outside play.

Although adaptations of this nature may be made specifically to benefit a student having visual difficulties, they also can benefit other students. Students without disabilities may find that visual adaptations (e.g., greater contrast, brighter colors, movement) are more interesting. Again, such adaptations can serve to bring children together, which is another goal of inclusive education.

Adaptations for Hearing Impairments

For many students with severe sensory and multiple disabilities, teachers will also need to modify instructional strategies or environmental arrangements to facilitate hearing and listening skills. For example, part of the curriculum may incorporate teaching basic signs to everyone in the classroom. All of the students and adults may have name signs as well as learn to use basic signing vocabulary. These name signs, plus fingerspelling the alphabet and basic vocabulary, could be incorporated into classroom routines and activities (e.g., spelling practice, attendance, requesting permission to go to the restroom).

In addition, adults and students in the setting will likely need to attend to the manner in which they interact with the student who has a hearing impairment. Students who have hearing impairments may need to be specifically prompted to attend to peers and adults who are speaking to them. Everyone should be encouraged to speak to the student at a normal rate; it is not necessary to speak unusually slowly. Communication partners should speak at normal levels at close range rather than attempting to talk to the student from across the room. Keeping mouths clear of obstructions (e.g., hands away) and facing directly toward the student also improve reception. The student will be better able to use residual hearing when the environment is quiet (i.e., background noise is minimized) rather than noisy. Therefore, adaptations to reduce noise levels by carpeting floors or using acoustic-enhancing ceiling tiles or wall panels are recommended (Prickett & Welch, 1995). Preferential seating (e.g., sitting closer to the teacher) also can help to increase volume and decrease background distractions. It may be easier for students with sensory and multiple disabilities to follow instructions when they are given verbally as well as paired with visual or concrete cues and/or natural gestures.

For students with the ability to understand some auditory information, assistive listening devices may be of value. The team audiologist can provide information concerning the types of assistive learning devices that may be helpful. If any amplification is used (e.g., hearing aids or FM systems), the adults in the setting will need to be familiar with the devices. Someone on the educational team should be trained in problem-solving (e.g., checking batteries, determining appropriate volume settings). With the help of the audiologist, the team also will need to understand the student's audiogram that provides information regarding what speech sounds the student can hear aided and unaided as well as those that the student will have difficulty hearing. This information can assist the teacher and inclusion facilitator to predict when auditory cues will need to be supplemented.

Even when the student cannot understand speech, an exaggerated tone of voice and pitch can help a student understand when a question is being asked or a direction is being given and some action is expected. Using sound to draw attention to important information may also help the student respond as expected. For example, tapping the item to be examined can draw the student's attention to the item even when speech cannot be understood sufficiently to add other information. Being directed to certain environmental sounds (e.g., doors slamming shut, children running, books being dropped) can alert the student to things happening around him or her. Using auditory information of this nature can help students understand events and act on them when necessary (e.g., move out of the way when someone is running toward you, or stop and pick up the book that has fallen).

Tactile Adaptations

For students who require tactile information either to supplement or substitute for visual and auditory information, adaptations may require even greater thought and preplanning. Touching and tactually examining objects being directly studied (e.g., sedimentary rock), as well as objects indirectly related to the topic (e.g, feathers, egg, and a nest in the study of birds), provide critical information and help to maintain interest. Obviously, allowing extra time for such examination is one needed adaptation.

However, the goal is not simply to provide tactile information, but to provide information that facilitates learning. Factors to be considered when adapting to the tactile mode are presented in Table 3.6. Because tactile information can be valuable for all students, considering the best way to incorporate it for the whole class should be addressed by the team during joint planning sessions.

Tactile information should be selected that is most relevant to the subject of study (Downing & Eichinger, 1990). Tactile representation of all aspects of the lesson may not be possible, but certain directly or indirectly related aspects could be presented tactually to add information. For example, a study of the desert could involve a terrarium of sand, rock, desert tortoise, and certain cactus plants, which would allow some careful tactile exploration. A unit on electricity could involve the use of a switch and a vibrating pillow or any appropriate device (e.g., fan, blender, radio). A history lesson on Christopher Columbus could involve a globe, a replica of a sailboat on water, or a tactile compass.

One caution needs to be mentioned. The use of miniatures to represent ideas, activities, and so forth, may *not* be the most meaningful approach for a given student, depending on their use. For instance, the study of animals (either at an elementary or secondary level in biology) is best done with real animals and not small plastic miniatures. The small size of miniatures makes it difficult to tactually discriminate one from the other, and they lack other relevant information, such as texture, smell, and movement. Miniatures, in fact, are very visual in the information they provide—not tactile. To try to convince a student with significant visual, auditory, and intellectual challenges that a 1"–2" plastic dog is a dog

Table 3.6. Factors to consider when adapting to tactile mode

1. Can some or all of the information for the lesson be presented tactually?

2. What aspects can be presented tactually?

3. How should some or all aspects be presented tactually in order to provide the clearest, most relevant information?

4. How will tactile information be used and when?
   • Does it truly benefit the student?
   • Does it benefit all students?

5. Obtain feedback from students for evaluation/modification.

would be confusing and impractical. When providing tactile information for any lesson, it is important to determine whether or not the information would clarify or confuse. Sometimes the object adds information for others in the class and can be held by the student who enjoys feeling it, whether or not it helps the student gain a better understanding of the subject. Letting the student be in charge of tactile items to show others and to hold during group instruction time could help create opportunities to practice appropriate social interactions and provide a calming activity (similar to doodling) until a more active response is required.

Adaptations for Physical Disabilities

Restrictions on a student's ability to move and manipulate items require that teachers facilitate these abilities as much as possible while finding alternative means for these students to actively participate in activities. Fortunately, there are many different accommodations that can be employed to assist a student who must deal with physical limitations. In general, these accommodations include physical positioning, assistive technology (both light and high technology), and an emphasis on expressive communicative abilities.

Physical Positioning   Campbell (1993) emphasizes the critical importance of effective physical positioning for students with physical disabilities. Teachers must ensure that students are comfortable and in a position that supports their ability to engage in meaningful activities. Students without disabilities change their bodily position almost constantly throughout each day; therefore, it is imperative that teachers remain sensitive to the need for students with physical disabilities to adjust their positions as well.

Adaptive positioning equipment allows students to sit, stand, kneel, and lie on their side, front (prone), or back (supine). Direct service providers must assume responsibility for assisting students into different positions throughout each day depending on the student's abilities, needs, physical limitations, and the demand or expectations of each activity. In addition, the physical position of students without disabilities will affect the decision regarding the appropriate position for a student with physical disabilities. For example, when young preschool or elementary students sit on the floor to listen to a story being read, the student having severe physical disabilities also should be on the floor in a supported sitting position as opposed to being placed in a wheelchair or bolster chair that elevates this student above the other children. Or, if students gather on the floor to work on a project, it may be a good opportunity for a student to be positioned prone on a wedge while working with this group.

At the preschool and elementary level it will be relatively easy to match the student's individual positioning needs since children at this age often work in a variety of positions during the school day. Fewer options may exist for secondary age students in middle and high school. At the secondary level, students may spend considerable time in wheelchairs since their classmates spend most of their time at their desks. During these school years, teachers and related service professionals will need to be particularly creative in ensuring that students experience different physical positions during each day. Arranging schedules so that students avoid taking numerous sequential classes that require the use of a wheelchair as the primary positioning equipment is one strategy. Such classes are best alternated with classes that permit a wider variety of positions. For example, a PE class would allow students to exercise on a mat in a prone or supine position, watch team sports on a bolster chair or in a standing table or a prone or supine stander, and participate in various activities by sitting or standing. Choir, art, drama, home economics, and woodshop, to name a few, also offer options for students to participate in class activities in a standing position versus sitting in a wheelchair. Because changing positions involves the use of various pieces of equipment, the educational team will need to come up with creative ways of getting the necessary equipment to the classes where it will be needed. Employing the assistance of classmates to address this potential difficulty can be very helpful to teachers and paraprofessionals who have several students to support.

Assistive Technology   Technology is pervasive in today's society, enhancing almost everyone's life in some manner (Inge & Shepherd, 1995). The use of assistive technology for students with severe and multiple disabilities has contributed significantly to their ability to participate in typical environments. A wide range of assistive technology from simple or light technology to complex or high technology is available to support students having severe and multiple disabilities. Educational team members need to be aware of available technology to ensure the greatest level of student participation.

Light Technology   Assistive technology does not have to be expensive or complex to be highly useful. Almost any adaptation to material or an entire activity can fall under this category. Many adaptations or examples of light technology can be readily purchased from common retail stores (e.g., pencil grips, step stools, Handitak to hold objects, signature stamps, headphones, calculators with extra large numbers). Other relatively simple types of adaptive technology are commercially available via companies producing specialized equipment for individuals with disabilities (e.g., adapted spoons, nonslip placemats, pictorial communication systems, orthotic splints, bolsters, simple switches). A wide variety of switches can be activated with various body parts and require varying amounts of pressure for activation. For example, plate switches in the form of lever, disc, or membrane switches can be positioned so that any part of the body can activate the switch (e.g., hand, elbow, back or side of the head, knee, foot). Some switches can use air pressure (e.g., the sip-and-puff switch) for activation. Mercury switches can be attached to the head (e.g., on an age-appropriate hat or hair ribbon) and the switch activated with head movements. A final example involves a switch activated by the child's voice. The type of switch and the body part used to activate the switch will be determined by the child's educational team, with input from a person with expertise in motor skills.

Many adaptations, which are not complex in nature, can be made by family members, teachers, volunteers, and other students. Examples of handmade light technology could include pressure switches, jigs to perform different jobs, adaptive mitts, handles for a variety of objects, bags to attach to wheelchairs or walkers, pictorial conversation books, and page fluffers.

Light technology can help a student perform more efficiently in almost any daily activity and can be specifically designed to the individual's needs. This type of technology facilitates communicative interactions, task performance, and care of one's personal needs. The effective use of light technology demonstrates the creativity of the educational team in resolving potential barriers.

High Technology   This area of technology has grown substantially since the 1980s and continues to make progress in addressing human needs. High technology is considerably more complex than light technology and usually carries a higher price tag as well as a need for training in its use. Careful assessment of an individual student's needs and careful analysis of how that student's needs would be most effectively and efficiently addressed by a given piece of technology are needed to avoid purchasing the expensive, yet wrong, equipment.

The personal computer has revolutionized the way people interact with one another. It has opened countless doors for individuals with severe physical disabilities. Software programs with voice output, adapted keyboards, and touch windows have enabled students to participate in a wide range of activities using computers. Students of any age can learn about the relationship between their movements and related consequences (cause and effect) using software programs that create colorful and changing designs or that allow creative musical expression. Aspects of such programs are fascinating to anyone of any age, and therefore the teacher does not have to worry about using software that is age-inappropriate for older students.

The field of high technology has had a major impact on the development of augmentative communication systems for individuals with severe physical disabilities. Numerous electronic communication systems are available and can be adapted to meet individual student needs (see Goetz & Hunt, 1994; Romski & Sevcik, 1988). For example, Zygo's Macaw and Prentke Romich's Introtalker (and Touch and Light Talkers) allow for a wide range of symbols (e.g., objects, pictures, photographs) to be used with these systems. In addition, digitized speech for these products creates a natural sounding voice to accompany a selection. These electronic systems continue to decrease in size, allowing them to be more easily portable.

Communication as an Emphasis Although a physical disability may limit a student's ability to move and handle objects, meaningful participation still can occur in school activities when the student's ability to convey information is emphasized. The student will be a part of whatever activity is occurring for the class, but will capitalize on the ability to make choices, reject or request actions or items, and express opinions instead of participating in the actual manipulation of materials. Other students will make the actual products, while the student with severe and multiple disabilities that includes a severe physical disability will direct, decide, and comment.

The major accommodation that must occur is for those without disabilities (students and teachers) to provide the opportunities to allow the student unable to move well to be an active participant. Too often students with severe and multiple impairments will be physically close to the other students, but merely passive observers. No expectation is present for these students to participate. This situation can be changed to include any student when those without disabilities take the time to offer choices ("would you like Aaron or Jonah to mix the chemicals?"), ask for direction (e.g., "Where should I put this?" or "What's next?"), request feedback (e.g., "Do you like it this way?", "Is it better with yellow or black?"), or allow a comment (e.g., a student vocalizes and looks interested in a mural being made, and his peer responds with, "Yeah, Tracy, I like that too").

Many options exist for students with severe and multiple disabilities to communicate, including highly symbolic means via the use of high technology and nonsymbolic means via the use of facial expressions, vocalizations, or slight body movements (Mirenda & Iacono, 1990; Siegel-Causey & Guess, 1989). The important point to remember is that everyone has something to say, even though it may prove very difficult to say it. Expecting each student to express himself or herself through whatever means is available is the key. The next step is to provide each student with the most appropriate means to communicate and to give that student time and supportive instruction to be successful. The examples across age ranges provided in Chapters 4, 5, 6, and 7 of this volume highlight the importance of expecting students to communicate their thoughts, despite an inability to use speech or other symbolic means.

Adapted Activities

If students with severe sensory and multiple disabilities cannot perform all aspects of a given activity, then adaptations will need to be made that allow participation based on the students' strengths. Adaptations can take many forms and can be simple or complex as suggested in the previous sections. The critical point is to recognize when adaptations are necessary and to be able to apply them as effectively as possible. Instead of excluding these students because they cannot do certain steps (even major steps) in an activity, teachers and other team members can identify the steps that provide the most appropriate learning opportunities. Sometimes steps can be skipped altogether and another student can complete them as a partner to the student with a disability.

For example, removing a sheet of cookies from an oven during home economics class may not be possible for a student who is deaf-blind and has severe physical limitations. A classmate does that step for him or her. Or, in physical education (PE) class during a softball game, a student may be supported in a standing position while he or she hits the ball off a batting tee, but a team member may then run the bases. In other instances, students with severe sensory and multiple disabilities can perform the activity, but in a different manner. For example, Sharon gives her report in English class using a switch, cassette recorder, and prerecorded report. Sometimes students participate in the activity, but use different materials. James may do his mathematics problems using a talking calculator. Sometimes rules can be modified to allow for the participation of all students. For example, during sustained silent reading, one student is permitted to read quietly to a classmate who is unable to read. During basketball practice, a student with multiple disabilities is allowed to move as close to the basket as she desires instead of having to stay at the free throw line. Considerable information exists on ways to adapt activities to more effectively include all students in school activities (Brown & Lehr, 1993; Ford, Davern, & Schnorr, 1992; Gee, 1995; Hamre-Nietupski, McDonald, & Nietupski, 1994; Ryndak, 1995). In determining adapted activities, the team is limited only by their own creativity.

SUMMARY

This chapter has examined educational strategies for working with students in preschool through high school who have severe sensory and multiple disabilities. Emphasis has been placed on first determining who the student is (identifying strengths, hopes, interests) and then assessing the student within typical activities and environments that lead toward the goals that the student and/or parents have targeted as priorities. Helping the student acquire needed skills according to individual interests, strengths, and limitations, as well as the demands of the environment, is done in a positive and least intrusive way. Respect for the student is shown, first, by recognizing that individuals learn differently and require varying support across different activities; and, second, by providing as many options as practicable and giving each student as much decision-making power over educational goals and methods of attaining them as possible.

REFERENCES

Bailey, B.R., & Downing, J. (1994). Using visual accents to enhance attending to communication symbols for students with severe multiple disabilities. *RE:view, 26*(3), 101–118.

Brown, F., & Lehr, D. (1993). Making activities meaningful for students with severe multiple disabilities. *Teaching Exceptional Children, 25*(4), 12–17.

Brown, R., & Snell, M. (1993). Measurement, analysis, and evaluation. In M. Snell (Ed.), *Instruction of students with severe disabilities*, (4th ed., pp. 152–183). New York: Macmillan Publishing Co.

Campbell, P. (1993). Physical management and handling procedures. In M.E. Snell (Ed.), *Instruction of students with severe disabilities* (4th ed., pp. 248–263). New York: Macmillan.

Demchak, M. (1990). Response prompting and fading methods: A review. *American Journal on Mental Retardation, 94*(6), 603–615.

Downing, J. (in press). *Assessment of the school age student with dual sensory and intellectual impairments*. Monmouth, OR: Traces Technical Assistance Project.

Downing, J., & Bailey, B. (1990). Developing vision use within functional daily activities for students with visual and multiple disabilities. *RE:view, 21*, 209–220.

Downing, J., & Bailey, B.R. (1993). *Helping young children with visual impairments make use of their vision*. Terre Haute, IN: Indiana State University, Blumberg Center for Interdisciplinary Studies in Special Education.

Downing, J., & Eichinger, J. (1990). Instructional strategies for learners with dual sensory impairments in integrated settings. *Journal of The Association for Persons with Severe Handicaps, 15*, 98–105.

Downing, J., & Perino, D. (1992). Functional versus standardized assessment procedures: Implications for educational programming. *Mental Retardation, 30*, 289–295.

Ford, A., Davern, L., & Schnorr, R. (1992). Inclusive education: "Making sense" of the curriculum. In S. Stainback & W. Stainback (Eds.), *Curriculum considerations in inclusive classrooms: Facilitating learning for all students* (pp. 37–61). Baltimore: Paul H. Brookes Publishing Co.

Fox, T., & Williams, W. (1991). *Implementing best practices for all students in their local school: Inclusion of all students through family and community involvement, collaboration, and the use of school planning teams and individual student planning teams*. Burlington: University of Vermont, Center for Developmental Disabilities.

Gee, K. (1995). Facilitating active and informed participation and learning in inclusive settings. In N.G. Haring & L.T. Romer (Eds.), *Welcoming students who are deaf-blind into typical classrooms: Facilitating school participation, learning, and friendships* (pp. 369–404). Baltimore: Paul H. Brookes Publishing Co.

Giangreco, M.F., Cloninger, C.J., & Iverson, V.S. (1993). *Choosing Options and Accommodations for Children: A guide to planning inclusive education*. Baltimore: Paul H. Brookes Publishing Co.

Goetz, L., & Hunt, P. (1994). Augmentative and alternative communication. In E.C. Cipani & F. Spooner (Eds.), *Curricular and instructional approaches for persons with severe disabilities* (pp. 263–288). Boston: Allyn & Bacon.

Hamre-Nietupski, S., McDonald, J., & Nietupski, J. (1994). Enhancing participation of a student with multiple disabilities in regular education. *Teaching Exceptional Children, 26*(3), 60–63.

Haney, M., & Falvey, M.A. (1989). Instructional strategies. In M.A. Falvey (Ed.), *Community-based curriculum: Instructional strategies for students with severe disabilities* (2nd ed., pp. 63–90). Baltimore: Paul H. Brookes Publishing Co.

Inge, K.J., & Shepherd, J. (1995). Assistive technology applications and strategies for school system personnel. In K.F. Flippo, K.J. Inge, & M. Barcus (Eds.), *Assistive technology: A resource for school, work, and community* (pp. 133–166). Baltimore: Paul H. Brookes Publishing Co.

Kelley, P., Davidson, R., & Sanspree, M. J. (1993). Vision and orientation and mobility consultation for children with severe mutliple disabilities. *Journal of Visual Impairments and Blindness, 87,* 397–401.

Kennedy, C.H., & Haring, T.G. (1993). Combining reward and escape DRO to reduce the problem behavior of students with severe disabilities. *Journal of The Association for Persons with Severe Handicaps, 18,* 85 92.

Levack, N. (1994). *Low vision: A resource guide with adaptations for students with visual impairments* (2nd ed.). Austin, TX: Texas School for the Blind and the Visually Impaired.

Linehan, S., Brady, M., & Hwang, C. (1991). Ecological vs. developmental assessment: Influences on instructional expectations. *Journal of The Association for Persons with Severe Handicaps, 16,* 146–153.

Mirenda, P., & Iacono, T. (1990). Communication options for persons with severe and profound disabilities: State of the art and future directions. *Journal of The Association for Persons with Severe Handicaps, 15,* 3–21.

Orelove, F.P., & Sobsey, D. (1991). *Educating children with multiple disabilities: A transdisciplinary approach* (2nd ed.). Baltimore: Paul H. Brookes Publishing Co.

Prickett, J.G., & Welch, T.R. (1995). Adapting environments to support the inclusion of students who are deaf-blind. In N.G. Haring & L.T. Romer (Eds.), *Welcoming students who are deaf-blind into typical classrooms: Facilitating school participation, learning, and friendships* (pp. 171–194). Baltimore: Paul H. Brookes Publishing Co.

Romski, M.A., & Sevcik, R.A. (1988). Augmentative and alternative communication systems: Considerations for individuals with severe intellectual disabilities. *Augmentative and Alternative Communication, 4,* 83–93.

Ryndak, D.L. (1995). Adapting environments, materials, and instruction to facilitate inclusion. In D.L. Ryndak & S. Alper (Eds.), *Curriculum content for students with moderate and severe disabilities in inclusive settings* (pp. 97–124). Needham, MA: Allyn & Bacon.

Schnorr, R.F. (1990). "Peter? He comes and goes...": First graders' perspectives on a part-time mainstream student. *Journal of The Association for Persons with Severe Handicaps, 15,* 231–240.

Schwartz, I.S. (1995). Using social-validity assessments to identify meaningful outcomes for students with deaf-blindness. In N.G. Haring & L.T. Romer (Eds.), *Welcoming students who are deaf-blind into typical classrooms: Facilitating school participation, learning, and friendships* (pp. 133–142). Baltimore: Paul H. Brookes Publishing Co.

Siegel-Causey, E., & Guess, D. (1989). *Enhancing nonsymbolic communication interactions among students with severe disabilities.* Baltimore: Paul H. Brookes Publishing Co.

Snell, M., & Brown, F. (1993). Instructional planning and implementation. In M. Snell (Ed.), *Instruction of students with severe disabilities* (4th ed.). New York: Macmillan Publishing Co.

Sobsey, D., & Wolf-Schein, E.G. (1991). Sensory impairments. In F.P. Orelove & D. Sobsey, *Educating children with multiple disabilities: A transdisciplinary approach* (2nd ed., pp. 119–154). Baltimore: Paul H. Brookes Publishing Co.

Turnbull, A.P., & Turnbull, H.R. (1990). *Families, professionals, and exceptionality: A special partnership.* Columbus, OH: Charles E. Merrill.

Wolery, M., Ault, M.J., & Doyle, P.M. (1992). *Teaching students with moderate to severe disabilities.* New York: Longman.

Chapter 4

THE PRESCHOOL CHILD

MaryAnn Demchak and June E. Downing

For young children, the first educational experiences should be centered on play, which is young children's "work." When approached as play, learning has a greater impact on a young child's development and is more enjoyable for the child (Burton, 1991). Early childhood education should involve active learning that consists of choice making, abundant materials for children to manipulate in various ways, and an emphasis on language development (Tompkins, 1991). Active learning can occur in various types of play: 1) dramatic play or role play, in which children pretend; 2) constructive play, in which children use materials to make something; 3) exploratory play; and 4) play with various board, card, and action games (Rogers, 1991). Through play, young children learn about objects and events and the language for talking about them, in addition to developing a variety of interaction skills (Lifter, Sulzer-Azaroff, Anderson, & Cowdery, 1993). Play also contributes to cognitive, social, and physical development on an incidental, or informal, basis in numerous areas, including object permanence; memory; attention; cause-effect; problem solving; color, shape, and size identification; grasping and manipulation; gross motor skills; turn taking; and expressive and receptive communication skills.

A typical schedule for a preschool program includes, first and foremost, a generous amount of play time (inside and outside) stressing free play as well as planned activities at centers and play in small and large groups. In addition, the schedule typically includes greeting time (i.e., morning circle), snacktime, story time, and closing circle at departure time. These various activities allow young children to learn the skills previously identified, as well as to learn about self and others, to participate in a group, to follow directions, to complete self-help skills, and to respect the property of others.

EDUCATING YOUNG CHILDREN TOGETHER

The current emphasis in early childhood special education is a play-based, child-centered, and teacher-facilitated program (Hanline & Fox, 1993; McLean & Odom, 1993; Weber, Behl, & Summers, 1994). The practices valued by early childhood special education are also those valued by early childhood education in general (Fox, Hanline, Vail, & Galant, 1994). This compatibility is important, in that there is increased emphasis on educating young children with disabilities in inclusive settings. Buysse (1993) summarized the benefits of educating young children with disabilities with their typical peers as including: 1) more positive interactions with peers, 2) increased verbalizations directed toward peers by children with disabilities, and 3) greater levels of social participation. Buysse (1993) also cited what is perhaps a more important result of inclusive education for young children—the reciprocal friendships that develop between young children with and without disabilities.

The activities that occur in typical preschools are perfectly suited to the needs of young children with multiple and sensory impairments. Young children with such impairments usually are learning to communicate, to take care of bodily functions, to play appropriately with toys, to interact with others their age, and to follow the rules of social conduct. If young children with disabilities are placed in a homogeneous group according to ability (or rather disability), lack of appropriate role models will hinder the development of targeted skills and place the burden of teaching on a few adults. Being surrounded by appropriate role models at a very young age and experiencing typical expectations for behavior can set a critical foundation for future learning. Therefore, it is imperative that preschoolers with and without disabilities be educated together.

BARRIERS TO INCLUSIVE PRESCHOOL EDUCATION

Perhaps the biggest barrier to inclusive education for preschool-age children with disabilities is the lack of public preschool programs for typical children (Odom, McConnell, & Chandler, 1993). Children without disabilities receive early childhood education and child care in a range of programs that includes 1) in-home care by others, 2) family child care, 3) nursery schools, 4) child care centers, and 5) federal Head Start programs. Unfortunately, many preschoolers with disabilities do not have access to peers without disabilities because they receive their early education in separate schools or separate classes in public schools. The youngest children in most public schools are in kindergarten. Nonetheless, there are options for educating preschoolers with disabilities in the typical settings previously listed. For example, early childhood special education teachers may collaborate with local private preschools (e.g., Montessori preschools or others) or with public programs for at-risk preschoolers (e.g., Head Start). In some instances a school district may choose to open its own preschool program for all children or may rent space to a private preschool on an elementary campus. Inclusion of young children with disabilities has occurred successfully within existing child care and preschool options (Klein & Sheehan, 1987). However, it is likely that the early childhood special educator and the early childhood general educator will need to collaborate to ensure that necessary adaptations are implemented for young children with multiple and sensory impairments. The adaptations to be implemented should be developed by the educational team, which includes family members, and should be linked to the goals and objectives specified in the individualized education program (IEP).

Despite the benefits documented for young children with severe and multiple disabilities in inclusive preschool settings, children with more severe disabilities tend to be educated in specialized settings to a greater degree than children with milder disabilities (Buysse, Bailey, Smith, & Simeonsson, 1994). Therefore, few early childhood teachers have had the opportunity to teach a child with a severe disability. Naturally, fear and apprehension could exist on the part of these teachers, especially when children have complex health needs in addition to sensory and other disabilities. These teachers will need to receive sufficient information and support to ease concerns and feel comfortable including a child with this disability label.

Although young children tend to be quite accepting at this age, when a classmate does not respond or behave as expected, children may opt to avoid this child. In addition, children at this young age are just developing skills of sharing toys and engaging in cooperative and interactive play. Their typical level of development in play skills (especially for 3-year-olds) may make interactions with a child having complex special needs all that more challenging. These children will need to be given specific guidance to encourage interactions and ensure that they are positively reinforced for their efforts (Fad, Ross, & Boston, 1995).

Although there are barriers to inclusive preschool education, all of these barriers can be overcome. Preschool children with severe disabilities should be educated with their peers without disabilities. The IEP is a key means for the educational team to address some of the barriers that may be present.

DEVELOPING THE PRESCHOOL CHILD'S IEP

The IEP is developed by an educational team comprising family members, relevant professionals, and paraprofessionals. The educational team should collaborate in targeting IEP goals and objectives that are meaningful and appropriate for a preschooler. Any areas that were identified as priorities by the family should be targeted within the IEP. The various professionals involved with the child should write IEP objectives that address basic skills (e.g., motor, communication, vision, and hearing) in the context of meaningful activities. Each professional is *not* allotted a separate section within the IEP; rather, there is a common set of IEP goals and objectives. Notari-Syverson and Shuster (1995) provided guidelines for developing IEPs that address real-life skills needed by preschoolers. The targeted skills should be functional in that they should increase children's abilities to interact with others in their natural environments, as well as address behaviors that would otherwise need to be targeted by someone else. The targeted skills also should address generality by 1) focusing on general concepts, 2) allowing for adaptations, and 3) focusing on behaviors needed across settings, materials, and people. The skills targeted in the IEP should be those that can be taught in a naturalistic manner in ongoing routines. As is true for any age student, the targeted skills should be directly observable and measurable and should have specific criteria delineated. Finally, short-term objectives should be hierarchically related to the long-term goals; that is, achieving an objective should be directly related to attainment of the goal.

The following objective demonstrates the incorporation of these guidelines as well as collaborative efforts by the educational team: "When greeted by name, Seth will respond by looking at or turning toward that peer or teacher in 9 out of 10 opportunities." Seth's teacher had identified greetings as an important aspect of the arrival routine, and the parents had indicated that greetings were a priority for them. The communication specialist collaborated regarding the meaningful use of greetings, while the hearing specialist provided guidelines to facilitate the likelihood that Seth would hear the greetings (in addition to subsequent communications). Finally, the physical therapist provided input regarding appropriate positioning to enable Seth to turn his head in response to greetings. A similar process is followed in developing all goals and objectives for the preschooler with severe sensory and multiple disabilities.

Table 4.1 lists skills that could be targeted to the IEP and the manner in which they can be incorporated into the ongoing preschool routines. The actual IEP objectives are written to reflect the class activities and routines in which the objectives can be meaningfully addressed. Writing IEP objectives in this manner leads to targeting of skills in a relevant fashion throughout the day, rather than in isolation.

POTENTIAL ADAPTATIONS

A variety of relatively simple adaptations can be incorporated into a typical preschool schedule to facilitate the purposeful participation of children with disabilities. (Although the examples discussed here focus on preschoolers, it should be noted that many of these adaptations cross ages and are relevant to older children as well.) Due to limited sensory input and possible physical limitations, one critical and relatively simple adaptation may involve allowing children with multiple and sensory impairments more time to explore the learning environment. This may be particularly important when a child has both a visual and physical impairment. Adaptations may require collaboration between professionals from various disciplines to ensure that a specific child's needs are met. For example, early childhood educators and early childhood special educators may work with occupational and/or physical therapists to address motor impairments.

In some instances, adaptations are incorporated into numerous, if not all, activities throughout the day, rather than being limited to one particular activity at a specific time. For example, equipment allowing for proper positioning to enable a child to interact and stay involved in the learning activities to the greatest extent possible will be used throughout the day. This equipment could include corner chairs, bolster chairs, prone standers, wedges, bolsters, sidelyers, standing tables, or other equipment as recommended by physical and/or occupational therapists. The therapist(s) will assist in deciding what adaptive equipment will be necessary and in acquiring the equipment. In general, the equipment needed by an individual student is determined both by physical strengths and limitations as well as by functional needs to interact with others most efficiently.

The goal of using any type of adaptive equipment should be to increase meaningful and active participation in ongoing activities and routines within the classroom (Rosenberg, Clark, Filer, Hupp, & Finkler, 1992). Equipment should

Table 4.1. Sample preschool schedule with skills to meet IEP objectives

Activity	Potential IEP objectives
Arrival and greeting	Greet peers Respond to peers' greetings Mobility (e.g., use walker) Assist with removing coat/jacket Anticipate next activity using object calendar (e.g., toy car and ramp)
Free play	Choose activities, partners Maintain head control Maintain balance Grasp and manipulate objects (e.g., toy cars) Anticipate next activity using object calendar (e.g., cassette)
Good morning circle and music	Maintain sitting posture Grasp and manipulate objects Activate a switch (e.g., to turn on a cassette recorder) Anticipate next activity using object calendar (e.g., clay, blocks)
Center time	Maintain head control, balance, sitting posture Choose activities, partners Grasp and manipulate objects (e.g., blocks) Interact with peers (e.g., pass items) Mobility (e.g., use walker to move between centers) Anticipate next activity using object calendar (e.g., beanbag)
Active play	Use walker Maintain head control and balance Grasp and manipulate objects (e.g., bean bags) Choose activities and partners Interact with peers (e.g., pass balls, beanbags) Assist with putting coat/jacket on for outdoor play Assist with removing coat/jacket after outdoor play Anticipate next activity using object calendar (e.g., cup)
Snacktime	Maintain head control, balance, and sitting posture Choose food, drink, and who is to help Self-feeding and drinking Interact with peers (e.g., request snack food or pass objects) Personal hygiene (e.g., wipe face, bathroom break) Anticipate next activity using object calendar (e.g., book)
Story time	Maintain head control, balance, and sitting posture Grasp and manipulate objects (i.e., those related to the story) Anticipate next activity using object calendar (e.g., backpack)
Closing circle and departure	Respond to peers' good-bye Communicate good-bye to peers Mobility (e.g., use walker) Assist with putting on coat/jacket Anticipate trip home using object calendar (e.g., part of a seat belt)

not be used solely to achieve an alternate position for some specified time period. A child positioned in a piece of adaptive equipment without concern for meaningful interaction or participation in ongoing class activities can become bored and frustrated and miss valuable learning opportunities. A more appropriate use of adaptive equipment is provided in the following example. If children are playing on the floor, positioning equipment (e.g., a corner chair) may allow the child with severe sensory and multiple disabilities to also play on the floor. The child's position is determined by physical needs as well as the activities in the classroom and where those activities occur (i.e., on the floor, at a table, or standing). Table 4.2 shows examples of incorporating the use of adaptive equipment into ongoing class activities.

Adaptive devices also are available to help young children with fine motor tasks (e.g., grasping and maintaining that grasp) with which they might otherwise have difficulty. For example, a mitten with Velcro attached enabling the hand to be shaped into a fist can help a child to hold and examine a doll, pinwheel, kaleidoscope, or any other object that a strong extensor pattern and/or floppy tone might hinder grasping.

Switches and environmental control units can be used to allow the student with motor impairments access to and control of various items in the classroom that might otherwise not be possible. For example, the frequent repetition of familiar songs or the use of predictable books facilitates the use of augmentative communication devices that allow a child to press a switch to participate vocally with peers (see Musselwhite & St. Louis, 1988; Schweigert, 1989). Switches allow the child to learn the impact of his or her actions on the social environment as well as participate more meaningfully in class activities. An additional benefit is that the use of switches can be fascinating for typical peers. This fascination results in young children gathering around the child using the switch (he or she may be less able to move toward them). Moreover, when all students are allowed to share a switch to activate a toy or appliance, it helps to validate for the student with disabilities that such an adaptation is accepted and even valued by others. (Chapter 3 discusses a variety of switches that can be activated with various body parts.)

Not only is it important to adapt activities to accommodate motor impairments, but it is essential to make the appropriate modifications to address vision and hearing impairments. Chapter 3 discussed potential adaptations for accommodating deficits in vision and hearing. In general, activities involving use of vision and hearing should be meaningful and functional as well as incorporated into regular preschool routines. For example, it is *not* meaningful to remove the

Table 4.2.   Sample preschool schedule incorporating adaptive equipment

Activity	Potential adaptive equipment
Arrival and greeting	Adapted wheelchair Walker
Free play	Supported sitting device on floor Prone over wedge Sidelyer
Good morning circle and music	Supported sitting device on floor
Center time	Adapted wheelchair Stander Corner chair Bolster chair
Active play	Adapted wheelchair Walker
Snacktime	Adapted wheelchair Bolster chair
Story time	Supported sitting device on floor
Closing circle and departure	Adapted wheelchair Walker

child from classroom activities to locate fabricated sounds, such as a drum being hit behind him or her. The child must learn to hear the sound for a purpose that has relevance for the child in the classroom setting. That is, a functional listening activity can involve asking the child to respond to sounds relating to the task at hand. Responding when the teacher calls a child's name is one obvious example that can occur many times a day. Musical chairs is another common example, since it requires all children to use their hearing and to respond according to the presence or absence of sound. The teaching staff will direct the child's attention to other environmental sounds that occur on an incidental basis (e.g., classroom telephone ringing, school bell) and will instruct the child to respond differently to each sound. Incorporating activities that involve vision and listening into the ongoing preschool routines provides the child with numerous worthwhile opportunities to practice the skills in a distributed fashion throughout the day.

MEETING INDIVIDUAL STUDENT NEEDS THROUGHOUT DAILY ROUTINES

The need for specified adaptations is contingent on individual student strengths and needs. When a child's particular learning needs require adaptations, these are brought to the child and incorporated into meaningful activities throughout the day. This section reviews typical activities from an inclusive preschool schedule in order to provide examples of the manner in which adaptations can be incorporated.

Arrival and Greeting

As children arrive at the classroom, it is important to facilitate the child's greeting of peers on a one-to-one basis by encouraging individual children to come together long enough to exchange a look, touch, and/or verbalization. This informal interaction helps to ensure that the children are aware of one another. In addition, the child with severe sensory and multiple disabilities should be encouraged to greet the teacher. If the child has extremely limited vision and hearing, it is important for each person to have a unique name sign or object cue so that the child will know with whom he or she is interacting. For example, if a particular staff person always wears a certain ring, that staff person may always initiate interactions with the child by having the child feel the ring as a way of identifying himself or herself. Similarly, other staff and peers should have unique ways of identifying themselves. One little boy, for instance, frequently wore a baseball cap with an insignia patch on the front. This patch came to represent this boy to his classmate who did not see or speak. Another patch glued to a small piece of cardboard became this student's means of requesting interactions with his peer.

Free Play

Frequently, preschool activities begin with free-time activities for children as they wait for the other children to arrive. To facilitate independence at this time, materials for all children should be easily accessible and visible (i.e., *not* hidden away in cabinets) and have a specific place where they can be found. Brightly colored toys with interesting sounds and textures may encourage children with multiple and sensory impairments, as well as children without disabilities, to explore the toys. A sufficient number and variety of toys should be provided. Toys that may be used alone (e.g., puzzles, clay) as well as those that encourage cooperative play (e.g., balls, wagons, puppets) should be available. All children should be allowed to pick their desired activity. Some children will choose without prompting, whereas others will need minimal prompts such as the models provided by other children choosing activities. Children may also need simple gestures that direct their attention to what other children are doing or verbal prompts such as "Susie is playing with the dolls. Would you like to join her?" Other children will need to have their choices provided in a more structured format. A child may choose an activity after being provided with actual objects or parts of objects used in the activity or after being shown picture cues representing the available activities. For example, Seth, who has a mild hearing loss and cortical visual impairment as well as mobility and cognitive impairments, uses actual objects to choose his free-time activity. Seth is typically given two activities to choose from at a time—for example, headphones (to represent listening to preferred children's music) and brightly colored bristle blocks that self-stick. Seth's choices are presented to him separately, several inches apart from each other and tacked on a contrasting background, and he has a chance to explore each one tactually. Seth is then asked to look at first one object and then the other before expressing his preference. When Seth chooses to listen to songs, he also is taught to activate the tape player with a switch. The choices provided should allow for independent play as well as play with other children. The teaching staff may need to carefully balance the time the child plays with other children and the time spent playing alone, so that the child does not spend more time playing alone than other children do.

Good Morning Circle and Music

The songs, nursery rhymes, and rhythmic activities that are frequently part of circle time and other activities are excellent activities for teaching children with hearing impairments about the rhythm and structure of spoken language. Turn-taking activities and games also permit the child to learn about the "give and take" of communicative exchanges. In group activities, where various children are taking turns, the teacher can develop a procedure that allows the child to know who is taking a turn or contributing to an activity and when it is the child's turn (Luetke-Stahlman, 1994). For example, a peer may tell the child where to look.

To help maintain attention and interest, all children should be actively involved in the morning circle. Children frequently sing the same "good morning songs" in unison each morning. The child with severe sensory and multiple impairments might be taught to use a switch to activate a prerecorded song to sing with the other children. If other children choose songs to sing, the child with disabilities can also choose a song through picture or object cues. Providing all children with rhythm instruments to play with the music involves everyone. The child with multiple and sensory disabilities can choose his or her instrument by using picture or object cues and can then be encouraged to play the instrument. If necessary, the occupational therapist might provide suggestions regarding assisted grasping. During this circle routine, the class also frequently sings a special song of greeting to each other. To facilitate the participation of the child with sensory and motor disabilities, the teacher may choose two or three preferred friends of the child and provide tactile and/or visual cues to name cards. The child with disabilities can hold the name cards, explore the cards tactually, and respond to peers by passing the name cards as requested.

For the child with motor impairments, it is important that the child be positioned on the floor close to the other children and the teacher. In some cases, it may be necessary to use specialized equipment such as a corner seat to allow the child to sit without adult assistance. Using equipment allows the child to be as independent as possible during the activity and frees the adult to assist with the activity in other ways.

Center Activities

A variety of center activities are typically available in any preschool. These frequently include: art, dramatic or dress-up play, books or reading, fine-motor manipulatives (e.g., building blocks, puzzles, sticker play, magnet play), water play, sand play, and others. In some preschools the available centers may be related to a thematic unit that is incorporated throughout all preschool activities. For example, in the spring a unit may involve plants and flowers. Thus, the book center may include books about plants. The sand area may be replaced by one that allows the children to plant seeds. The art center may provide the children with materials to create artistic "plants." Regardless of the types of centers available and whether or not thematic units are used, children with multiple and sensory impairments can be involved meaningfully.

As with choosing free-time activities, all children should be provided with choices regarding center activities. When the child with sensory and multiple disabilities is instructed to choose a center activity, the early childhood educator may speak to the child as well as provide him or her with objects representing each center. Thus, the child is given auditory input and visual information as well as a concrete object that can be explored tactually. Prior to giving the auditory and visual cues, it is important to also use language that stresses hearing and listening (e.g., "Listen to Anna. She is calling your name and asking you to play with her" or "Listen, Jake is making car sounds"). Using such vocabulary combined with gestures (e.g., pointing to your ear) can help to prompt listening behaviors (Flexer, 1994). When asking the child for a response, it is essential that the child be given sufficient time to respond (Halle, 1987). If teachers expect responses too quickly and step in to complete activities for children rather than allowing them to respond independently, children may feel their communicative efforts are not really valued.

Once the child has chosen a center, the child becomes actively involved in manipulating, exploring, and passing objects to peers. For example, art activities allow the child to make multiple choices regarding the medium to be used, where artwork is to be located on a piece of paper, or the implement to be used. Art activities allow the use of materials of varying textures (e.g., various fabrics, colored sand, rice, play dough) that some children will enjoy tactually exploring. If the child with disabilities is working on paper, the paper may be taped to the table top or wheelchair tray to keep it from being pushed off by accidental, involuntary movements. Materials may be placed on nonslip placemats or on trays or pans with raised edges to confine the materials. For other activities, adapted scissors or easy-to-use glue bottles (e.g., those that simply require tapping on the paper rather than squeezing) may be provided. The final product does not need to look like that of other children. Of primary importance is that it is the child's work, not the teacher's or the teaching assistant's. All children can be recognized for their unique and creative work.

In a book center, all children will be given choices of books. The child with sensory and multiple disabilities can be provided books with accompanying tapes. Page fluffers, which elevate individual pages with varying thicknesses of foam, may be used to assist the child in turning pages. Tactile books (with braille or raised drawings) can be used that allow the child to tactually explore the page. For the child for whom hearing is a strength, books that allow the child to press a button to hear the page read aloud or to hear particular sounds related to the story may encourage greater involvement. For the child with vision impairments, it may be beneficial to provide books with pictures that are clear and uncluttered and that have contrasting backgrounds. In some instances, books may be made that incorporate specific visual adaptations. A slant board with small ledges to hold objects in front of the child can assist in providing access to information (e.g., looking at a book).

Various adaptive skills can be incorporated into center activities. For example, prior to completing an art activity, all children may be expected to put on a smock. For the child who has such an activity targeted in the IEP, this activity provides a natural opportunity to work on putting on an oversized shirt or smock and later removing it. Similarly, the dramatic or dress-up center gives children a chance to practice putting on oversized clothing of various types (e.g., shirts, dresses, hats, gloves). In addition, many art activities, sand play, water play, and other activities will require that the children wash and/or dry their hands following completion of the activity.

Addressing all of the potential activities that can occur in centers is not possible within the confines of this chapter. However, it is essential to ensure that the child with severe sensory and multiple impairments is actively involved in any center in which the child chooses to participate. Involvement is limited only by the creativity of the educational team.

Active Play

Most preschools include gross motor activities, or active play, both indoors and outdoors. Once again, the child with sensory and multiple disabilities can be given choices of activities as previously discussed. Whenever possible, peers can be encouraged to provide the child with his or her choices. For the child with physical disabilities, it is essential to encourage interactions with peers during active play so that the child's active play does *not* consist of only being pushed in a wheelchair around the playground by an adult. In order for the child to participate on the playground, it may be necessary to make physical adaptations (e.g., adapted swings). In some activities, the child may participate in the same activity but in a different way (e.g., pushing a ball off a wheelchair tray rather than throwing it).

Active play is a prime opportunity for the physical therapist to incorporate hands-on activities with the child who has physical impairments. For example, the physical therapist can add "therapy equipment" (e.g., large bolsters, therapy balls) into the active play area of the classroom, and all children can be encouraged to use them. Thus, all children can have fun with the equipment, and the preschooler with motor impairments is not singled out in any way. In addition, the physical therapist should share with the staff information on ways to incorporate activities into the ongoing routines of the class (e.g., the manner in which the child sits on the floor, how the child moves from sitting to standing).

Outdoor active play provides an opportunity to work on self-dressing skills, depending upon the weather and climate. For example, the child may need to put on a jacket or coat, hat, gloves, and boots. If the child cannot perform such tasks independently, then partial participation is encouraged (e.g., the student pushes an arm into a coat sleeve that is held for her). Students who have very limited physical movement can participate by deciding which coat belongs to them and requesting help to get it on. Obviously, upon returning to the classroom, the child can then assist in removing these items of clothing and/or ask for help to do so.

Snacktime

The impact of motor difficulties may be evident at snacktime, and some children may benefit from the use of adaptive equipment at this time. The specific equipment to be used is determined by student need, with input from an occupational therapist. Equipment that may be used at snacktime includes

1. Nonslip placemat: Holds plate or bowl in place
2. Plate guard: Allows child to scoop food against it
3. Scooper bowl: One side is built up to assist with scooping
4. Utensils with built-up handles: Allows a better gripping surface
5. Utensils with Velcro cuffs: Assists child in maintaining grasp
6. Nonmetal or coated utensils: Recommended for children with feeding problems (e.g., bite reflex)
7. Weighted utensils: Recommended for children with a tremor or sensory integration problems
8. Cutout plastic cups: Children can drink without extending neck
9. Two-handled mugs: Allows for two-handed grasping

Regardless of the adaptive equipment employed, it is imperative that the child be positioned correctly so that he or she can appropriately manipulate the adaptive equipment and participate more meaningfully at snacktime. A physical therapist should consult with the educational team to provide recommendations regarding positioning for snacktime.

The child also works on communication skills by being allowed to make choices throughout the activity, as appropriate. For example, the child can be given the choice of where to sit, what to eat and drink, and who is to help. Since snack- and mealtimes tend to be social occasions, communicative and social exchanges between peers can be targeted for instruction. All children should be encouraged to talk to one another, to request more of the snack or drink, and so forth. For example, Anna is a very social young girl who has limited verbal communication skills and some motor impairments as well as visual impairments. At snacktime she uses a simple augmentative communication device that allows her to choose one of four messages. Each quadrant of the device is a different color (permitting her to use her limited vision to aid in making her choice) and is paired with a line drawing representing the communicative message. The device requires minimal pressure, and Anna is able to use a device with voice output to ask for more snack or drink as well as to talk to her peers. Similarly, if necessary, some children might use any of the switches previously discussed that are connected to augmentative communication devices to activate prerecorded messages. Other children may be encouraged to use pictures or sign language to communicate at snacktime. The speech-language pathologist, along with teachers and teaching assistants and other therapists (e.g., vision, occupational therapist), should discuss options as a team to determine the communication demands of the situation, the current communicative skills of the child, and the need to find an alternative or augmentative mode of communication. What is effective in one situation may not be as effective in another, reflecting the dynamic nature of communication and interactions in general.

Snacktime also provides an opportunity for all the preschool children to work on various adaptive skills. For the child with multiple and sensory impairments, some of these skills may be targeted within the child's IEP. For example, all children are typically asked to wash and dry their hands prior to snack. Following snack, the children are likely to be asked to once again clean up. Depending upon the snack, they may be asked to wash and dry both their faces and hands when finished with snack. At this time, it may also be appropriate to target participation in toothbrushing as part of the ongoing snack routine. These adaptive skills involve all the children and do not single any one child out, but may involve different levels of participation depending on the child's abilities. A child with disabilities who can physically perform the task can either partially participate (e.g., grasp the toothbrush) or indicate choices involving the task (e.g., choosing a flavor of toothpaste).

Story Time

As the daily schedule is winding down, the class may move to a quiet activity such as story time. As in the morning circle, the child with disabilities should be assisted to sit on the floor close to peers and the teacher, supported either by positioning equipment or by adult staff. For example, Tracy, who has limited vision, is given preferential seating so that she is able to see the pictures. Teachers can use "big books" that are commercially available and thus enhance the likelihood that Tracy (as well as the other children) will be able to see the pictures. If big books are not available, an effort should be made to show Tracy each picture. For example, a peer may have a duplicate copy of the book and can be encouraged to show her each picture. The teacher also may attempt to select books that have pictures with contrasting backgrounds and/or pictures that are relatively uncluttered visually.

Similarly, the teacher may provide the child having hearing impairments with preferential seating so that the child is more likely to use any residual hearing that is present. If the child uses assistive listening devices, these should be in place for story time. In some instances, it may be appropriate for the child to listen to a prerecorded story on tape with headphones.

If children assist with turning pages of the story, the child with physical disabilities may use the earlier-mentioned page fluffers. The child also can participate by asking what will happen next, using augmentative communication devices (e.g., prerecorded loop tapes or prerecorded messages such as those described for snack). Similarly, if the teacher periodically asks the class questions regarding the story, the child may have a prerecorded answer on an augmentative communication device so that he or she can participate in this part of the activity as well.

As with other activities, active involvement should be encouraged whenever other children are also actively involved. For example, when particular stories are favorites and are read repeatedly, the class may begin to "read" along with the teacher. In this instance, the child with multiple disabilities may be asked to use a switch to activate a prerecorded tape of the story. Or the child may be asked to activate a tape that tells the rest of the class "Ready? Begin reading!" Thus, the child provides the cue to begin the activity. The child can be cued by peer or teacher, requiring the child to respond to a specific request. In some instances, children may be provided with objects or items related to the story. For example, when reading a story related to puppetry, the children may be provided with puppets that they are expected to hold up or manipulate at various points in the story. The child with multiple and sensory impairments also will be provided with an item and given time to explore it. The child will then receive instruction on how to respond similarly to the other students.

Closing Circle and Departure

The child with severe sensory and multiple disabilities needs to be encouraged to say good-bye to peers in a similar manner in which greetings were facilitated. Once again, the child can be positioned on the floor close to peers and the teacher, as opposed to in a wheelchair at the back of the group. Saying good-bye could mean waving, lifting an arm partway, looking at a peer, or raising one's head. These behaviors can be cued by the teacher, teaching assistant, or classmate. If the class sings a farewell song, the child can use a switch to activate a prerecorded tape of the song. Involvement in any songs sung at this time can be similar to involvement discussed for the good morning circle.

Summary

Although the preschooler with severe sensory and multiple impairments may have numerous needs as well as many professionals involved on the educational team, it is important to remember that the child must be treated in a holistic fashion. That is, the team members must work together collaboratively to meet the needs of the whole child. Team members share roles and move beyond traditional discipline boundaries to facilitate addressing the needs of the whole child. Such an approach also will have value for all children, who have different needs even if not related to a disability.

GENERAL GUIDELINES TO ENHANCE INTERACTIONS

General modifications to the classroom setting can establish occasions for children with multiple and sensory impairments to interact with their peers without disabilities. For example, the early childhood educator can provide materials that encourage more than one child to play together simultaneously. Martin, Brady, and Williams (1991) recommended using "social toys" (e.g., balls, dress-up clothes, puppets) to facilitate interactions between preschoolers with and without disabilities. In addition, it may be necessary to teach children both with and without disabilities specific skills to initiate and maintain interactions. Demchak and Drinkwater (1992) described activities that can be done prior to as well as after enrolling a child with sensory and multiple disabilities to facilitate interactions with children without disabilities. For example, activities previous to enrollment can include 1) discussing concepts of similar and different with the children without disabilities, 2) talking about various disabilities with the children, 3) conducting simulations of these disabilities and discussing the children's reactions, 4) watching a videotape of the child to be included, and 5) a visit to the preschool by the child's mother or father to "introduce" their child to the class (Raab, Nordquist, Cunningham, & Bliem, 1986). These types of activities can assist in providing a setting that enhances development of interactions after the child is enrolled. After enrollment, specific prompting and reinforcing of interactions can be done if more general and nonintrusive procedures are insufficient to encourage interactions between children with and without disabilities. If necessary, adults can take a more facilitative role by suggesting activities, directing children to play together, recommending sharing of toys, or other similar suggestions. At this age, both children with impairments as well as those without disabilities need to be encouraged in such activities; it is insufficient to promote one-sided interactions.

PLANNING FOR DAILY TRANSITIONS

Following a clear routine that does not change considerably from day to day will help children of all ages anticipate events and order their world. Access to a pictorial or object schedule prior to and following each activity can help reduce anxiety regarding transition times and facilitate communication (Rowland & Schweigert, 1989; Writer, 1987). Table 4.1 provides examples of incorporating an object schedule throughout the school day. Use of either an object schedule or a picture schedule typically involves providing the child with a concrete representation of the next activity in which that child will be participating. If an object schedule is being used, the child might be asked to hold onto an object as he or she moves to the next activity, thus helping to clarify the representative role of the object. For example, if a small car is used to represent free play, Seth would then use that car at least part of the time during free play. Subsequently, the child would be asked to place the object in a "finished" or "done" location to indicate for the child that the activity has ended and that it is time to move to a new activity. This type of object representation works well so long as children remain in one classroom. When they move from class to class, as at the secondary level, a more portable object system must be developed (e.g., small parts of objects can be placed in a small book). The use of a picture schedule provides a more abstract method of teaching the same skills and concepts (e.g., anticipating the next activity, moving to that activity, completing it, and anticipating the following activity).

Object and picture schedules can serve a communicative purpose if there is an expectation for active involvement on the part of the child (Rowland & Schweigert, 1989). For example, the child may indicate that an activity is completed by giving the symbol for the activity to someone or placing it in the finished bin. When the child is presented with the calendar or schedule, the child would be expected to point to, pick up, or touch the next symbol. Subsequently, the child might be expected to move in the direction of the activity indicated by the symbol, to look in that direction, to indicate preference for that activity (e.g., smiling, frowning), or to gather materials to participate in the activity. The use of such a system is essential in assisting children with sensory and multiple disabilities to understand and anticipate what is happening to them and around them.

PROVIDING INSTRUCTIONAL SUPPORT

The interaction styles that the adults in the setting use with the child with severe sensory and multiple impairments will likely influence the way in which peers interact with that child. For example, the adults should not baby or interact with the child with disabilities in an infantile manner. Sometimes adults interact in such a way unintentionally based on the child's disabilities or because the child is so much smaller in stature than the other children. The adults in the setting should interact with and talk to the child with disabilities in the same manner they would with others who are the same chronological age. However, adults in the preschool setting should remember that there is typically a 2- or 3-year age range within the setting. The manner in which they interact with 3-year-olds will be different from that used with 5-year-olds.

In addition, the manner in which instructional support is provided must be monitored and should facilitate the child's ability to interact with peers, engage in active play, and learn specific critical skills. At this age, the child is learning how to function as part of a larger social group. Overdependence on a special caregiver/instructor will teach the child to look to this individual for direction and assistance and not toward the true leader of the class. Systematic fading techniques must thus be applied appropriately so that the child can learn to respond as others in the class respond. Considerable finesse and skill are required to ensure that the necessary support is provided as needs arise without dominating the child's attention with an adaptation or unwittingly dominating the class with the child's needs. There is a fine line between providing too much support and not enough. Too often a child may be separated from other children in the classroom by a well-meaning special educator or teaching assistant. For example, a young child is sitting on the lap of a teaching assistant behind the other children and farthest away from the teacher when a story is read to the class. This adult may be trying to provide the necessary adaptations and instruction unaware of the separation being created. Using adaptive equipment that supports this child in a sitting position near the teacher and other children will reduce this separation.

Providing too much support to the child can also negatively influence peers' perceptions of that child. Too much assistance or hand-over-hand manipulation might lead to peers viewing that child as less competent or as the "baby of the class" (Drinkwater & Demchak, 1995). Children with sensory and multiple disabilities should be encouraged to be as independent as possible. For example, if children are moving independently from center to center, the child with impairments should also be encouraged to move as independently as possible, using adaptive equipment if necessary (e.g., a walker). In general, when teaching the child new skills or expanding on previously taught skills, overmanipulation of the child should be avoided. The physical manipulation (hand-over-hand guidance) of children draws the child's attention to the stimulation of being manipulated rather than to the activity itself. Where and how adults physically manipulate a child to perform an activity may actually create an adverse response (e.g., a startle response and extension reaction) to the targeted behavior. For instance, manipulating a child to grasp a toy or spoon by placing a hand over the child's hand may cause the child to extend his or her hand and not maintain the desired grasp. Instead, it may be more efficient and much less intrusive to have the adult use one finger to press the item more firmly against the child's palm to stimulate the desired response (Klein & Delaney, 1995). This strategy allows the child to experience what a grasp is and receive the necessary proprioceptive feedback. Physical and occupational therapists can assist all direct service providers in the most efficient ways to provide the needed physical support without overmanipulation.

Although a temptation may exist to manipulate a child through various activities, especially the child with vision loss, an effort should be made to manipulate the learning activity and items used in the activity, rather than manipulating the child. The goal is to shape the desired behavior in a more subtle and less intrusive way. For example, when children are playing with building blocks, instead of using hand-over-hand guidance to produce the desired behavior, children can be placed close together, materials can be placed close to all children, and peers can be encouraged to touch a block to the child's hand to cue the child to grasp it. Using brightly colored materials and materials that are interesting to touch will facilitate the child's interest in the play. Guiding the elbow forward can assist in a pass to another student or in releasing the item where needed. (Magnetic building materials can be very helpful for the child with little or no vision.) The adult can concentrate on providing only the needed verbal and physical cues to enhance active participation without disrupting a typical play scenario.

Naturalistic Teaching Procedures

Naturalistic teaching procedures are prime methods to use in preschool environments for facilitating acquisition and maintenance of targeted behaviors for all children without disrupting play. Naturalistic teaching procedures are those that occur in the natural environment, are brief and interspersed throughout the day, are child initiated, and use natural consequences (Fox & Hanline, 1993). Naturalistic teaching procedures include incidental teaching and naturalistic time delay.

Incidental teaching procedures involve the specification of a target behavior (e.g., use of an augmentative communication device) and an initiation by the child (e.g., child points to a snack and begins to cry). If the teacher decides to use this situation as a teaching opportunity, the teacher asks the child for an elaboration (e.g., "I'm not sure what you want; where's your card?") and allows time for the child to respond. When the child responds, the teacher provides a snack. If the child does not respond or responds incorrectly, the teacher provides a prompt that will elicit the desired behavior (e.g., a model).

An example of the naturalistic time delay is applied to teaching Jacob to use a line drawing to ask for help (i.e., the targeted skill). At predetermined times when Jacob is likely to need help (e.g., putting coat on, taking coat off, getting a drink, reaching for items out of reach), the teacher approaches Jacob, withholds assistance, and looks at him with a questioning or "expectant" look. The teacher waits for at least 5 seconds to give Jacob an opportunity to respond. If Jacob responds appropriately (i.e., points to the help picture on his communication card), the teacher provides natural consequences by providing the assistance needed. If no response or an incorrect response occurs, the teacher provides a prompt (e.g., a model) and again waits for at least 5 seconds. Assistance (i.e., the natural consequence) is provided when Jacob responds following the prompt.

Naturalistic teaching procedures have been used to teach a variety of functional communication behaviors to young children with disabilities (Wolery, Ault, & Doyle, 1992). In addition, Fox and Hanline (1993) used naturalistic teaching procedures to teach a preschooler with multiple and sensory disabilities, within the context of play, to put objects in a container, give objects to peers, and manipulate objects with both hands. These procedures are developmentally appropriate in that they respond to the child's interests and intent, occur within the context of ongoing routines, and use natural consequences.

TRANSITION FROM PRESCHOOL TO KINDERGARTEN

Transitions from one learning environment to another are challenging for most students of any age. The unfamiliarity of the new physical and social environment creates an adjustment period that may result in undesirable behaviors. The child who requires more time to learn about any environment due to severe sensory, intellectual, and physical limitations will need a carefully planned transition when the learning environment changes significantly (O'Shea, 1994). Several months before the child is to attend kindergarten, the receiving and sending teams need to confer on the most appropriate and effective transition plan. Obviously, the parents need to be actively involved in the transition process. Moving from preschool to kindergarten is a major life transition and can be as difficult for the parents as for the child. Keeping everyone informed of options and encouraging parents to spend time visiting different kindergarten classrooms will help. The child and the parents need to visit the new environment, meet the new teacher, and spend time in a positive and interactive activity in the new setting. During the summer months, family members may wish to allow the child time to play on the playground at the new school and help the child to become accustomed to the physical layout of the school. Learning the route (if physically possible) from the car or bus drop-off location to the kindergarten classroom is one transition skill that could be acquired prior to the beginning of the new school year.

Assessing the Next Environment

Knowing what skills will be expected in the next environment will facilitate the adjustment process when the student enters the new learning environment. These expected skills can also guide the learning activities in the present environment before the transition occurs. Children in kindergarten are expected to function in large groups, demonstrate a longer attention span, initiate interactions, and show greater independence (Salisbury & Vincent, 1990). Being aware of such differences in expectations can help to alter both the content and method of instruction during the last year of preschool to ease the transition to kindergarten. The transition to kindergarten and resulting changes in expectations can be particularly difficult for the young child with severe sensory and multiple disabilities. This child needs considerable learning opportunities to understand these new expectations and to participate to the maximum extent possible in kindergarten activities.

Assessing the next environment is *not* for the purpose of determining the readiness of the child with disabilities to enter kindergarten (Hains, 1992). Rather, the purpose is to increase the likelihood of success for the transition by planning appropriately and by specifying adaptations that may be needed. The kindergarten assessment entails examining the supports and teaching strategies that will be needed for new activities in the new setting (Salisbury & Vincent, 1990). Planning and support are essential for any transition to be successful.

Developing a Portfolio to Assist in Transition

A portfolio is a systematic approach for keeping important current and historical information regarding a student in a concise, user-friendly format. Any transition can be exciting as well as stressful; a portfolio can assist in making the transition less stressful. The portfolio is developed by the preschooler's educational team, which should include family members, the sending and receiving general education teachers, and special education personnel (e.g., teachers, therapists). The information included in the portfolio should address some of the following areas (Demchak & Greenfield, 1995):

1. Communication: Touch and object cues used, nonconventional forms of communication (e.g., challenging behaviors) and their meaning, specifics regarding the child's augmentative/alternative communication system
2. Medical needs: Emergency contacts, allergies, medications administered and potential side effects, seizure history, situations that constitute an emergency
3. Strategies and adaptations needed for accomplishing IEP objectives in the context of the general education classroom: Positioning, curriculum/instructional adaptations and supports, vision and hearing adaptations
4. Behavioral support and reinforcement strategies: Form of the problem behavior, purpose of the behavior, intervention strategies, previously successful reinforcers

Other areas can be included in the portfolio as specified by the educational team. Every portfolio is student-specific and individualized to that child.

As part of the team developing the portfolio, the kindergarten teacher will have the opportunity to learn important information about the child prior to the start of the next school year. The portfolio provides the teacher with a permanent record of the information exchanged at the transition meeting. This record will likely prove invaluable at the beginning of the school year. The kindergarten teacher may also request to observe the child in the preschool setting or to view a brief videotape of the child in the preschool class. All of these strategies increase the likelihood that the transition from preschool to kindergarten will be conducted efficiently and effectively.

REFERENCES

Burton, L.H. (1991). *Joy in learning: Making it happen in early childhood classes.* Washington, DC: National Education Association of the United States.

Buysse, V. (1993). Friendships of preschoolers with disabilities in community-based child care settings. *Journal of Early Intervention, 17,* 380–395.

Buysse, V., Bailey, D.B., Jr., Smith, T.M., & Simeonsson, R.J. (1994). The relationship between child characteristics and placement in specialized versus inclusive early childhood programs. *Topics in Early Childhood Special Education, 14*(4), 419–435.

Demchak, M., & Drinkwater, S. (1992). Preschoolers with severe disabilities: The case against segregation. *Topics in Early Childhood Special Education, 11,* 70–83.

Demchak, M., & Greenfield, R. (1995). *Developing portfolios to facilitate inclusive education of students with disabilities.* Manuscript submitted for publication.

Drinkwater, S., & Demchak, M. (1995). The Preschool Checklist: Integration of children with severe disabilities. *Teaching Exceptional Children, 28*(1), 4–8.

Fad, K.S., Ross, M., & Boston, J. (1995). We're better together: Using cooperative learning to teach social skills to young children. *Teaching Exceptional Children, 27*(4), 28–34.

Flexer, C. (1994). *Facilitating hearing and listening in young children.* San Diego: Singular Publishing Group.

Fox, L., & Hanline, M.F. (1993). A preliminary investigation within developmentally appropriate early childhood settings. *Topics in Early Childhood Special Education, 13,* 308–327.

Fox, L., Hanline, M.F., Vail, C.O., & Galant, K.R. (1994). Developmentally appropriate practice: Applicability for young children with disabilities. *Journal of Early Intervention, 18,* 243–257.

Hains, A.H. (1992). Strategies for preparing preschool children with special needs for the kindergarten mainstream. *Journal of Early Intervention, 16,* 320–333.

Halle, J.W. (1987). Teaching language in the natural environment: An analysis of spontaneity. *Journal of The Association for Persons with Severe Handicaps, 12,* 28–37.

Hanline, M.F., & Fox, L. (1993). Learning within the context of play: Providing typical early childhood experiences for children with severe disabilities. *Journal of The Association for Persons with Severe Handicaps, 18,* 121–129.

Klein, M.D., & Delaney, T.A. (1995). *Feeding and nutrition for the child with special needs: Handouts for parents.* Tucson: Therapy Skill Builders.

Klein, N., & Sheehan, R. (1987). Staff development: A key issue in meeting the needs of young handicapped children in day care settings. *Topics in Early Childhood Special Education, 7*(1), 13–27.

Lifter, K., Sulzer-Azaroff, B., Anderson, S.R., & Cowdery, G.E. (1993). Teaching play activities to preschool children with disabilities: The importance of developmental considerations. *Journal of Early Intervention, 17,* 139–159.

Luetke-Stahlman, B. (1994). Procedures for socially integrating preschoolers who are hearing, deaf, and hard-of-hearing. *Topics in Early Childhood Special Education, 14,* 472–487.

Martin, S.S., Brady, M.P., & Williams, R.E. (1991). Effects of toys on the social behavior of preschool children in integrated and nonintegrated groups: Investigation of a setting event. *Journal of Early Intervention, 15,* 153–161.

McLean, M., & Odom, S. (1993). Practices for young children with and without disabilities: A comparison of DEC and NAEYC identified practices. *Topics in Early Childhood Special Education, 13,* 274–292.

Musselwhite, C.C., & St. Louis, L.W. (1988). *Communication programming for persons with severe handicaps: Vocal and augmentative strategies.* Boston: Little, Brown & Co.

Notari-Syverson, A.R., & Shuster, S.L. (1995). Putting real-life skills into IEP/IFSPs for infants and young children. *Teaching Exceptional Children, 27*(2), 29–32.

Odom, S.L., McConnell, S.R., & Chandler, L.R. (1993). Acceptability and feasibility of class-room-based social interaction interventions for young children with disabilities. *Exceptional Children, 60,* 226–236.

O'Shea, D.J. (1994). Modifying daily practices to bridge transitions. *Teaching Exceptional Children, 26*(4), 29–35.

Raab, M.M., Nordquist, V.M., Cunningham, J.L., & Bliem, C.D. (1986). Promoting peer regard of an autistic child in a mainstreamed preschool using preenrollment activities. *Child Study Journal, 16,* 265–284.

Rogers, A. (1991). Settings for active learning. In N.A. Brickman & L.S. Taylor (Eds.), *Supporting young learners: Ideas for preschool and day care providers* (pp. 151–157). Ypsilanti, MI: High/Scope Press.

Rosenberg, S., Clark, M., Filer, J., Hupp, S., & Finkler, D. (1992). Facilitated active learner participation. *Journal of Early Intervention, 16,* 262–274.

Rowland, C., & Schweigert, P. (1989). Tangible symbols: Symbolic communication for individuals with multisensory impairments. *Augmentative and Alternative Communication, 5,* 226–234.

Salisbury, C.L., & Vincent, L.J. (1990). Criterion of the next environment and best practices: Mainstreaming and integration 10 years later. *Topics in Early Childhood Special Education, 10,* 78–89.

Schweigert, P. (1989). Use of microswitch technology to facilitate social contingency awareness as a basis for early communication skills. *Augmentative and Alternative Communication, 5,* 192–198.

Tompkins, M. (1991). Active learning: Making it happen in your program. In N.A. Brickman & L.S. Taylor (Eds.), *Supporting young learners: Ideas for preschool and day care providers* (pp. 5–13). Ypsilanti, MI: High/Scope Press.

Weber, C., Behl, D., & Summers, M. (1994). Watch them play—watch them learn. *Teaching Exceptional Children, 27*(1), 30–35.

Wolery, M., Ault, M.J., & Doyle, P.M. (1992). *Teaching students with moderate to severe disabilities: Use of response prompting procedures.* New York: Longman.

Writer, J. (1987). A movement-based approach to the education of students who are sensory impaired/multihandicapped. In L. Goetz, D. Guess, & Stremel-Campbell (Eds.), *Innovative program design for individuals with dual sensory impairments* (pp. 191–224). Baltimore: Paul H. Brookes Publishing Co.

Chapter 5

THE ELEMENTARY SCHOOL CHILD

June E. Downing

This chapter addresses issues of inclusion facing the child from kindergarten through sixth grade. Public school children from 5 years of age to 11 or 12 years of age typically remain in one classroom for the majority of the day and follow the directions of one classroom teacher. There is a strong sense of belonging to one group of children and one teacher for the entire year. Although the class may benefit from a music teacher, physical education teacher, and art teacher, the primary instructor for the group is the teacher for that particular grade. The child with severe disabilities, including a sensory impairment, will be placed with same-age peers in the appropriate classroom of his or her neighborhood school or preferred magnet school and provided with whatever additional supports may be necessary to ensure learning. In other words, the student is not placed in an existing special program; rather, an appropriate program is built around the student's individual needs. The student is not just physically integrated into the classroom, but receives necessary support in terms of personal assistance, adapted materials, equipment, and instruction so that learning as part of a larger group can and does occur.

TRADITIONAL FORMAT OF ELEMENTARY CLASSROOMS

Children from kindergarten through sixth grade are typically not ready to spend long time periods at their desks doing seat work. They need to be more actively engaged in their learning (Katz, 1988; Kovalik, 1993). Classroom teachers who recognize this need alternate between independent sedentary seat work and active small-group instruction with plenty of movement and hands-on learning. With the acceptance of cooperative learning (Johnson & Johnson, 1989; Johnson, Johnson, & Holubec, 1990; Putnam & Spenciner, 1993) as a viable mode to promote learning, the traditional emphasis on quiet, independent paper and pencil work has evolved into a more active and child-centered approach. Teachers initially may present information (in longer periods as children reach the higher grades), demonstrate the desired behavior to follow the presentation, and then encourage students to work singly, in pairs, or in groups to accomplish their tasks. During the elementary school years, children learn the critical skills of reading, writing, and mathematical calculations. With these basic learning tools, they can explore various topics of interest. The typical curricula for these grades not only cover reading, writing, and mathematics but also science, computer technology, social studies, health, art, music, and physical education. The skilled classroom teacher employs a variety of teaching techniques to meet all the individual learners' needs in the classroom.

ADAPTATIONS FOR STUDENTS WITH SEVERE SENSORY AND MULTIPLE IMPAIRMENTS

To include the child with severe sensory and multiple impairments in this type of learning environment, the educational team for each child must approach typical classroom activities with a slightly different perspective. Guiding each child's educational program is the clear identification of skills that the child already possesses and the skills that will be needed in present and future environments. Although many standardized and formal assessment instruments exist to determine skills and deficits of various children with disabilities, an alternative approach may be to look at quality-of-life indicators for all children and use those as guideposts for intervention planning. As described in Chapter 3, the goals and aspirations of the individual and family members take precedence over standardized assessment tools (Giangreco, Cloninger, & Iverson, 1993). Quality-of-life indicators such as friendship development and the social and communicative skills that such development requires, health, safety, ability to earn money to obtain desired goods, and social acceptance in one's community may help keep the focus away from isolated skills measured by assessment tools that may have limited bearing on one's life. Most children can benefit from learning how to interact with peers and adults, follow directions, and creatively explore and manipulate objects for information and/or enjoyment. The child with a severe intellectual and sensory impairment may have considerable difficulty learning some of these skills and will need assistance to recognize what is expected and possible in various situations. Individually designed support provided for these children addresses these issues.

Because children with severe sensory and multiple disabilities typically do not have strengths in reading, writing, and arithmetic, the traditional focus of most classrooms at this age appears at first to create a barrier to inclusion. This perception must be replaced with the goal of identifying what skills the child has and needs to learn and how these can be met within this typical context. One way to create the necessary curriculum adaptations is to view the academic skills of reading, writing, and arithmetic from a functional perspective. That is, the educational team must determine what level of academic skills will best meet the present and future needs of the student. For instance, one student may benefit from learning one-to-one correspondence and counting, in order to be able to set the table and play board games with his family and friends. While adding, subtracting, multiplying, and dividing may be learned by other students, the student with severe multiple disabilities can learn one-to-one correspondence and counting. Different aspects of the *same* activity can be used to address all learning needs. There is no need to separate students because learning objectives are different. For example, four fifth graders are playing a game designed by their teacher to determine the probability of a certain number on a dice being rolled. One of the students needs to learn the four basic mathematics skills just mentioned as well as some basic interaction skills. He will learn these skills by counting the number of times that the dice is rolled, presenting the dice in front of each student for his or her turns, and taking his turn as well. Students participate at different levels to master the skills they individually need to meet life goals. Table 5.1 features a list of some of these lifelong skills that occur across subject areas.

The following sections address, from a functional perspective, the academic areas that typically occur in elementary schools. Specific suggestions are made in each area for students with severe sensory and multiple impairments. These suggestions are meant to serve as catalysts for educational teams who are presented with the opportunity to educate diverse learners together. Academic, instead of nonacademic, subjects have been targeted, owing to the tendency to exclude students from academic areas if they are not performing at grade level. Adaptations and a focus on various skills needed by students (e.g., communication, social interaction, dexterity) should be considered in nonacademic areas as well.

Reading

Reading is one academic skill that may require a somewhat broader definition to allow for all students to participate and learn. Traditionally, reading has been considered the ability to recognize, decode, and comprehend the written word (Adams, 1990). However, for some students who have no or limited vision, reading occurs by tactile recognition, decoding, and comprehension of the braille code. For students with a severe visual and/or hearing disability as well as a severe intellectual impairment, neither the written word nor the tactile code of braille will facilitate the skill of reading. This does not mean that reading is not important, but that it must be targeted in another way. Reading also can be defined as including recognizing and comprehending the meaning of photographs, pictures, or parts of objects. In fact, those who can read the printed word

Table 5.1. Basic skills learned across subjects

Attending to teacher
Following directions
Getting out materials
Putting materials away
Using materials appropriately
Requesting attention
Responding to direct questions/comments
Socially interacting with classmates
Attending to a task
Decision making
Problem solving
Reading
Writing
Mathematics or using numbers

also obtain considerable information and enjoyment by simultaneously experiencing other visual as well as tactile information. For instance, many people browse through clothing catalogs, furniture catalogs, and a variety of magazines on sports, famous people, and gardening, in addition to comic books. These same individuals also may enjoy touching sculptures, various textures, seashells, and an array of interesting objects to add to their visual understanding of the written word.

Teaching students with severe sensory and intellectual impairments to obtain information and entertain themselves by "reading" alternative formats is valuable instruction that can occur while other students are concentrating more on the recognition and decoding of print. Students who can receive auditory input can benefit from learning how to hold a book appropriately, listen to a classmate read to them, respond to their cue to turn the page, and follow along by looking at relevant pictures in the book or from other sources. In Figure 5.1, a second grader receives information from a classmate who reads to him. This same form of auditory reading can be accomplished via tape-recorded information and headphones. If allowed, students can choose to listen to a taped story, recorded message from a parent or other family member, or a taped letter from a friend. These choices are provided by color coding or tactually coding the different tapes.

When students receive information via the auditory mode, it is critical to check for some level of comprehension. Although the social aspects of being read to by a peer are present, learning how to attend to, enjoy, and obtain information via the auditory mode also is important. Therefore, being a passive recipient of

Photograph courtesy of Ed Waller

Figure 5.1.   A second grader reads information to her classmate.

the reading process is insufficient. A common strategy to check for comprehension of material is to ask questions regarding content, tone, relationship to other information, and so forth. Although the student with severe sensory and multiple impairments may have difficulty expressing thoughts concerning auditory information, an effort should be made to encourage some kind of response. For a student with visual abilities, pictures from the book or another source can be used to check for comprehension. Depending on subject matter, use of objects or parts of objects also can aid the student in responding to simple questions about the reading material. Clear choices are provided for the student to use in responding (i.e., yes/no responses). Even without pictures or objects, students can be asked if they like the story, if they think it's boring or exciting or important, or whether or not they agree with the information. Students need to learn that they will be expected to respond in some manner to questions, that their opinion is important and will be sought, and that listening to material requires active involvement on their part. Such interaction between teacher and students is typical, happens frequently during each school day, and provides an opportunity to support the development of conversational skills.

Some students have sufficient vision to see print. These students may acquire some sight word vocabulary and/or individual letter recognition that is paired with the information they more readily perceive (e.g., pictorial and tactile). Whole-language instruction as an approach to reading holds considerable promise for students with various severe disabilities in general education classes. Making sure the student has access to the printed word in the natural environment and encouraging the student to associate these words with pictures or items of interest expose the student to a whole-language approach to reading. The whole-language approach rejects labeling learners and assumes that *all* students can participate in emergent literacy (Smith-Burke, Deegan, & Jaggar, 1991). As discussed in Chapter 2, the whole-language approach is based on the notion that learning is interactive; thus, the approach lends itself to some of the critical skills needed by students with severe disabilities (e.g., to be aware of and respond to the environment). Tefft-Cousin, Weekly, and Gerard (1993) documented the use of this approach for some of these students. The technique of pairing the written word with pictorial and/or tactile information can be used effectively across activities and settings. For example, students can read their schedules of pictorial/word combinations to organize their day. Pictures have been used successfully to teach students with multiple disabilities to perform different tasks as well (Roberson, Gravel, Valcante, & Maurer, 1992). This reading can occur for a few minutes at the end of each activity or period to see what has happened and what will happen. If the schedule is tactile and the student has no usable vision, printed words help to clarify for classmates what the student has done, wants to do, or needs to do. Table 5.2 contains an example of materials used for one tactile schedule. Table 5.3 presents examples of alternative ways to "read." The aim is to be creative and flexible so that desired outcomes can be reached (e.g., following written/pictorial instructions for greater independence or learning ways to entertain oneself) without excluding students from the frequently occurring activity of reading. The student is not denied access to reading instruction, but is expected to partially participate in the activity to reach individually determined goals that may or may not resemble reading mastery. Encouragement from peers can facilitate skill acquisition, as depicted in Figure 5.2.

Table 5.2. Sample tactile schedule for fifth grader

Activity	Representation
1. Opening[a]	Cross piece of flag pole
2. Mathematics	Small calculator
3. Reading	Cassette tape
4. Physical Education	Wristband
5. Lunch	Plastic wrap
6. Science	Magnet[b]
7. Writing	Padded sticker (same as one on student's writing book)
8. Art	Clay[b]

Note: These items are placed in order on separate cardboard pages in a small (4-inch-by-6-inch) three-ring binder. The schedule is read at the beginning and end of each activity.

[a] Numbers (1–8) are tactually represented as glue dots.
[b]Item changes with the topic.

Writing

Similar to adaptations needed for reading instruction, writing is approached from a somewhat different perspective as well. It may not be possible for many students with severe sensory and multiple disabilities to write using a pen/pencil or traditional keyboard. However, writing is a form of self-expression that can take multiple forms. When students in various grades are engaged in writing activities, the student with severe sensory and multiple disabilities can be provided alternative writing media from which to choose, including pictures, photographs, small objects, parts of objects, textures, stamp pad designs, stickers, paint, wide felt-tip pens, and so forth. For students without vision, a brailler can be used to create a tactile design, or a mesh screen can be used with thin paper and a blunt pointed instrument (pen, knitting needle) to make tactile creations. Regardless of the medium used, students should be encouraged to express themselves in much the same way that writing can be encouraged as a form of expression. The printed word or words are added to this form of expression, either by a classmate or an adult. Later, this written work can be "read" by the student with the help of a peer. Even if students cannot physically manipulate the different media to express themselves, they can still choose from various symbols offered to them while a classmate or adult affixes those chosen symbols to the paper.

General education classes offer many opportunities to help students develop their creative writing or creative expression skills. Due to physical limitations, however, students may need to use adaptive writing tools (Wisniewski & Anderson, 1995). Simple adaptations such as putting a pencil through foam, clay, or rubber ball can allow a student easier means of grasping a writing tool. An

Table 5.3. Ideas for including students in reading activities

Students read their pictorial/word or tactile/word schedules before and after every activity.
Students read pictorial/word menus before lunch (if they buy lunch).
Students are read a chosen library book by a volunteer or older student.
Student listens to information on tapes.
Student reads pictorial/word or tactile/word directions prior to performing steps in a familiar activity (e.g., recycling, getting ready to go home).
Students reread stories/reports they have created with pictures/words and/or tactile items/words.
Students read photograph albums of family or school outings.
Students read pictures in the newspaper, comic books, or magazines.

Photograph courtesy of Pat Danielle Smith

Figure 5.2. A first grader receives help from her classmates to read certain words.

empty roll-on deodorant bottle filled with paint can be easy to grasp and be-comes an easy-to-roll applicator. Also, a T-shaped pencil or pen holder can be obtained commercially or made by melting the writing or painting instrument into and perpendicular to a wide glue stick (i.e., for a hot glue gun). The student grasps the glue stick and pushes the pen or pencil forward. For students unable to use their hands, a head or mouth stick might be more appropriate. The paper for these students will need to be elevated on a slant board for easier access. Wearing 1- or 2-lb. weighted cuffs also can be used for some students to help stabilize arms and arm movements. Additionally, paper may need to be firmly anchored to a table or wheelchair tray by being taped down, placed on Dycem, or held by a clipboard.

Access to a computer may be the most effective means by which some stu-dents express themselves during writing activities. Switch devices and adaptive keyboards may be needed to use the computer. Obviously, software programs that have colorful graphic symbols to choose from for students who have some vision will be preferred. Auditory feedback for students without vision is another option.

Students using alternative means of writing can serve as illustrators of their own work or of a peer's written work. They can also be paired with a peer and assume the responsibility for choosing the topic to be written about (for an entire story, paragraph, or even sentence by sentence). For example, two boys in a third-grade class are given the assignment to write a story. One boy, Mike, has severe and multiple disabilities, although he does have vision and is learning to use it.

Mike is offered three pictures to select the topic for the story. He chooses a picture of several different animals; his partner then gives him three different animal pictures to select which animal they are to write about. Mike picks a dog picture. His partner offers him different dog pictures to choose from for different pages of the story. Mike responds to each question from his partner and chooses what pictures to use, what color paper for each picture, where on the page to put the picture, and the order of the pictures. His partner writes a sentence or two per picture to create a story as determined by the order of the pictures. Mike adds page numbers using number stamps or numbered labels. This situation forces Mike to make multiple decisions and respond appropriately and consistently to his partner. It also forces Mike's partner to creatively produce a story that will fit with the pictures. This interplay can be challenging and can also be very helpful to a student who cannot decide what to write. An added benefit is the camaraderie that can occur between the two students as they respond to each other's comments and decisions. Creative works should be maintained so that the students can be paired up again to add to or reread the work. Sending work home also provides family members with a practical means of discussing activities that happened during the school day. Of course, work always has the student's name on it. Signing one's name (or part of one's name) can be done with any writing instrument, a signature stamp (with adapted handle if necessary), individual rubber stamp letters, braille labels, or self-adhesive labels with the name printed on it. There are many opportunities during each school day for students to practice "writing" their name.

Spelling

Learning to spell is a typical activity of most elementary classrooms. Sometimes this lesson is integrated into other curricular areas such as reading, writing, science, and social studies. Some teachers treat this as a more separate skill area. In either case, adaptations are needed to include students with severe sensory and multiple disabilities in spelling activities.

For students with severe disabilities who are learning to recognize some letters or words, participation in spelling activities can be similar to that of students without disabilities. Students can be helped to pick a few words most relevant to their learning needs from the list of spelling words for the class, using a picture or object that matches the word. Students can learn to match the picture or object to the word, or match the same words, or match the first letter of the word to the whole word. Color cues can be added for ease of teaching (to clarify the matching task) and then can be faded as the child begins to cue into the printed word (Jan & Groenveld, 1993; Kelley, Davidson, & Sanspree, 1993). The student can study with a peer who works on the entire spelling list but who also asks the student to do one or more of the matching tasks just described for the few words that are the student's. During the spelling test, the student with severe disabilities may be asked to identify the correctly written word that is on a separate card and to glue that word to the paper to be handed in with the other tests (a matching test). The person supporting this student can decide if the choice is from a field of two words, three words, or any number of words depending on the student's ability. Another option is for the student to identify the first letter of the word to be spelled from a variety of letters offered and glue that letter onto the correct space on the test paper (see Figure 5.3 for this ex-

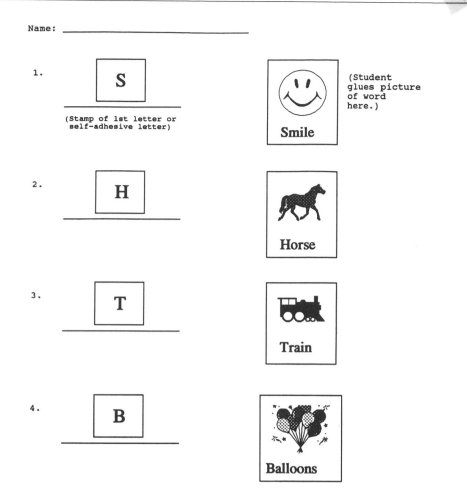

Figure 5.3. Example of an adapted spelling test. The student has previously chosen these words to learn.

ample). The student "signs" his or her name using a signature stamp or self-adhesive label and hands in the test with the others. The goal for this student is to match the picture to the word or vice versa, the object to the word, or to identify initial letters of words in preparation for more advanced reading skills.

For the student with no ability to use print, other adaptations will be necessary. Students who can hear may work on listening for the spelling word (again, words most relevant to the student's daily needs/interests) and identify the correct picture (with the word attached). Objects can also be used in the same manner. Three or four options can be provided per word, depending on the student's ability to discriminate across different options and make decisions. Classmates studying their spelling words with this student can ask the student to find the correct picture or object and then spell the word describing that object, write the word, and use it in a sentence. Students can pair up to create picture/object dictionaries that can be referred to when necessary.

Still other students may be asked to select a spelling word for their classmates to spell by feeling different objects, making a selection based on preference, and handing it to a peer. The peer will spell the word represented by the object (or that could describe the object), use it in a sentence, and spend a few minutes interacting with the student and the item as a form of social interaction. The goal for this student is to attend to a classmate, follow tactual, visual, and auditory cues, tactually discriminate among objects, handle objects appropriately, and socially interact.

The student with hearing, but who is unable to handle objects due to a physical limitation, may want to select the word(s) to be spelled by a peer by looking at the picture or actual object from a variety of possible choices. This student also could use a switch that would activate a tape recorder with the prerecorded spelling words on it. The goal for this student is to have an impact on the social environment through his or her actions. The student learns to respond to the prompts from classmates for the next word by looking at the desired picture or object or by activating the recorded spelling words. Greater fine and gross motor control can be developed if the switch is momentary and requires the student to maintain pressure long enough for each spelling word to be heard twice.

Mathematics

Mathematics provides a highly rich and diverse arena in which to accommodate individual students. Determining the individual student's needs is perhaps the most difficult part of any adaptation process. The educational team must continually strive to keep a clear perspective of the student's current strengths and what mathematics skills he or she will need to be as independent as possible in daily activities. Skills such as counting and one-to-one correspondence have ready application to a number of daily activities such as setting the table, buying a sufficient number of items, passing out school materials, handling money, playing a board or card game, and performing a variety of packaging tasks (as an adult). Number recognition and matching also are valuable lifelong skills that enhance the individual's ability to determine, for example, if enough money is available to make a purchase; play card and board games; or work in a library, retail store, or any place where numbers are used to organize items.

Basic mathematics skills such as these can be taught during any mathematics lesson, with some minor adaptations. To increase student motivation to learn, a calculator with large print numbers and possible voice output can be used to teach number recognition and matching, along with the appropriate fine-motor skills. Students with sufficient vision can use the calculator to check peers' work. This partnership not only epitomizes what is meant by inclusive education but is highly practical as well. Students can use the same textbooks and worksheets to work on their number recognition, counting, and number-matching skills. This eliminates the need to separate the student from the typical activity performed by the other students. Figure 5.4 provides one example of an adapted worksheet for mathematics, along with directions for use. The lesson using this worksheet addresses simple mathematics skills as well as name recognition, fine motor dexterity, and several other skills as described.

Manipulatives can and should be used to clarify the skills being taught. Students can use coins, playing cards, dominoes, Unifix Cubes, popsicle sticks, magnets, poker chips, marbles, building blocks, dice, stickers, toy soldiers, and so on (depending on what is appropriate for their age) anytime they are working

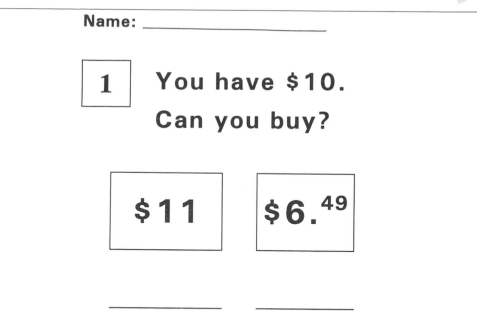

Name: _____

1 You have $10.
Can you buy?

$11 $6.⁴⁹

_____   _____

1) Student chooses from three name stamps (correct one is highlighted in bright yellow) or from three different names on self-adhesive labels with correct name in bright red, and "signs" name where indicated. (Skills: name recognition, fine motor dexterity, recognizing the word *name*, eye–hand coordination to place/stamp name on line.)

2) Student finds appropriate number to match number of sentence (uses number stamps or numbers on self-adhesive labels with cues as stated for name above) and places/stamps number in corresponding place on worksheet. (Skills: number recognition, fine motor dexterity, number matching, eye–hand coordination, number sequencing.)

3) Student is given specified amount of money (bills only) and asked to find the number on the bill. Student finds the same number on a number line (a large, clear, easy-to-read "ruler" with sufficient numbers sequenced to cover the given problem) and places the bill on the number. (Skills: number recognition, number matching, fine motor dexterity, eye–hand coordination.)

4) Student looks at first picture (or actual item) and finds price. Student is taught to look only at big number before the period (e.g., to look at the 9 in $9.48). Student matches price with number on number line and places picture or object there. (Skills: visual attention, number localization, number matching, fine motor dexterity.)

5) Student is told the rule and shown that "the money has to be on this side (right) of the picture/object to buy it." Student is asked if he or she can buy the item. This is modeled/demonstrated/cued as many times as needed until student answers correctly. (Skills: auditory and visual comprehension, attention to task, concept of more/less.)

6) Student finds yes or no self-adhesive label (color-coded) and applies to box under picture/item. (Skills: fine motor dexterity, eye–hand coordination to apply answer to space on sheet, recognition of words yes and no.)

7) Repeat steps until worksheet is completed or mathematics period is over. Peers who have completed their work can join the activity. Work not finished can go home as homework or be completed at a later time. (Skills: all skills mentioned in Steps 1–6, social interaction skills.)

Figure 5.4. Sample mathematics worksheet.

with numbers. Certain manipulatives—such as board games, cards, dominoes, and money—not only teach basic mathematics skills, like number recognition, matching, and sequencing, but also can teach typical leisure activities and appropriate social skills. This use of manipulatives benefits the entire class, making the mathematical concepts easier to understand and more motivating.

When students cannot use their vision well enough to engage in the basic arithmetic skills of number recognition and matching, the activity must be adapted somewhat to target counting real objects, as mentioned earlier. For example, students in a sixth-grade class are learning beginning algebra. They are learning to manipulate equations to determine missing numerical values. The teacher is interested in the thought process of how this occurs and is not particularly concerned with what numbers are used. The students are working in groups of three to figure out individual problems. Cyndi, for example, is assigned to one group. Cyndi has very limited vision, moderate hearing loss, and mild quadriplegia cerebral palsy. She also puts most objects in her mouth, has a problem with excessive drool, and is not very responsive to her peers. In this mathematics lesson Cyndi uses a magnetic wand to pick up magnetic bingo pieces (or paper clips). She pulls the objects off of the wand and is learning to hand them to a peer in response to their tactile and auditory request. The number of objects she hands them becomes one number in their equation. She does this twice per equation, while her peers figure out the third missing number. Cyndi is learning to handle objects appropriately and respond to her peers. She also enjoys the feel of the magnet's strength, and pulling the objects off the magnetic wand improves her fine motor control. The special education support teacher or assistant prevents her from putting objects in her mouth by simply blocking those movements and redirecting her to manipulate the objects with her hands instead. All students' needs are being met within this one activity. (Obviously, the same process could be used for basic addition, subtraction, multiplication, and division practice as well.)

Another example targets a fifth-grade classroom where students study the concepts of volume and weight through the use of popped popcorn. One fifth grader, Paco, has no vision or hearing and uses a wheelchair for mobility. The classroom teacher thought that using popcorn would make good use of Paco's olfactory abilities and would be fun for everyone. Students were assigned to groups of six and given popcorn, popcorn popper, oil, measuring tools, scale, and so forth. Paco delivers these items to each group using his tray and the help of a classmate. Classmates thank Paco by rubbing his arm, which Paco likes. With his own group, Paco explores the items tactually before helping to pour the popcorn into a measuring cup and then into the popcorn popper. (The popper is washed after Paco explores it.) Paco is learning to grasp and release items and to control his movements so as to better handle various items. Paco does this while members of his group decide how to determine the weight and volume of the corn once it is popped. Paco helps add oil and then uses a switch device to activate the popcorn popper. His classmates tactually cue him to start, maintain pressure, and stop when the popcorn is ready. Members of Paco's group calculate volume of popcorn and help Paco pour it into a bowl to weigh it. They fill out the worksheet accompanying the lesson while eating the popcorn. Paco is in charge of the salt shaker, and members of his group must tactually request it and then return it to him. Paco is learning to respond quickly and appropriately to all such requests. All groups report their findings while Paco and a few classmates clean up the materials. (A higher-grade level of students working on percentages and probability can engage in a similar activity by popping only a certain number of popcorn kernels at one time and trying to predict the probability of all kernels being popped and the percentage popped each time. This lesson provides opportunities for a student with a severe multiple disability to handle small items and count raw and popped kernels.)

Regardless of the materials used or how mathematics is targeted in a variety of activities, the emphasis should be on functionality for the learner as well as fun. Rote drill and practice, aside from being boring, may leave the student wondering how the information relates to anything meaningful. Teachers must be prepared to change activities frequently (still addressing the same or similar mathematics concepts, but in different ways). Whenever possible, students should be offered choices of materials, activities, partners, software programs, and so on, and the student should easily detect the element of fun. Because numerical concepts are prevalent in many games and enjoyable activities, keeping the learning of mathematics active and entertaining should not be overly difficult.

Science

As in the area of mathematics, science offers countless ways to actively include a wide range of diverse learners. Science activities typically involve hands-on manipulation of materials to determine the underlying principles being studied (Gurganus, Janas, & Schmitt, 1995; Mastropieri & Scruggs, 1995). Materials need to be gathered, arranged, and manipulated in such a way that an end result is attained. Some activities require that careful attention be paid to the precise manner in which materials are manipulated, whereas other activities allow more creative and independent actions. Either way, science activities offer numerous opportunities for students to learn how to properly handle a wide array of different items, follow directions, and work cooperatively within a social group.

As with the other academic areas, certain adaptations will be needed to allow for full participation and active learning on the part of the student with severe sensory and multiple disabilities. These adaptations will depend on the science activity, expectations for the entire class, the skills of the student in question, and the student's learning needs. Obviously, some activities will require more adaptation than others. For example, a fourth-grade class was studying dinosaurs, a theme that spans reading, writing, spelling, mathematics, art, and science. The class researched dinosaurs and created a 4-foot-by-6-foot replica of a likely scene from the Jurassic period. One student had 12-inch battery-operated plastic dinosaurs, which had been adapted to be switch operated and were the focal point for the replication. Students in the class used mud, clay, dirt, rocks, and a variety of art materials to create a living area for these two dinosaurs. The owner of the dinosaurs (who had severe sensory and multiple disabilities) assisted in the dinosaur research by choosing which book of two or three he wanted to have read to him (a communication objective) and by assisting in the creation of the replication (involving objectives for fine motor control and relaxation of overly tense muscles). He also chose different colors of paint for a peer to paint different parts of the replica (another communication objective). Finally, when the scenario had been replicated to size (involving considerable mathematics skills), this student received encouragement from his peers to activate the switches that moved the plastic dinosaurs within their "dinorama." Although this student may not have learned the same facts about dinosaurs as his classmates, or acquired the same mathematics skills that they practiced, he did have opportunities to practice his individualized education program (IEP) objectives, to remain a part of his learning group, and to enjoy the experience.

As another example, a first-grade class is studying aerodynamics—a topic that addresses reading, writing, mathematics, art, and science. As one part of this lesson, students are paired with a classmate and given a paper airplane that they will decorate. Each airplane has been designed differently for varying aerodynamic purposes. The intent behind the buddy system and the decorating of the planes is not only to have fun but to get students to share the decision-making process of how the plane should look. One student chooses how to decorate the shared plane by looking and reaching for a crayon (which her peer uses to color parts of the plane) and by selecting a variety of stickers that her peer puts on the plane for her. Once the planes are decorated, the paired classmates go outside to see how their model flies. One of the students just mentioned cannot throw a paper plane, and so a launcher has been designed for her that sits on the tray of her wheelchair. The launcher is essentially a piece of wood with a groove in it to hold the paper plane in the right position. A clothespin trigger with a rubberband is hit which in turn launches the airplane. The student who is unable to throw the plane must follow her peer's advice to visually find the trigger (clothespin) and apply sufficient strength to it to launch the plane. She then proceeds to launch all the planes, as one by one each couple places their plane on her launcher. This technique allows for a controlled way in which to see which aerodynamic design carries the plane the farthest, highest, or makes the most interesting maneuvers. In addition, it creates many opportunities for this young first grader to respond to her classmates via touch, gestures, and verbal encouragement. Following this activity, when her partner fills out the accompanying worksheet, this young girl chooses colors for the airplane illustration, assists in running a rubber stamp roller of an airplane design around the worksheet border, and writes her name in the appropriate place using a signature stamp with an adapted handle. She must choose her name stamp from one other to help her learn to recognize her name.

Other science topics that can easily accommodate the needs of a student having difficulty seeing, hearing, moving, and understanding abstract concepts include: magnetic fields, weighing items, identifying objects that float versus sink, plants, animals, recycling, gravity, categorizing items by unique characteristics, and materials that change form (e.g., ice to water). It would be difficult to identify a topic in science that would not provide a valuable learning experience for most students. Again, the objectives for the student with severe sensory and multiple disabilities may differ substantially from those for other students. However, all students can participate in learning, whether or not they attain the same end result.

Social Studies

The verbal nature of this topic poses more of a difficulty when attempting to include students whose verbal skills may be severely limited. However, adaptations can be made to successfully include students in these lessons and still meet individual needs. The team must be creative in working together to identify which parts of the lesson are most applicable, as well as the best way for the student to participate and learn.

Although reading about the topics typically addressed as part of a social studies curriculum is a common way to teach the information, creative teachers recognize the importance of hands-on, active learning experiences to teach their lessons. Teachers employ the use of films, field trips, guest speakers, and projects to maintain interest and heighten learning. These kinds of learning experiences are important to the student with severe sensory and multiple disabilities. Working collaboratively, the classroom teacher and inclusion support teacher can determine the most appropriate way to make the lessons worthwhile to the student with special needs, while at the same time maximizing instruction for all students in the class.

Depending on the grade level, social studies covers a wide range of topics, such as environmental issues, careers, citizenship, current events, historical time periods, and cultures of different countries. All of these topics can be taught using a multimedia approach as well as by engaging students in a variety of different activities. It is not possible within the confines of this chapter to describe ways to adapt every topic in social studies for the student with severe sensory and multiple disabilities; however, it is hoped that the four examples following—on environmental issues, historical periods, careers, and the history and culture of a country—will provide ideas for additional adaptations as needed across other topics.

Environmental Issues Environmental issues can be taught across grade levels and can involve a number of hands-on activities and informative field trips. For example, the class can request parents and neighbors to bring to school recyclable materials. Students sort and bag these materials and study future uses for them. Ryan, an active and creative fourth grader who cannot see or hear and has other learning difficulties, brings in recyclable items and helps classmates sort the items into appropriate bins. While classmates are discussing future uses for recyclable materials, Ryan continues to sort, crush aluminum cans, and organize materials for dropping off at the recycling center. In art, as part of this unit, students make sculptures out of wire, pop-tops from aluminum cans, and small cans. Ryan tactually examines several sculptures and then makes his own with assistance as needed from an inclusion support aide or parent volunteeer. The class also picks up litter around the school, sorts out the recyclable waste, and throws the rest away. Ryan uses the sighted guidance of a classmate and holds one of the garbage bags. He also participates in picking up the litter when there are several pieces of it in one spot and his sighted guide cues him to bend over and carefully feel for it. The class takes field trips to both a recycling center and a dump for waste. Ryan helps classmates unload the material they brought to these places and tactually explores containers and machinery that are safe to examine. Back in class, the students write reports sequencing the steps involved in either recycling or waste management. Ryan creates the design for the cover of a classmate's report using small pieces of recyclable materials (e.g., shredded paper, pop-tops, cardboard, and Styrofoam). Both boys put their names on the report, Ryan using a prebrailled sticky label. Although Ryan does not read braille, he does this as standard practice on all individual and shared work, so he can recognize his work and eventually learn to recognize his name.

Historical Period As another example of a social studies adaptation, as part of a sixth-grade unit on the "Old West," the class is engaged in playing the software program, "The Oregon Trail." They work in cooperative groups making the numerous decisions as teams. Shawna has a cortical visual impairment, seeing better on some days than others. She uses a wheelchair for support and mobility and has a difficult time holding objects or manipulating them for any length of time. Shawna responds best to movement and bright colors and appears to like to watch the computer screen as the images change. She also smiles when she hears various sounds that are part of the software program. Shawna uses an adaptive switch and keyboard to play with her teammates. They cue her to activate the switch when decisions are made, and they visually cue her to look at the screen as needed. As part of this unit, the class reads stories on the West and compares living conditions of the 1800s to the present. Students or volunteers read and tape short stories or parts of stories/reports so that Shawna can use her switch to activate the tapes at other times or play a section to the class when called upon by the teacher. When writing descriptions comparing the 1800s to the present, Shawna uses color-coded cards containing specific information that she matches using a rotary scanner and switch (see Figure 5.5). Information from her correct matches (using the color highlights) is added to the report. Reports are presented orally to the class by each team. Shawna's part is prerecorded by a teammate, and she activates the tape when cued, using her switch. To culminate the unit, the class reenacts a day in the "Old West" by dressing up in appropriate clothing, preparing food that might be eaten then, learning songs to sing, and staging other appropriate activities. Parent volunteers help with the cooking, and the first-grade classes are also invited. Shawna participates in all these activities: preparation, dress-up, role playing, cooking, and tasting of food. She indicates her choices by looking and touching pictures and objects that represent different activities/items of interest. Her learning goals target communication, social interaction, picture recognition, decision making, increased time on task, and appropriate object manipulation.

Careers   Awareness of different careers can and should begin early in the elementary years. A first-grade class learning about the different roles people play in their neighborhood and community engage in valuable hands-on activities as part of a social studies unit. Field trips are taken to local businesses and public service agencies. Photographs are taken of all of these places by the students, with help from the teacher and parent volunteers. Pamphlets, logos, and other information also are gathered and taken back to school. Exhibits and maps of parts of the community are recreated using the photographs and other graphic information to designate places, businesses, and community members. Software programs such as *KidArt* and *KidPix* (by Broderbund) allow children to create many computer-generated images of community helpers to supplement the other information on the community map. Stephen, a class member with moderate hearing loss and a visual impairment, is involved in all these activities. One of Stephen's strengths is his ability to move quickly and efficiently and manipulate items easily. He also has a short attention span and exhibits disruptive behaviors (destroying materials, throwing items, and screaming). He wears hearing aids and glasses, but he takes these off and throws them when frustrated or angry.

Stephen attends all field trips and is provided additional support by the inclusion support teacher, who clues him in to critical information, directs and redirects his attention, and simplifies the information using visual cues and fewer words. She also anticipates and blocks attempts on Stephen's part to destroy items or to run off. He collects information like the other children and puts them

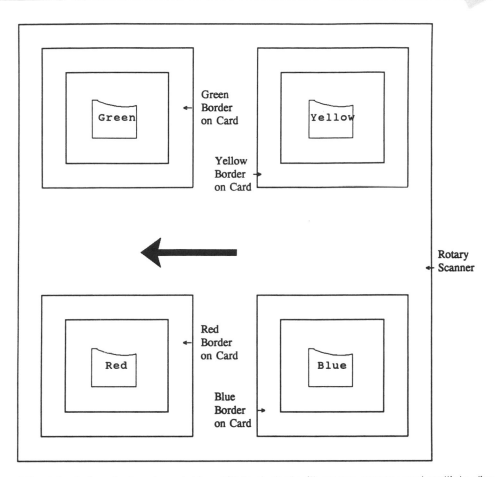

Figure 5.5. Adaptations to teach matching skills to student with severe sensory and multiple disabilities in sixth-grade social studies unit on the "Old West." *Use of Scanner:* Student is shown separate card with one of the four colored borders on it. On the card is one theme discussed during the Old West unit (e.g., transportation, clothing, trade). Student uses a touch-sensitive switch to activate the scanner until it stops at the matching colored square. A classmate then selects a card from the card holder attached with Velcro in this square and must answer a question pertaining to that theme.

in a zippered fanny pack to avoid tearing them or throwing them away. In school, Stephen uses a keyguard on the computer to help him avoid hitting several keys at once and to encourage him to look at specific keys before touching them. Only keys needed to run the software program are left uncovered.

As a part of this unit, parents and other family members come to school to tell the class what careers they have chosen and what that involves. When Stephen's parents come in, Stephen introduces them to his classmates using signs for "mother" and "father." On another day, the teacher reads stories to the class about different occupations, which the librarian reinforces when the class goes to the library. Stephen sits close to the person telling the story and occasionally is requested to hold the book toward the class so everyone can see the pictures. Sometimes Stephen needs to sit close to an adult (who rubs his shoulders) or in a big beanbag chair for additional sensory input and physical support, while he looks through his own copy of the book being read. If particularly energetic, he may be given a small rubbery ball to hold and squeeze to calm him and help him attend to the story. When the teacher asks questions about the stories, Stephen uses pictures (choosing from one of two options) and holds one up as his response. The questions are simplified to assist in his understanding of the expected response. For example, instead of asking the question, "Who puts out fires?" the inclusion support aide or teacher might offer Stephen two pictures and ask, using the sign for firefighter, "Which one is the firefighter?"

This study topic also involves written assignments. Worksheets can be adapted to allow Stephen to demonstrate skills and to hand in his work like the other students. These worksheets involve the use of pictures to write with as well as adapted means of writing numbers and one's name. Figure 5.6 provides an example of one such worksheet and the accompanying explanation.

Finally, children choose their favorite occupation and dress up accordingly for an "our town" simulation. Stephen is given specific things to do in his role of mailman (a role he chose) to help him avoid becoming overstimulated. Be-

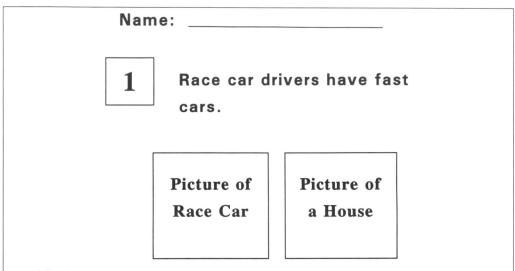

Name: _____

1 **Race car drivers have fast cars.**

| Picture of Race Car | Picture of a House |

1) Student chooses from three name stamps (correct one is highlighted in bright yellow) or from three different self-adhesive labels with correct name in bright red, and "signs" name where indicated. Peer adds name as well, if both are turning in paper together. (Skills: name recognition, fine motor dexterity, recognizing the word *name*, eye–hand coordination to place/stamp name on line.)

2) Peer writes sentence related to unit of study. Student finds appropriate number to match number of sentence (uses number stamps or numbers on self-adhesive labels with cues as stated for name above) and places/stamps number in corresponding place on worksheet. (Skills: number recognition, fine motor dexterity, number matching, eye–hand coordination, number sequencing.)

3) Student chooses from among two or three pictures the most appropriate one to describe the sentence that the teacher or peer writes and reads to him or her. For initial teaching, the teacher cues by bringing correct picture closer, tapping it, and/or preventing the student from picking up the incorrect picture by keeping the teacher's hands on it. (Skills: auditory comprehension, visual discrimination, recognition of pictures, matching auditory information to pictorial information, and responding to a peer or teacher.)

4) Student uses glue stick to adhere correct picture to spot below sentence and places picture with the correct visual orientation on the page. (Skills: fine motor dexterity, visual recognition of picture and picture orientation, eye–hand coordination.)

Figure 5.6.   Sample social studies worksheet. The student selects the appropriate illustration for each sentence.

cause the activity can be somewhat noisy and confusing, at times Stephen is taken out in the hall to calm him down for a few minutes before returning to the activity. The classroom teacher and special education support person determine when this becomes necessary. Either person may help Stephen to calm down, while the other adult remains in the classroom.

Studying a Country This final example of a social studies unit describes a third-grade class study of the history, culture, language, and geography of Mexico. Students are grouped in fours to research various aspects of the country, each group deciding what they wish to research. They go to the library, listen to stories read on Mexico, and obtain their own books. The teacher brings in different guest speakers (some of whom are parents of the children) to learn about the dress, music, customs, food, crafts, and folklore of Mexico. As part of the unit, students reproduce some of the folk art in art class, learn some Mexican folk songs in music, and play games in physical education that are common to Mexico. As a bilingual class, they are already learning Spanish, which is woven throughout all lessons. Mathematics, reading, spelling, and writing also are integrated throughout activities involving this unit on Mexico. At the end of the unit, each team of four makes an oral report to the class on the information they have obtained. They use visual media as well, to illustrate their points.

Certain accommodations need to be made for Carlos, who is a member of this class and has significant challenges that interfere with his learning. Carlos is beginning to say a few words in English and Spanish (e.g., "hi," "bye," "no," and "ok") when appropriate. He is also beginning to ambulate with a walker, although he uses a wheelchair for most mobility purposes. Carlos is totally blind and likes to find out about things by putting them in his mouth. He screams when frustrated, bored, or desires attention.

Carlos is engaged in all learning activities. He chooses what peer reads to him, often preferring someone who can read to him in Spanish, the primary language spoken at home. He may not understand everything being read, but when the reader pauses, he does indicate by vocalizing and hitting the book that he wants the reader to continue. He also listens for longer periods of time when allowed to hold objects related to the unit (e.g., a gourd or onyx piece of artwork). He is prevented from putting objects in his mouth by the inclusion support aide, who uses her arm to block this movement. She immediately redirects him to explore the items with his hands only, but does not draw any negative attention to this behavior. He chooses topics for peers to help him investigate by indicating "no" or "ok" when asked.

Carlos practices walking with a walker from one work area to another in the classroom, and stands for added weight-bearing practice during some activities (e.g., cooking and art activities). For several activities, he is given different materials that are needed and is taught to respond to his classmates' requests for the materials. In this way he is learning the names of some objects, how to handle objects appropriately, how to respond to specific requests, and how to tactually differentiate one item from another.

TARGETING INDIVIDUAL STUDENT NEEDS ACROSS EACH DAY

The preceding examples demonstrate ways in which all children can and do learn together across different subject areas. The educational team takes advantage of typical daily classroom activities, focusing on student strengths and adapting as appropriate to meet individual needs. As described in Chapter 3, an activity analysis is done for each student with disabilities to identify when specific IEP objectives will be targeted across different activities (an activity analysis for a first grader with severe sensory and multiple impairments is presented in Table 5.4). Such analyses clarify for all team members how skills will be addressed during the day. They also help to clarify that content mastery may not be the primary objective, but that participation in the same activities as the other students does provide sufficient opportunities to practice crucial skills. Once this analysis has been done by all team members, the daily schedule can be devised with the special and general educators, clarifying how desired outcomes will be addressed on a daily basis.

Analyzing the entire school day's activities needs to occur so that everyone involved in a student's education can see how, when, and where critical skills from IEP objectives will be taught and who can provide the necessary instruction and support. Not all of a student's IEP objectives can be met in one activity. However, seeing how the entire day unfolds aids the team in collaborating to ensure a comprehensive and coordinated program. Figures 5.7 and 5.8 provide examples of two students' daily schedules, specifying adaptations to enable each student to participate according to his or her strengths and identifying those available to provide support. Both students are full-time class members who receive all of their support services within their typical classrooms.

TRANSITION TO MIDDLE SCHOOL

Expectations for secondary school students can differ substantially from those for elementary school students (McKenzie & Houk, 1993). Students typically do not remain with the same teacher and peer group for the majority of the day, but instead take several classes from different teachers and interact with different classmates. Although cooperative planning by the educational team needs to occur as the child moves from grade to grade in elementary school, the learning arrangement in secondary school places new demands on students and may be particularly challenging for some students, especially those with severe sensory and multiple disabilities. Thus, the need to actively plan the transition from elementary to middle school is extremely important.

Due to a limited ability to receive visual or auditory input or both and to process that information easily, students with severe sensory and multiple disabilities will need an opportunity to become familiar with their new school prior to attending it. They need the chance to physically explore the next environment in order to gain some comfort level with the actual physical transition. Supported by family members, this familiarization can take place at the new school in the months before summer break or during the summer months. As with all decisions, the way in which the transition occurs represents a team decision that best meets the student's and family's needs. A student's classmates can be a major asset to a successful transition (see Bishop & Jubala, 1994).

The receiving team also needs time to prepare for a smooth transition. They need information about the student (e.g., likes, dislikes, strengths, limitations), what the student needs to learn, and how the student learns. Written as well as videotaped information as part of a portfolio assessment must be shared with

Table 5.4. Activity analysis for first grader

Student: Joshua is 6 years old, is eager to learn, and likes being with other children. He is totally blind and has developmental delays, and cerebral palsy. He uses a wheelchair.

Goals	A.M. Storytime	Spelling	Math	Science	Reading	Writing	Physical education
1. Increase comprehension skills	Ask who, what, when, where, and how—give choices for answers.	Define spelling words (says yes or no to meanings provided). Peer puts word in sentence and Joshua says yes or no if it makes sense. Identifies first letter of word.	In 1:1 correspondence, simple story problem. Joshua makes up problem using different items for peers to add together (e.g., coins, popsicle sticks).	What happened first, second, third... last? What materials were used? Who did what? (Give choices; Joshua confirms or denies.)	Ask one of the five w's. Give choices, choose book or program, tell story (sequence), and ask Joshua to confirm or deny order.	Peers write sentences and Joshua confirms or denies whether they make sense or are funny, scary, and so forth.	What's going on in PE? Who's on what team? Who's the captain? What are the rules? What equipment is needed? Give limited choices for his answers.
2. Addition/subtraction by 1	Ask number of people/animals/items in stories. Add/subtract these people by having them come together or leave (use manipulatives).	Count number of words, children in group, then add set; count letters in words.	Use manipulatives (cubes, beads, raised number line), work on some math problems in book using talking calculator.	Count objects used in experiment, take 1 away, add 1. Count students in group.	Computer math program using manipulatives, number the questions of story: #1, Who—$1 + 1 = 2$; #2, What—$2 + 1 = 3$; #3, Where—....	Label number of sentences written by peer, using braille sticky labels.	Keep score, count students on each team, count warmup exercises.
3. Increase expressive communication; increase social skills with peers	Respond to questions about story (one word or yes/no).	Joshua asks peer to explain words used in spelling ("What?").	Tell answer to teacher by raising card with answer on it after confirming/denying it is correct.	Work with peer, ask peer to explain, ask question of peer, make comments (one word).	Work with peer who is finished working; ask for clarification from peer ("What?").	Pass brailled notes back and forth (underlined for classmates and spoken to Joshua).	Pair with peer who pushes wheelchair, thank peer, comment on game, cheer classmates.
4. Braille readiness	Follow along on brailled story, turn page at end, find top of page.	Braille words, line up paper in brailler, braille name to paper.	Count small manipulatives, count number of braille words per line, count braille designs per line.	Read brailled number 1 (first), number 2 (second)...for assignments in science. Add brailled name to assignment.	Follow along in braille book, brailled keyboard for computer, feels brailled question.	Braille name, spelling words, braille first letter of words written by peer.	Feel braille label on door.
5. Increase orientation and mobility	Have Joshua trail walls to go places in the room, explain where he is, tell him who's to left and right, where teacher is; give directions to get himself there.						

Student: Celia is a young girl with strong preferences, good use of her hands, and a wonderful giggle. She appears to have much to say, but has a difficult time doing so and may scratch or bite her arm when frustrated. Celia has no vision and uses a wheelchair.

Typical activities		Adaptations for Celia
8:00 A.M.	Enter class, greet teacher/peers, put things away in cubby, go to desk, stand for pledge of allegiance, listen to morning teacher announcements.	Sixth-grader (neighbor) pushes Celia in wheelchair into room and helps her put things away after she identifies her own cubby tactually. Teacher and peers prompt Celia to greet them (a vocalization or head up). She listens to pledge of allegiance and announcements, but is allowed to fiddle with onyx pieces that she collects. Aide goes over daily schedule with her.
		Goals: greater independence in daily routines, social interactions with peers, and receptive and expressive communication.
8:20	Reading groups—students move from independent reading centers to reading group with teacher.	Teacher assigns Celia to a group, which assumes responsibility for getting her from one center to the next. The group reads to her, asking her to indicate (by touching) which child she wants to read out loud. Teacher reads for Celia in her group. Celia indicates who goes next.
		Goals: decision making, attending to task, listening
8:40	Creative writing—students work in small writing groups to create an ending to a story.	Supported by aide, Celia chooses between different objects she wants to incorporate into her story (to be read by peer when finished).
		Goals: decision making, receptive and expressive communication
9:00	Transition time—clean up work, put away.	Aide helps her to go to bathroom. Celia partially participates in this activity.
		Goal: increase independence in daily activities
9:05	Music	Celia goes to music room with peers, vocalizes, holds instruments, chooses where to sit.
		Goals: decision making, following directions, appropriate use of items.
9:45	Mathematics —Students receive large-group instruction, then work in small groups. —Cooperative learning groups on addition/subtraction word problems.	Aide and teacher work with entire class; fifth grader having trouble in math assists Celia and others. Celia plays board games that incorporate counting, making purchases (handling money, exchanging money for items).
		Goals: Functional math skills, following directions, receptive and expressive communication.
10:30	Recess	Celia is helped outside by peers and plays with two best friends. She decides where to play and with what.
		Goals: friendship development, decision making, receptive and expressive communication

(continued)

Figure 5.7. Sample daily schedule for second-grader.

Figure 5.7. *(continued)*

Typical activities	Adaptations for Celia
10:50	Science —Large-group instruction —Cooperative learning groups of four do experiment, write results, report to class.	Depending on unit studied, Celia follows directions from peers, holds objects (animals, plants, magnets, etc.), recognizes similarities, differences, characteristics of items.
		Goals: following directions, decision making, receptive and expressive communication, social interactions, appropriate use of items.
11:30	Lunch	Aide assists and physically supports Celia while eating with peers in lunch room. Celia chooses food/drink items. She responds to comments and questions from friends.
		Goals: decision making, social interactions with peers, independence in daily activities.
12:00 noon	Recess	As before, aide assists Celia in bathroom before going to recess.
12:15 P.M.	Library—listen to story from librarian; check out book, read.	Teacher assists Celia while listening to story. Celia holds objects related to story and later listens to her own chosen book on tape.
		Goals: attending to task, appropriate use of items.
1:00	Computer lab	Volunteer assists Celia to access computer with speech output—musical program.
		Goals: decision making, attending to task, appropriate use of computer.
1:50	Prepare to leave school with class. Get belongings from cubbies. Say good-bye to teacher/peers.	Peers help Celia get her things, say good-bye; neighbor helps her home.
		Goals: social interaction, decision making, appropriate handling of items.

Notes on Related Service Support:
- On Mondays at 10:50 A.M. during science, the teacher certified in visual impairments works with Celia in the classroom, teaching her to make good use of her tactile discrimination skills and monitoring this part of the program. This teacher also works with Celia on Wednesdays at 8:20 A.M. during reading and assists the classroom teacher in promoting Celia's comprehension of aural material.
- On Tuesdays and Fridays, the physical therapist works with Celia at 9:05 A.M. during physical education (this class alternates with music and art). The therapist has Celia do exercises (stretches and range of motion) on a mat, usually with two or three other students, and then adapts and supports her participation in the class activities.
- On Wednesdays, the speech-language pathologist works with Celia on clarifying her communicative intent during mathematics (9:45 A.M.) and on Mondays during creative writing (8:40 A.M.).
- On days when related service professionals work with students, the teaching assistant or special education support teacher works with other students in other classrooms, helps the classroom teacher with other students in that room, or consults with the specialists.

the receiving educational team (e.g., general educator, special education support teacher, administrator, counselor) well before the student plans to attend the new school. The sending team can answer questions regarding expectations for behavior, while the receiving team may have questions regarding the most effective ways to interact, expectations for the student's performance, and potential problem areas or issues for the student. Sharing this type of information with even some of the future team members can help to alleviate fears and ensure the most effective transition. Transition planning should begin no later than March for the

Student: Michael has many skills, such as verbal comprehension, some verbal expression, and good fine motor skills. He also has no vision, some echolalia, and mental retardation.

Time	Sample daily activities
8:00 A.M.	Morning announcements over public address system. Daily oral language—peer reads sentence to be grammatically corrected to Mike. Mike tells classmate what the sentence means to him, with help from teaching assistant. Peer corrects the sentence. (Goals: auditory comprehension, verbal expression.)
8:15	Reading—Mike reads library book with peer, who reads it out loud. Mike tapes his book report while others write theirs. Teaching assistant facilitates Mike's verbal expression. (Goals: auditory comprehension, verbal expression.)
9:00	Science—continuing unit on insects. Mike helps to get materials needed and work area set up for group of four. Peers perform dissection, telling Mike what they're doing and helping him tactually explore. Peers and teaching assistant help him with recording findings on a tape recorder. (Goals: social interaction with peers, tactile discrimination, organizational skills, verbal expression.)
9:45	Physical Education—Mike uses cane to walk to PE and then warms up with class, following directions from the teacher. He runs laps using peer as sighted guide. Adaptations are used when and where needed to allow full participation (e.g., Mike uses batting tee and runs with a runner during softball). (Goals: physical development, following directions, social interaction, learning rules of common sports.)
10:30	Mathematics—unit on fractions. Individual numbers from the mathematics text have been brailled for some problems. Mike is learning to identify numbers and find them on his talking calculator. Peers help with function keys ($\times$, $+$, $-$) and ask him to check their work. Mike also responds to peers' requests to roll a dice, count the dots when rolled, and report that number to peers for numerator/denominator in problems they are creating. Special education support teacher instructs Mike and other students. (Goals: tactile discrimination of braille numbers, counting, use of a calculator, responding appropriately to peer requests.)
11:15	Free time to read or finish work from morning. Special education support teacher helps Mike finish math or earlier work.
11:30	Lunch—Mike uses cane to walk with peers to lunch room, where he makes choice of chocolate or white milk when asked by lunch assistant. Peer or parent volunteer helps Mike carry tray to table. He eats and socializes with classmates.
12:00 noon	Recess—Mike plays tether ball with peers or walks around playground with group of kids from class.
12:30 P.M.	Social studies—unit on maps. Teaching assistant helps Mike create a tactile map of the school and his neighborhood using cardboard and string or pipe cleaners to delineate markers and boundaries. Mike brailles some words to label the map. (Goals: tactile discrimination, spatial awareness and organization, general knowledge of maps and map making, braille writing.)

(continued)

Figure 5.8. Sample daily schedule for fifth-grader.

Figure 5.8. *(continued)*

Time	Sample daily activities
1:15	Creative writing—students read part of a story and then write the ending. Peer reads to Mike. Mike either records his story on a tape recorder or relays his thoughts and ideas to peer with help from teaching assistant. They cowrite the ending. Students share their stories with rest of class. (Goals: listening skills, creativity, problem solving, cooperation with peer, verbal expression.)
2:00	Art—Mike participates in all art media. He listens to directions and background information. Then he creates artwork using materials others are using, unless materials are visual only. As necessary, adaptations are made (e.g., when students draw, Mike uses paper on a mesh plastic screen and a dull pointed tool to create tactile designs). Teaching assistant supports Mike as needed. (Goals: creative expression, listening skills, fine motor development, tactual discrimination.)
2:45	Students finish up work, gather materials, and get homework. Mike uses cane to get to school bus. He socializes with peers on the way home.

Notes on Related Service Support:
- On Tuesdays the teacher certified in visual impairments works with Mike on recognizing braille numbers during mathematics (10:30 A.M.). This teacher also works with Mike on his listening skills and verbal expression on Thursdays during creative writing (1:15 P.M.) and on Fridays during reading (8:15 A.M.).
- On Mondays and Wednesdays the speech-language pathologist works with Mike on his comprehension and verbal expression skills during reading (8:15 A.M.).
- The orientation and mobility teacher works with Mike on Mondays going to PE and on Thursdays going to lunch. This teacher has assessed Mike's skills, has developed programs to teach him his daily routes, and monitors his progress throughout the year.

following school year. Again, cooperative planning for transition will be important as the student progresses through each secondary grade level.

REFERENCES

Adams, M.J. (1990). *Beginning to read: Thinking and learning about print.* Urbana-Champaign: University of Illinois.

Bishop, K., & Jubala, K. (1994). By June, given shared experiences, integrated classes, and equal opportunities, Jaime will have a friend. *Teaching Exceptional Children, 21*(1), 36–40.

Giangreco, M.F., Cloninger, C.J., & Iverson, V.S. (1993). *Choosing Options and Accommodations for Children (COACH): A guide to planning inclusive education.* Balimore: Paul H. Brookes Publishing Co.

Gurganus, S., Janas, M., & Schmitt, L. (1995). Science instruction: What special education teachers need to know and what roles they need to play. *Teaching Exceptional Children, 27*(4), 7–9.

Jan, J.E., & Groenveld, M. (1993). Visual behaviors and adaptations associated with cortical and ocular impairment in children. *Journal of Vision Impairments and Blindness, 87,* 101–105.

Johnson, D.W., & Johnson, R.T. (1989). *Cooperation and competition: Theory research.* Edina, MN: Interaction Books.

Johnson, D.W., Johnson, R.T., & Holubec, E. (1990). *Cooperation in the classroom* (rev. ed.). Edina, MN: Interaction Books.

Katz, L. (1988). Engaging children's minds: The implications of research for early childhood education. In C. Warger (Ed.), *A resource guide to public school early childhood programs* (pp. 32–52). Alexandria, VA: Association for Supervision and Curriculum Development.

Kelley, P., Davidson, R., & Sanspreer, M.J. (1993). Vision and orientation and mobility consultations for children with severe multiple disabilities. *Journal of Visual Impairments and Blindness, 87,* 397–401.

Kovalik, S. (1993). *Integrated thematic instruction: The model* (2nd ed.). Oak Creek, AZ: Susan Kovalik & Associates.

Mastropieri, M.A., & Scruggs, T.E. (1995). Teaching science to students with disabilities in general education settings: Practical and proven strategies. *Teaching Exceptional Children, 27*(4), 10–13.

McKenzie, R.G., & Houk, C.S. (1993). Across the great divide: Transition from elementary to secondary settings for students with mild disabilities. *Teaching Exceptional Children, 25*(2), 16–20.

Putnam, J.W., & Spenciner, L.J. (1993). Supporting young children's development through cooperative activities. In J.W. Putnam (Ed.), *Cooperative learning and strategies for inclusion: Celebrating diversity in the classroom* (pp. 123–143). Baltimore: Paul H. Brookes Publishing Co.

Roberson, W.H., Gravel, J.S., Valcante, G.C., & Maurer, R.G. (1992). Using a picture task analysis to teach students with multiple disabilities. *Teaching Exceptional Children, 24*(4), 12–16.

Smith-Burke, M.T., Deegan, D., & Jaggar, A.M. (1991). Whole language: A viable alternative for special and remedial education. *Topics in Language Disorders, 11*(3), 58–68.

Tefft-Cousin, P., Weekly, T., & Gerard, J. (1993). The functional use of language and literacy by students with severe language and learning problems. *Language Arts, 70,* 548–556.

Wisniewski, L., & Anderson, R. (1995). Managing the needs of students with physical and health challenges in inclusive settings. In D.L. Ryndak & S. Alper (Eds.), *Curriculum content for students with moderate and severe disabilities in inclusive settings* (pp. 243–268). Needham, MA: Allyn & Bacon.

Chapter 6

THE MIDDLE SCHOOL
AND HIGH SCHOOL STUDENT

June E. Downing

Compared with the elementary school years, the secondary school years feature considerably more complex academic work and subject-based learning. At the secondary levels, students are expected to obtain information more through a lecture and note-taking format, supplemented by textbooks, than through active, hands-on approaches. The emphasis on paper and pencil tasks at this level can pose a considerable barrier to the inclusion of students with significant sensory and cognitive disabilities. In addition, teachers are pressured to bring their students to a level of mastery on national standardized tests that can interfere with the need to individualize instruction and accommodate differences in learning styles (Campbell & Olsen, 1994). As a result, the educational team must take even greater care to ensure that the match between typical classes and the individual student's needs is a good one.

Both middle and high school students take a variety of courses requiring movement from one room to another and from one teacher to another. Not all students take the same courses; rather they follow a more individualized schedule. During the middle-school years, students may follow a block schedule and be grouped for certain academic courses (language arts, science, mathematics, and social studies) so that they can relate to a smaller group of students and experience a more integrated curriculum. During high school, each student's schedule becomes more diversified depending on the student's needs and future goals. It is possible for a student to take courses with different students in each class, with minimal overlap. The sense of belonging to a specific classroom as in elementary school is replaced (it is hoped) with a sense of belonging to a particular group of students within a class or grade level (freshman, sophomore, junior, senior). Although students must complete a certain number of required courses, a degree of flexibility is allowed to foster individual preference and need. For instance, not all students will take German, physics, choir, or photography.

Some courses offered during the secondary age range involve more sedentary instruction, whereas others are more active and encourage movement and more hands-on learning by all students. Teacher style and philosophy of learning determine to a great extent how a given topic is addressed and what student expectations will be. Considerable diversity among teachers exists in secondary schools (as in elementary schools), and this factor must be considered when including students who have severe sensory and multiple impairments. Again, placement in a typical classroom is determined not by developmental or performance level but by the careful and creative blending of individual needs with the learning opportunities in a given classroom. These learning opportunities could be academic, communicative, social, or motoric. Just physical placement in a typical classroom is not inclusion. There must be an expectation that the student will learn, and attention must be paid to how the student will be actively involved in the learning process.

ANALYZING THE LEARNING ENVIRONMENT TO ACCOMMODATE MIDDLE AND HIGH SCHOOL STUDENTS WITH SEVERE AND MULTIPLE IMPAIRMENTS

As for the elementary-age student, participation for secondary-age students (those in middle school and high school) focuses on instructional adaptations to meet individual needs within the context of typical classrooms. These adaptations may look much like those designed for the younger-age student, except that the materials and activities selected and the manner in which they are presented are appropriate to the secondary levels. Age-appropriate materials and activities reflect the chronological age of the student, do not draw negative attention to the student because they are too juvenile in nature, and are such that others of the same age feel comfortable sharing the materials and engaging in the activity. Adaptations will involve both instructional procedures and materials and can make use of a number of potential assistants in the learning process.

Because many classes at this age are academic in nature, the process of including individual students requires thoughtful analysis of the goals of the general education curriculum and how they relate to the student with severe sensory and multiple impairments. The following steps are suggested to assist in the problem solving that must inevitably occur.

- First, the team must decide the underlying importance of the lesson to the student's everyday life. In other words, what parts of the general topic of study relate to the individual student's present and potential future needs?
- Second, the team must analyze how the classroom teacher is instructing the students to arrive at the overall goal for the lesson. It is vital to know the teacher's mode(s) of instruction to determine if that format is beneficial for the target student. For example, a straight lecture format will present significant barriers for the student who has no hearing or vision.
- Next, the team will determine how to adapt the materials and instruction to address the underlying theme and highlight its im-

portance for the target student while meeting individually determined educational objectives.

- Finally, the team must determine ways of allowing students at considerably different learning levels and learning objectives acquire
the necessary skills and knowledge during the same (or essentially
the same) activity.

An example may help to clarify the preceding steps. A 10th-grade science
class is studying plant physiology. The students' primary objective is to identify
plant parts and their function in photosynthesis and why that process is important. The teacher lectures for approximately 20 minutes to explain what is in the
textbook and then assigns students activities related to the lecture. Students may
work independently or in small groups. For Lance, a determined and eager student who has severe sensory impairments and a significant intellectual impairment, the team decides that the importance of the topic for his everyday life
focuses on the appreciation of plants, how they add to people's lives, and how
to obtain and adequately care for them. Adaptations for Lance involve using
several real plants, a watering can or something suitable, plant food, a water-
measuring device to avoid overwatering, and advertisements from stores on
plants and plant prices. During the lecture portion of the class, Lance is assisted
by a peer tutor (a work-study high school student) who teaches Lance how to
discriminate between pictures of stores that do and do not sell plants and that
it requires money to obtain plants. The tutor uses pictures to explain the differ-
ence between large and small plants as well as various types of plants to teach
awareness of preferences. This instruction occurs quietly at Lance's assigned seat,
using pictures to identify and categorize plants by similarity and a wallet with
a variety of bills to practice the necessary money exchange. During the remainder
of the class, three classmates work with Lance to label parts of the plant and
discuss photosynthesis. Lance learns to check on and take care of the plants and
seedlings in the classroom, including use of the necessary plant care equipment.
As part of his community-based instruction, which occurs during another seg-
ment of his school day, Lance has gone to plant stores to find preferred plants
and has purchased plants, seeds, and the necessary materials to maintain these
plants. The community-based instruction supports what Lance is learning in science class. The skills he learns can continue at home with his parents, who have
verified that having and caring for plants is a normal occurrence and pastime
for the family. Furthermore, Lance can use these skills upon graduation and upon
leaving home, when he lives on his own, with a roommate or with more formal
support.

The process of analyzing activities that typically occur during the secondary
school years remains essentially the same regardless of the activity. In general, it
should be fairly apparent how the topic of study for the day, week, or longer
period relates to the learning needs of the student requiring extra support (see
Table 6.1, for example, for an analysis of the skills that could be learned during
a high school biology class). However, when the analysis reveals that little of the
topic pertains to the individual student's life or that a meaningful adaptation
would be difficult to achieve, then the team must consider alternatives. An alternative could mean taking another class. Since earning all the required credits
for graduation may not be the goal for a given student, less attention needs to

Table 6.1. Identification of outcomes and skills within a 10th-grade biology class

Outcomes and specific underlying skills	DNA	Plants		Insects	Mammals		Birds	Fossils
	Building models using color and shape Differences	Planting	Care of plants	Dissection	Dissection	Categorization (color, size)	Categorization (color, size)	
1. To have friends/social relationships								
Greet peers and respond to greetings	✓	✓	✓	✓	✓	✓	✓	✓
Share materials during laboratory activities	✓	✓	✓	✓	✓	✓	✓	✓
Request help if needed	✓	✓	✓	✓	✓	✓	✓	✓
Respond to directions from laboratory partners	✓	✓	✓	✓	✓	✓	✓	✓
Ask to see what others are doing	✓	✓		✓	✓		✓	✓
2. To have control over certain aspects of life—to make decisions								
Decide to participate in class activities	✓	✓		✓	✓		✓	✓
Decide what needs to happen first, second, third, and so on in each task	✓	✓	✓	✓	✓	✓	✓	✓
Decide what materials are needed	✓	✓	✓	✓	✓	✓	✓	✓
Determine same/different	✓	✓	✓	✓	✓	✓	✓	✓
3. To get a preferred job								
Follow directions given by classroom teacher	✓	✓		✓	✓		✓	✓
Attend to task for duration of activity	✓	✓	✓	✓	✓	✓	✓	✓
Obtain necessary materials for task	✓	✓	✓	✓	✓	✓	✓	✓
Handle materials appropriately	✓	✓	✓	✓	✓	✓	✓	✓
Work cooperatively with others	✓	✓	✓	✓	✓	✓	✓	✓
Put materials away	✓	✓	✓	✓	✓	✓	✓	✓

be paid to "required" courses, and more freedom and creativity can be demonstrated in the development of the student's schedule. In other words, a student may choose to take two earth science courses, drama, woodworking, and art because those classes offer the means of instruction and subject matter that most closely pertain to the individual's learning needs. The same student may not take English, history, or physical education, which would all normally be required for a high school diploma, but which do not meet either the student's instructional needs (e.g., active, hands-on learning in cooperative groups of peers) or do not easily permit adaptations of topic matter to make it relevant to the student's life. The activity/individualized education program (IEP) objective analysis (first described in Chapter 3 and again illustrated in Chapter 5) is applicable to the older student as well. Table 6.2 contains an example of such an analysis for an 11th-grader.

INCLUDING SUGGESTIONS FOR MIDDLE AND HIGH SCHOOL STUDENTS IN GENERAL EDUCATION CLASSES

Many of the adaptations described in the previous chapters are appropriate for secondary school students as well. Approaches for teaching basic reading, writing, and mathematics to a young adult with severe sensory and multiple disabilities can closely resemble those discussed in Chapter 5. One word of caution is in order, however. Materials used at the secondary levels must not reflect negatively (e.g., in a juvenile manner) on the student. For example, pictures used should come from magazines geared to the appropriate age group, and pens or felt-tip markers should be used in lieu of crayons and stickers. Software programs clearly designed for young children would not be appropriate. The following sections describe several different middle school and high school classes (both academic and nonacademic) and the way in which certain students' learning needs were addressed within those classes.

Seventh-Grade Mathematics Class

Mr. Webber, a mathematics teacher, starts class by having his students exchange homework papers and correct them as he reads off the answers. Kim is paired with a classmate for this activity. Kim is agile, moves quickly, and loves to draw and manipulate small items. She has severe myopia (nearsightedness), a mild hearing loss for which she wears a hearing aid, significant cognitive disabilities, and behavioral outbursts. She can engage in self-injurious behavior when upset.

Kim sits at the front of the class to be close to the teacher. Although Kim cannot do the same homework assignment as the rest of the class, she is expected to listen to the teacher and identify each mathematics problem the teacher is correcting by pointing to that particular number. Kim has a large number line (like a ruler) on her desk, and as Mr. Webber states the number of the problem he taps that number on the number line as he reads off the answer. This visual cue helps to draw Kim's attention to the task. Kim then finds the number on the homework sheet, and her classmate provides her with a positive acknowledgment when she is correct or positive corrective feedback when she makes a mistake. Kim is learning to follow directions, to match numbers, and to sequence numbers. With these skills, she may be better able to use a calculator while

Table 6.2. Activity/IEP objective analysis for an 11th-grader

Student: Travis is 17 years old, curious, persistent, and active. He is deaf, has mental retardation, has very limited communication skills, and has difficulty with self-control.

Objectives	PE/weight training	Photography	Keyboarding	Chemistry	Art/drawing	Careers
1. Remains on task until completion.	Works with partner. Has pictorial routine of weights to do. Checks off weights he does on laminated sheet.	Stays with lab group or partner and does not wander off.	Stays at computer and finishes predetermined amount of work (data entry).	Stays with lab partners at table until assignment is completed or bell rings.	Finishes one assignment before starting another. Stays at work table throughout the period and does not roam.	Stays with large group for discussions instead of running around room. Looks at magazines with appropriate pictures.
2. Expresses his needs without getting angry.	Uses a card (attached with Velcro to a wrist sweatband) that says, "Leave me alone." When Travis holds the card toward someone, that person leaves him alone.	Gets someone's attention and signs HELP when he needs help. Does not throw equipment.	Signs BREAK or uses break card to indicate need to stop working.	Raises hand instead of running up to teacher when he wants to do the experiment or hand out papers.	Signs HELP when frustrated, rather than tearing up paper.	Requests attention by appropriately touching classmate or teacher or by raising his hand instead of biting his hand.

114

3. Gets along with others.	Works cooperatively with partner during weight-training. Together they decide who goes first and amount of weight.	Shares equipment with classmate and decides with classmate what to photograph.	Follows directions from chemistry teacher; classmates share materials.	Sits close to other students at art table, not by himself. Responds to their requests (via pointing and gestures) for materials he has.	Shares materials (books, magazines) when doing a project such as a collage on possible careers. Does not hit or bite others.
4. Easily makes the transition from one task to the next.	Uses pictorial schedule to determine when one activity is completed and what happens next. Is given reminder of approaching transition 5 minutes before class ends. Is learning to match clock time with time on schedule.				
5. Initiates interactions with others.	Approaches classmate and gives him or her a pictorial card that asks, "Want to work with me?" (part of his weight training routine).	Signs HI to teacher and to at least one classmate. Asks that student's opinion of his (Travis's) photograph by pointing to it and using facial expressions.	Turns in software program to teacher when leaving class and signs BYE. When appropriate, asks other students if he can see what they are doing. He extends a pictorial/written card for this ("What are you doing?").	Signs HI to chemistry teacher and signs HELP when he does not understand what to do.	Uses pictorial card ("What are you doing?") or points and uses facial expressions to ask other students about their projects (life goals). Pictures used to clarify understanding.

shopping. She also may obtain a job that involves stocking shelves by matching stock numbers or doing data entry. During the activity of correcting homework assignments, Kim receives support from both the classroom teacher and her classmates. This allows a special education support person to spend more time with another student who needs physical assistance when using the restroom.

After the homework has been corrected, the papers are passed to the front and Kim is asked to collect them and place them on Mr. Webber's desk. This task gives Kim the chance to follow directions from the teacher and to interact briefly with a few students (e.g., attend to their verbal cues of "Here, Kim," reach out to take the papers). Then Mr. Webber has the class (as a whole) work on the manipulation of numbers and functions. He draws a square on the blackboard and asks students to raise their hands and give him a number less than 10. Kim is supported by the special education support person (assistant or teacher) to choose a number card (index cards) from three presented and wave it in the air to be called on. Kim and five other students are called on, and the six numbers are placed in strategic places around the figure on the blackboard (top, bottom, left, right, middle, and on one line). The same figure and numbers are drawn in black felt-tip pen by the support person for Kim to have at her desk. The teacher then calls on students to make up problems by using words, not numbers from the figure (e.g., "top minus bottom times line"). Kim cannot do the mathematics involved, but instead works on her objectives of following directions and number recognition. She follows the directions of classmates (and the teacher, who repeats the question) and points to the stated location. Using her number line or from a choice of three separate index cards with numbers, she matches the number on the figure to the appropriate number. She does the first part of the different problems that the students invent—the ones she hears or attends to. The teacher touches her on the arm to focus her attention before he repeats the question that a student has created. Kim's support person also assists other students around her who appear to be having difficulty following the class or performing the mathematics functions.

Eighth-Grade Physical Science Class

Carina attends Colter Junior High as an eighth grader. Carina has a great smile, likes to be around people, and responds quickly to familiar voices. Carina has limited vision in her left eye, although it is uncertain what she sees and understands. She may have a mild hearing loss, but responds to most frequencies. She has extremely minimal movement of her head and arms and has significant cognitive disabilities. Carina indicates "no" by slightly turning her head away from an item (e.g., food) and tightening her arms next to her side. She smiles and vocalizes to indicate "yes," "I like this" and "more."

Carina enjoys physical science class because many of the activities involve small groups of students. Examples of study units include rotational motion, structural soundness of buildings, and efficiency of machinery. These units typically involve some reading, lectures, and hands-on experimentation. When there is a lecture or when group instructions are being given that may last for 10–15 minutes, Carina uses her Walkman, which she activates with a switch positioned near her right cheek to listen to her choice of music or taped material.

During the active small-group time periods, Carina, who uses a wheelchair, is helped by her lab mates. For a 3-week unit on structural soundness of buildings, students work in groups of four or five, constructing miniature towers and bridges from a variety of different materials (e.g., drinking straws, paper clips, tape, string). The students are to collaborate in the building and testing of these structures and in preparing their findings in a final report. Carina's teammates show her materials (two choices at a time) and ask for her decision regarding which material to use at different times during the construction. Carina responds by looking at one of the offered choices held against a pale blue backing (to eliminate extraneous visual information). Sometimes her teammates tell her and show her that they are using a specific material such as plastic drinking straws. Then they ask her to select that particular material, again from a choice of two. Once the structure is complete, Carina participates in testing its strength by using her momentary switch to activate devices that put pressure on the structure. For example, Carina activates a switch-adapted fan to apply wind pressure. Her teammmates cue her to apply this force with verbal and tactile cues and then record the results. The final report contains both sentences written by her lab partners as well as pictures and object cues (e.g., pieces of straw) that Carina decides upon.

Carina is working on understanding how she can affect her environment through the use of switches and decision making. She also is learning to respond to her peers, to use her vision to make choices, and to match spoken words to objects.

Ninth-Grade Woodshop Class

Stephen has a wonderful sense of curiosity. He uses his hands to accomplish many activities using small items. He can be totally absorbed in activities of choice (e.g., woodburning, rolling stacks of coins in wrappers). He responds to a few (five) tactile signs and cues. He has no vision or hearing and usually conveys his intent through body movements, facial expressions, and manipulation of different objects.

Stephen is a student in Mr. Jamison's 9th/10th-grade woodshop class. He has a work partner who sits at his table. Stephen helps Mr. Jamison with all of the demonstrations and explanations at the beginning of each class. He hands Mr. Jamison pieces of wood or equipment and turns equipment on and off as directed. Participation of this nature helps Stephen stay more focused with the group and provides him more information and practice anticipating cues than if he were just sitting at his table. Mr. Jamison uses touch cues and objects to communicate with Stephen, and a teaching assistant or special educator is present to assist when Stephen has difficulty.

Following the demonstration with Mr. Jamison, Stephen works with his work partner (if a joint project), or he works with a teaching assistant on independent projects. He enjoys this class and can perform most steps after tactually being shown what to do and examining a finished product. Stephen does not participate in written examinations or lectures. Since he takes more time to finish projects then students without disabilities, he uses times of exams or writing assignments to continue working on projects. There is thus no need to rush Stephen through projects, and he can see each project through to completion, working at his own pace.

Stephen's goals are to follow tactile (touch and object cues) and occasionally signed instructions, handle materials appropriately, and remain on task for a specified time period without engaging in self-stimulatory behavior (e.g., head tapping), which interferes with his performance.

Tenth-Grade Drama Class

Ben, a student in a 10th-grade drama class, often follows verbal directions, takes good care of his own materials, and performs many tasks involving fine motor skills without assistance. Ben has been blind since birth, with a mild hearing loss. He also has significant cognitive impairments and can exhibit severe behavioral outbursts when frustrated (e.g., does not get his way). Ben is ambulatory and uses the sighted guide technique as well as a cane (diagonal technique) for walking in familiar places. He has a few signs that he uses spontaneously (EAT, MORE, FINISHED) and he vocalizes many sounds.

Ben's drama class offers him the opportunity to work on skills such as following directions, handling materials appropriately, expressing frustration in an appropriate manner, and interacting with same-age peers. Ben seems to enjoy role playing, during which students can practice different skills (e.g., getting in character, voice projection, changing voice style). When appropriate, Ben assumes roles of people who are either not vocal or have a few repetitive lines (such lines are prerecorded by a classmate, and Ben activates the cassette recorder on cue for the lines to be heard). Ben often plays the "straight man" in these skits. He also helps decide what props may be necessary and assists in obtaining or creating them. Ben is responsible for responding to classmates' or teacher's requests to get a certain prop for a scene as needed (e.g., chair, lamp, coffee cups).

To maximize Ben's opportunities to improve his skills, the support teacher, who works with the drama teacher, identifies the many situations that naturally exist as well as those that could be developed to enable Ben to receive sufficient skills practice. An activity analysis is completed for this class (as well as for all of Ben's classes), delineating how Ben's learning objectives are being addressed. This analysis clarifies expectations for everyone supporting Ben (drama teacher, classmates, special educator, speech-language pathologist, and teaching assistant).

Twelfth-Grade Life Enrichment Class

Sierra is a young woman of 18 who displays a love of music and a desire to be around her peers. Sierra can see very bright light or movement. She uses a wheelchair and has very slight movement of her head, which she uses to activate switches to control different appliances. She has considerable difficulty making basic needs known and has minimal responses under her control. As part of her school day, Sierra attends a life enrichment class (see Table 6.3 for a complete schedule of Sierra's school day).

Life enrichment is one part of a yearlong sequence of courses in home economics (foods and clothing). Considerable discussion of life issues occurs as part of this class, and the teacher frequently changes scheduled activities to follow the needs of individual students in the class who want to discuss personal problems. The focus on discussion makes it difficult for Sierra to participate, yet her classmates want her to continue to be part of the group and want her to listen. For many of the class periods, students engage in various creative activities, such as designing collages that reflect their present life, future dreams, ca-

Table 6.3. Sample schedule of 12th-grader

Student: Sierra (age 18) comes from a supportive family and has several friends. Sierra expresses herself by facial expressions and vocalizations. She loves to listen to others and to music. Sierra responds occasionally to very bright light and colors. She uses a wheelchair and activates switches with a slight movement of her head.

Typical activities	Adaptations/support
1st Period: Physical Education (PE) (soccer)	Sierra is taken to PE by a teacher assistant and is helped out of her wheelchair and onto mats. She is positioned prone on a slant board for drainage of bodily fluids. She receives her physical therapy while she watches her classmates play soccer. Students not playing sit next to her and converse.
2nd Period: Life Enrichment (class discusses issues relevant to their needs as young men and women)	Sierra's mother makes sure that she comes to class with photographs depicting trips taken and family members. These are used for discussions surrounding relationships, life goals, and so on.
	During class discussions (which often involve appearance), Sierra and her classmates experiment with putting on nail polish (Sierra both chooses color and indicates which hand by looking). She also responds to questions concerning how she wants her hair to look. Teaching assistant works with all students.
3rd Period: Art (learning about different art forms)	Sierra operates slide projector to show slides to class. When requested to do so, she turns on a switch by using slight head movement.[a] When producing art, Sierra uses her eyes to select color, texture, shape, tools, and so on, needed during the process. Teaching assistant, art teacher, and classmates provide instruction.
4th Period: Computers	Sierra uses a gurney during this class (for a change in position). She is assisted by an inclusion support teacher who has her select her software programs and sets up the touch-sensitive switch by her head. She also listens to music or books on tape (her choice) using a Walkman.
5th Period: Lunch	Sierra is pushed in her wheelchair to the cafeteria by a classmate she selects by looking. She is fed through a gastrostomy tube, which an adult sets up for her. She sits with her classmates from the life enrichment class.
6th Period: Choir	Sierra sits with classmates in choir after helping to pass out the books. She is to lift her head to look at each student when they say "Thanks, Sierra." She tapes segments that the teacher wants recorded (using her head switch) and plays them back when directed. A classmate provides additional support for her to pass out the books (they are placed on her tray) and to record and play back a practice segment.
7th Period: Computers	Sierra has two computer classes. She attends this one in her wheelchair. The teaching assistant supports her and all other students in this class. This class is more interactive than the previous computer class, and Sierra is more alert. Students check each other's work and offer suggestions. Sierra operates her software programs with her head switch and responds to peers when they ask her to show them what she is doing (age-appropriate musical, visual programs).

At the end of the day, classmates make sure Sierra has what she needs to take home. They help her get to the bus.

[a]Sierra uses same techniques to show her family at home what she has been doing at school. Slides have been taken (either by teachers or classmates) of Sierra's day. Explanations are sent home with the slides, and Sierra then has the opportunity to "discuss" her day using her head switch. Slides are updated periodically.

reer goals, and so on. Students work alone or in groups and are encouraged to interact during these projects.

Sierra is assisted by an inclusion support teacher or teaching assistant who offers her choices of brightly colored pictures or other materials to include in her collages. Classmates, too, occasionally find things they feel Sierra would like in her collages and present them as choices to her. Sierra makes her selection by looking slightly in the direction of the desired choice. When her choice is unclear, her peers choose for her, show her their choice, and ask her to tell them if she doesn't agree. Adult assistance is provided until classmates finish their own work and are free to work more with Sierra. When this happens, the adult fades out of the picture to help the teacher and other students as needed.

When students are working on projects, the teacher allows music to be played. If this is an option, Sierra controls the music via a momentary switch that she activates with her head. Classmates help her decide on the desired station and set the allowed volume. Classmates also remind Sierra to continue the music if she does not keep the switch on. This creates a teasing situation, which Sierra seems to enjoy.

Sierra is working on responding to her peers by turning her head toward them, making choices, and controlling the environment via switch activation. She benefits from the social stimulation in this classroom, since the effects of her medication make it very difficult to remain attentive and awake under less-stimulating circumstances.

DETERMINING WHEN COMMUNITY-BASED INSTRUCTION IS APPROPRIATE

Secondary school students quickly approach a time when they will be graduating and involved in nonschool activities. To complement the student's interests and abilities and make this inevitable transition as smooth as possible, teachers and parents must plan ahead (Szymanski, 1994; Wehman, Moon, Everson, Wood, & Barcus, 1988). Students at this age need experience in how to make use of public facilities, determine job preferences, obtain and keep jobs, gain access to community resources, and live safely and comfortably in a given neighborhood. The potential skills to be acquired before formal schooling ends are numerous and require considerable advance planning (Everson, 1995). The impact of community-based instruction on the student's ability to become a competent and actively involved community member should not be underestimated. Numerous benefits have been reported for secondary-age students who have received this type of instruction (McDonnell, Hardman, Hightower, Kiefer-O'Donnell, & Drew, 1993). Since the student with severe sensory and multiple disabilities may have had limited experiences and generally requires longer learning periods before skill mastery, the educational team must ensure that sufficient time and opportunities are provided to enhance the learning of these critical skills.

The most efficient environment for learning community-based skills is the environment in which they are required and expected (McDonnell & Ferguson, 1988; Moon, Inge, Wehman, Brooke, & Barcus, 1990). Therefore, at least a portion of the student's day should involve direct instruction in the community. The amount of time spent in such instruction typically varies with the student, as determined by individual and family needs and beliefs. However, because in most states formal educational services end for the student upon reaching age 22, as the student reaches this age, more and more time may be spent appropriately in community environments (Sailor, 1989; Sailor et al., 1986; Wehman et al., 1988). In addition, since most typical high school students have left school by age 17, students with special needs beyond this age are no longer with their peer group, and learning in the community is therefore perhaps more beneficial. Transition teams may thus wish to consider basing the student's entire educational program at a community college, university, vocational technology school, or place of employment.

Community-based instruction should not interfere with the student's sense of belonging to a school or specific class. For instance, if a student is appropriately placed in an English class that meets daily, it would be inappropriate to remove the student from this class for periodic community-based instruction. Rules for attendance should apply to all students equally. Rather, community-based instruction should occur on a daily basis for one or two consecutive periods during a time that does not interfere with any previously assigned class that also meets educational needs. An alternative option may be to have regularly scheduled, but not daily, instruction in the community, and on those days when community instruction does not occur, the student could be assigned to a study hall or job training at the school. An important consideration is that students with severe and multiple disabilities have similar schedules to those students with no disabilities. Because students at the secondary level follow highly individualized schedules, based on both required and elective coursework, students with severe and multiple disabilities who take some classes on campus and some "classes" off campus will not draw undue attention. They will not be pulled from a particular class to receive special instruction. Sowers and Powers (1995) suggest the use of instruction for parents and home assistance providers, and minimal in-school training to support community-based instruction without interfering with inclusive educational programs. Table 6.4 provides a sample schedule for a middle school student as one example of integrating both school and community-based learning.

PLANNING COMMUNITY-BASED INSTRUCTION

As with all instructional planning, decisions related to where instruction will occur, how it will occur, and what skills will be taught are made by the educational team. Family members obviously play a critical role in planning community-based instruction, since they are most knowledgeable about the community environments that are frequented (or need to be frequented) by the student (e.g., grocery store, convenience store[s], clothing stores, fast-food and sit-down restaurants, movie theaters, laundromat). Although all teaching may not occur in these most commonly accessed environments, it may be preferable for initial instruction to occur in these places so that the student is given opportunities to practice skills after school and on weekends with family members. Once the student is familiar with the physical layout of such commonly used environments and demonstrates appropriate skills there, teaching in other similar environments to broaden skill acquisition and use will be necessary (Browder, Snell, & Wildonger, 1988). For example, one student lives down the block from a convenience store frequently used by his younger brothers and parents. Although this student

Table 6.4.　Sample daily schedule for seventh-grader

Student: Sandi has many strengths such as effective use of her eyes for communication, some hearing, and a very social nature. She also has a moderate hearing impairment with her hearing aid, significant cognitive delays, and severe quadriplegia cerebral palsy.

Time	Sample daily activities
8:00–8:25 A.M.	Homeroom. Announcements over public address system. Discussion of news (school, local, state, and national). Sandi goes over daily pictorial/word schedule with inclusion teacher to better understand her day. She refers back to this schedule following every period as a reading skill. She brings in a local paper for discussion of news and indicates by looking at one of two pictures what topic she would like to address. (Goals: develop pictorial/sight word-reading skills; number recognition; concepts of before and after, first, second, third, etc.; decision making.)
8:30–9:20	Social Studies (unit on civil rights in different countries). Students read a section of the text on this topic and watch a short video on the subject. They make lists and compare what rights are important to each of them, how these rights can be lost, and how they compare with others. Sandi participates in all these activities, but has a peer read to her and explain what is read in terms related to her life. Inclusion support aide uses pictures and simple phrases to help her understand; the aide asks her to choose what rights she wants for herself and what she does not want. (Goals: develop pictorial/sight word-reading skills, receptive communication, peer interactions, decision making, self-advocacy.)
9:25–10:15	Mathematics (computing areas of different geometric shapes, making comparisons, and relating findings to day-to-day situations [e.g., computing amount of paint needed to paint a house or amount of carpet needed for various rooms]). Sandi is shown what numbers to input into her calculator (calculator is large, with speech output). She inputs one of three numbers (given physical support) while her peers input the others to speed up the process. Sandi is working with two other students (one of these has a learning disability). Extra help is provided to all three students by the inclusion teacher or mathematics teacher (who alternate monitoring the class and providing more in-depth instruction). As homework, two friends who are class members go to Sandi's home to measure rooms in her house. In class they determine how much carpet her family needs. Using carpet samples, Sandi chooses her favorites based on texture and color, and her friends calculate the price. Using an adapted number line, Sandi determines the most/least expensive carpet. (Sandi leaves early with inclusion support teacher to use the restroom.) (Goals: decision making, concepts of more/less, number recognition, use of a calculator.)
10:20–11:10	Language Arts (unit on discrimination). Class reads stories and a film on individuals facing discrimination. Class discusses issues. Students try to determine how additional factors could have affected the various stories of discrimination. Using pictures and/or sketches, Sandi indicates the sequence of different stories (e.g., what came first, second, third, etc.). Inclusion teacher helps Sandi to choose color of paper to use for her report as well as who will help her prepare it. The chosen peer puts report on the computer using Sandi's sequenced pictures as a guide. Sandi chooses graphics to add to report. (Goals: enhance receptive communication, decison making, communication with peers.)

(continued)

Table 6.4.   (continued)

Time	Sample daily activities
11:10–12:00 noon	Science (unit on biological differences among species—relates to social studies and language arts units on civil rights and discrimination, respectively). Students categorize different species by certain characteristics, using actual cutouts and writing down characteristics of each group. Sandi uses her prone stander and chooses between two different forms to let the rest of her cooperative learning group know which form belongs to which category. (Goals: recognize concepts of same and different, communicate with peers, improve physical strength and endurance.)
12:00–12:30 P.M.	Lunch. Classmates ask Sandi whom she would like to push her wheelchair to the cafeteria. Sandi chooses by looking and they go together. Her friends put her food on her tray as they push her through the line. She chooses items by looking at one option more than another. An inclusion support aide helps her eat, once she is seated next to friends. Sandi tells this assistant what she wants to eat or drink by looking at one of three choices offered. Her friends engage her in conversation by referring to teen magazines. She responds by looking at different pictures and using her facial expressions to convey her reactions. (Goals: choice making, responding to peers.)
12:30–12:45	Break time. Sandi goes to restroom to clean up after lunch. Sometimes a friend or two goes with her to socialize and discuss makeup.
12:50–1:40	Physical Education (PE) (Monday, Wednesday, Friday) or Music (Tuesday, Thursday). Since PE usually involves many team sports, Sandi receives her physical therapy (range of motion, stretches, etc.) at this time. She is on mats on the side and can watch the class play. She has access to a switch device that allows her to send vocal messages to classmates during their game (e.g., "Way to go!"; "Alright!"). Anyone not playing sits with her and draws her attention to the game or otherwise converses. Physical therapy is done by a teaching assistant or physical therapist. Sandi is much more involved in certain PE units like swimming. In music, Sandi uses her prone stander during class to listen to classmates sing. She uses a head switch to turn on the metronome for everyone to keep the beat. Sometimes the switch activates a cassette recorder and she tapes the songs the class is learning. A peer hits the appropriate buttons (record, rewind, or play) and asks Sandi to turn on the recorder according to the teacher's direction. (Goals: greater comfort and use of her body, social interaction skills, enhanced physical strength, following directions.)
1:45–3:00	Community-Based Instruction (Monday, Wednesday, Thursday). Sandi goes with another student who has Down syndrome, a peer without disabilities, and the support teacher or aide to the mall to window-shop, make purchases, get a snack, and learn about job opportunities. On Tuesdays Sandi goes to Student Council with peers. On Fridays Sandi works on the school paper making decisions about layout, paper color, and graphics. (Goals: decision making about purchases, foods, and jobs; familiarity with public facilities.)

has limited vision, no speech, and a label of mental retardation, his parents feel he could use this store on his own or with a friend, given the necessary adaptations (e.g., sufficient money in an adapted wallet that gives written instructions to the cashier). Community-based instruction, therefore, will occur at that convenience store for this particular student. When skills have been mastered (or nearly mastered), the student can receive training at other convenience stores in the community.

Community-based instruction (CBI) is highly individualized and should not be confused with large-group awareness outings (e.g., a 12th-grade government class visiting a political campaign headquarters). Of course, if a student with severe and multiple disabilities is a member of a class scheduled to go on a field trip, that student would accompany classmates. Due to the highly individualized nature of CBI, the number of students with disabilities learning in a given environment would be small (one or two). In this way, individual needs for instruction can be met without drawing a lot of attention from the general public. Students without disabilities could provide additional support for instruction while receiving work-study credit.

BLENDING GENERAL CLASS
PLACEMENT WITH COMMUNITY-BASED INSTRUCTION

Determining the most appropriate educational plan for a student is done on an individual basis and reflects a number of variables such as the student's age, present and future goals, abilities, needs, community, culture, and religion. As a result, no two students will have the same educational goals, daily schedule of activities, or amount of educational support. Some students will have minimal community-based instruction because their parents feel that such instruction is unnecessary and removes them from their peers (see, e.g., Sierra's schedule in Table 6.3). Other students will have considerable instruction in the community because, to reach their goals, this kind of instruction is critical. It is therefore difficult even to suggest guidelines for teachers at the high school and college levels. The critical goal is to find a balance between attending classes with peers who do not have disabilities and learning skills in the community for each individual student (Gee, Houghton, Pogrund, & Rosenberg, 1995). The following example of one high school student's schedule may help to clarify some of the decision-making processes that enter into a student's program.

Rick's Schedule

Rick is 16 years old and a junior in his local high school. He has a good sense of curiosity, is stubborn, likes to tease, and enjoys being with people. Rick uses a wheelchair and has a severe hearing loss even with bilateral hearing aids. He also has a visual field loss and is quite nearsighted. Rick uses his hands to grasp objects and then release them quickly. When interested in an object, he can maintain his grasp for a lengthy period. Rick is learning to make choices and to indicate his preferences using objects that represent items and activities.

Rick's daily schedule is as follows.

7:40–8:30 A.M.   Band. Rick chooses among different rhythm instruments. He grasps the instrument and keeps time with the band as they play their songs. He can hear the rhythm and appears to enjoy this class.

8:35–9:25 Home Economics. Rick participates in all aspects of food preparation. He locates utensils and food items and helps prepare the work area. He mixes and stirs ingredients with assistance from others in his group and uses a switch at times to activate a blender or mixer when needed. He also helps with all cleanup activities. When the teacher is giving a lecture or when the class is involved with written tasks, Rick gathers the used, dirty linen and washes it in the washing machine, then puts it in the dryer. He also unloads the dishwasher and puts items away that are within his reach. He does this by visually matching the item to be put away with others already in their place.

9:35–10:25 Art. Rick enjoys this class because it is so active and involves many different textures and objects. Rick participates in all class activities: obtaining materials, working on projects, cleaning up, and putting materials away. He particularly likes sculpting with clay and wire, but also likes painting and collage. When lectures occur or considerable verbal information is shared by the teacher, Rick helps set up the work area and begins his projects earlier than other class members.

10:30–11:20 Woodshop. Rick likes the loud sounds and vibrations from the tools used in this class. He also likes working with different kinds of woods and stains, experiencing their feel and smell. Rick partially participates in all of the activities of this class, although, like art, his finished products may look uniquely his own.

11:30–12:10 P.M. Lunch. Rick eats in the cafeteria with at least one classmate from his morning classes. He is working on making choices as he goes through the lunch line, keeping his food on the tray, eating with a spoon without excessive spillage, responding to peers, and cleaning up when finished. On Tuesdays and Thursdays he occasionally goes out into the community earlier and has lunch at a fast-food restaurant. He is sometimes accompanied by one of his classmates who wants to go.

12:15–1:05 School Job. Rick has several different jobs on the school campus. On Mondays he works in the library, putting books that are lying on tables and shelves in a large bucket to be reshelved. He also waters the plants for the librarian and helps to open new shipments of books as they arrive. On Wednesdays he works in the administrative office, helping with mailings, putting messages in staff boxes, and making copies. On Fridays he volunteers in the school's recycling program by helping to sort items collected and crushing cans and plastic bottles. On Tuesdays and Thursdays he goes into the community for the last two periods of the day, exploring—or actually training at—places of employment. For example, he works at a pet store bagging animal feed, checking water in the pet cages, and stocking shelves with pet food. (Rick has at least four job internships a year, in order to provide him with the necessary experiences he needs to determine his strengths and preferences.)

1:10–2:00 Study Hall (Monday, Wednesday, and Friday). When Rick finishes with his jobs around school, he ends his day in study hall. He goes over his schedule of the day (object representation) in preparation for telling his parents when he arrives home. He has a choice of listening to music using headphones or creating object and part-of-object books to serve as conversation tools during lunch or other classes. Sometimes other students work with him if appropriate. They show him how to operate the cassette recorder, adjust volume (loud), and choose desired tapes and help him compile his conversation books by adding appropriate phrases. On Wednesdays and Fridays Rick leaves school early to receive physical therapy at home. (Therapy is also embedded into many activities throughout each day.)

Care has been taken in developing Rick's schedule to build on his strengths and preferences (e.g., his social nature, his ability to see and grasp objects) so that he can use these skills in a variety of ways to achieve purposeful outcomes. He is supported by different team members throughout the day as determined by his needs. Each year Rick and his educational team will need to choose specific courses and evaluate alternative options to allow him to continue to develop useful skills. The teachers of these courses, as well as course format and structure, will determine the appropriateness of fit to Rick's needs. In addition, the amount of time Rick spends learning in the community (i.e., at various places of employment, public facilities, community college) will depend on a number of factors, including Rick's health, his changing preferences, his increased abilities, and his personal goals. For Rick, therefore, as for high school students with disabilities in general, coordinating learning time at school with time away from school in the community does not follow a predetermined plan. Rather it is highly individualized and dynamic as the student's skills and goals change.

TRANSITION TO ADULT LIFE

By age 16, students with special needs are required by law (Individuals with Disabilities Education Act) to have a formal transition plan as part of their individualized education program. The importance of such a plan cannot be overemphasized for a student with severe sensory and multiple disabilities. These graduates may well require ongoing support in most areas of adult life (work, home, recreation, and community involvement) (Everson, 1995). They will require time to adjust to new expectations beyond school. And they need opportunities to make decisions about their adult life so as to maintain as much control as possible over the quality of their lifestyle. As stated previously, during high school each student with severe sensory and multiple impairments needs to have exposure to several different job or volunteer options in order to make an informed choice about future work goals. Each student also needs to experience as many leisure and recreational pursuits as possible to determine those which he or she most enjoys. Students with limited or no reading skills cannot easily explore career and recreational options unless they have the opportunity to actually experience them. The transition plan for each high school student with severe disabilities, especially when those disabilities involve sensory impairments, must allow for hands-on experiences to which the student can respond.

Transition plans build on skills acquired during the school years. Therefore, the importance of an appropriate school program that continues to plan ahead for its students is obvious. The inclusion of students with severe and multiple disabilities in typical activities with others who do not have disabilities, as described in this chapter, should not end with graduation, but needs to be continued in the years following. Young adults with severe sensory and multiple disabilities, like other graduates, should have the opportunity to move into typical places to live, work, and recreate as determined by individual preferences, and not by the availability of existing *programs*. To this end, the creativity, problem-solving skills, and commitment of individual team members will continually be challenged to ensure successful transitions for students with severe sensory and multiple impairments.

REFERENCES

Browder, D.M., Snell, M.E., & Wildonger, B.A. (1988). Simulation and community-based instruction of vending machines with time delay. *Education and Training in Mental Retardation, 23*(3), 175–185.

Campbell, P., & Olsen, G.R. (1994). Improving instruction in secondary schools. *Teaching Exceptional Children, 26*(3), 51–54.

Everson, J.M. (Ed.). (1995). *Supporting young adults who are deaf-blind in their communities: A transition planning guide for service providers, families and friends.* Baltimore: Paul H. Brookes Publishing Co.

Gee, K., Houghton, J., Pogrund, R.L., & Rosenberg, R. (1995). Teaching orientation and mobility: Access, information, and travel. In N.G. Haring & L.T. Romer (Eds.), *Welcoming students who are deaf-blind into typical classrooms: Facilitating school participation, learning, and friendships* (pp. 307–346). Baltimore: Paul H. Brookes Publishing Co.

Individuals with Disabilities Education Act of 1990 (IDEA), PL 101-476. (October 30, 1990). Title 20, U.S.C. 1400 et seq: *U.S. Statutes at Large, 104*, 1103–1151.

McDonnell, J., Hardman, M.L., Hightower, J., Kiefer-O'Donnell, R., & Drew, C. (1993). Impact of community-based instruction in the development of adaptive behavior of secondary-level students with mental retardation. *American Journal on Mental Retardation, 97*, 575–584.

McDonnell, J.J., & Ferguson, B. (1988). A comparison of general case in vivo and general case simulation plus in vivo training. *Journal of The Association for Persons with Severe Handicaps, 13*, 116–124.

Moon, M.S., Inge, K., Wehman, P., Brooke, V., & Barcus, J.M. (1990). *Helping persons with severe mental retardation get and keep employment: Supported employment issues and strategies.* Baltimore: Paul H. Brookes Publishing Co.

Sailor, W. (1989). The educational, social, and vocational integration of students with the most severe disabilities. In D.K. Lipsky & A. Gartner (Eds.), *Beyond separate education: Quality education for all* (pp. 53–74). Baltimore: Paul H. Brookes Publishing Co.

Sailor, W., Halvorsen, A., Anderson, J., Goetz, L., Gee, K., Doering, K., & Hunt, P. (1986). Community intensive instruction. In R. Horner, L. Meyer, & H. Fredericks (Eds.), *Education of learners with severe handicaps: Exemplary learning strategies* (pp. 251–287). Baltimore: Paul H. Brookes Publishing Co.

Sowers, J., & Powers, L. (1995). Enhancing the participation and independence of students with severe physical and multiple disabilities in performing community activities. *Mental Retardation, 33*, 209–220.

Syzmanski, E.M. (1994). Transition: Life span and life-space considerations for empowerment. *Exceptional Children, 60*, 402–410.

Wehman, P., Moon, M.S., Everson, J., Wood, W., & Barcus, M. (1988). *Transition from school to work.* Baltimore: Paul H. Brookes Publishing Co.

Chapter 7

THE IMPORTANT ROLE OF PEERS IN THE INCLUSION PROCESS

June E. Downing and Joanne Eichinger

Many schools and school districts, especially those in remote rural areas, may never have access to an adequate number of qualified and experienced teachers to support the inclusive educational process. When students have multiple impairments that include a severe sensory loss, obtaining knowledgeable educators for such schools is particularly difficult (Erin, 1986; Izen & Brown, 1991). As a result, school districts must look for other avenues of support to ensure the successful inclusion of these students. One resource for schools that is free and in abundant supply is their students. Capitalizing on the valuable resource that students without disabilities (or with lesser disabilities) represent is critical to the inclusion process (Ryndak, 1995; Villa & Thousand, 1992).

The use of peers to assist in including all students, regardless of the severity of their disability, has been well documented (Sasso, Hughes, Swanson, & Novak, 1987; Staub & Hunt, 1993; Staub, Schwartz, Gallucci, & Peck, 1994; Vacc & Cannon, 1991). Students have been used in the capacity of peer tutors, cross-age tutors, data collectors, and peer buddies or helpers. They have aided directly or indirectly in the instruction of gross and fine motor skills, communication skills, social skills, academic skills, and community living skills. Their impact has been impressive. The benefits that these peers have received are also innumerable (Giangreco, Edelman, Cloninger, & Dennis, 1993; Peck, Donaldson, & Pezzoli, 1990; Sasso & Rude, 1987). Including peers as active members in the education of their classmates having severe sensory and multiple disabilities is a critical component of full-time placement in the typical classroom. Yet it is not meant to be a one-sided benefit for students with disabilities. Learning and achievement are the goals of quality education for all students. Careful attention must be taken to ensure that learning together does not detract from any student's education and that it contributes to all. For example, a study by Hunt, Staub, Alwell, and

Goetz (1994) on the achievement of second-grade students learning mathematics in cooperative learning groups verified that all students did master learning objectives; the presence of a student with severe multiple disabilities as a member of the group did not interfere with other students' learning of mathematics.

RECRUITMENT OF PEERS

The process of soliciting the involvement of classmates will differ depending on the age of students and the specific class involved. In general, students of any age appear willing and able to offer assistance when needed. In fact, peers have been so enthusiastic and eager to assist, especially in the younger grades, that another problem arises—that of modifying their enthusiasm so it is does not interfere with any student's learning. However, not all students will feel comfortable interacting with a classmate who has obvious physical, sensory, and intellectual differences (although this may change with time). No student should ever be forced to help, and peer assistance should never be used as punishment. There are plenty of students who are interested in becoming involved with such a classmate, and therefore not all students in a given class or school are needed. There is no reason to expect that all students will want to be involved. In fact, it would be unusual in any school situation for all students to enjoy being with every other student. Students naturally choose their friends and study partners. This should be no different for the student with significant impairments, both sensory and intellectual. If interactions do not occur naturally, some suggestions for the more formal recruitment of peers are found in Table 7.1. For additional information, note that T. Haring, N.G. Haring, Breen, Romer, and White (1995) describe specific strategies for the selection and recruitment of peers in inclusive settings.

Elementary School Children

At the elementary school level, students usually express a desire to assist and work with a student with severe multiple impairments, and little formal recruitment is needed (Jorgensen, 1994; Staub et al., 1994). Students at this age are naturally curious about differences and are interested in discovering why such differences exist. Students can be encouraged to work together (e.g., in pairs, small groups, cooperative learning groups), and the teacher can ensure that all students have an equal opportunity to get to know one another. The students

Table 7.1.   Suggestions for recruiting peers to assist students with disabilities

1. Informally ask students if they would like to interact with a given student, and provide opportunities to do so.
2. Ask the teacher who might benefit academically, socially, and emotionally from working with a student having severe sensory and multiple impairments.
3. Ask the school counselor, especially at the secondary level, to identify students who may benefit from such interactions.
4. Assign students to the same cooperative learning groups for a few weeks to help establish relationships.
5. Have students with severe sensory and intellectual impairments join extracurricular activities and clubs.
6. Ask the student council or other school leaders if they are interested in getting to know or supporting some students.

who desire to work together and those who have the skills to do so become readily apparent. As much as possible, the student with severe sensory and multiple disabilities should be allowed to choose a work partner (especially if other students are allowed to do so). The student with disabilities can make this choice by looking at, reaching toward, or touching the desired partner or by using individual class photos. However, the same students should not serve as partners all the time. Students need to keep up with their own work and should not be relied upon to help another student for all assignments and activities. Some teachers rotate students so that everyone eventually works with everyone else. Other teachers allow peer tutoring or helping only by those students who are performing well with their own work. Being in a helping role thus becomes a privilege, not a duty.

Middle and High School Students

Pressure to be like everyone else, to be part of the "in" crowd, and to appear to defy adult authority may present some initial challenges when encouraging middle and high school students to become involved with a classmate who appears to be quite different. Despite this potential hindrance, finding interested students to become involved in another student's life has not been overly difficult (Haring, Breen, Lee, Pitts-Conway, & Gaylord-Ross, 1987; Peck et al., 1990; Strully & Strully, 1985; York, Vandercook, MacDonald, Heise-Neff, & Caughey, 1992). The greater difficulty, perhaps, is that of encouraging the paid adult support to fade out and provide opportunities for students to interact (Ferguson, Jeanchild, & Meyer, 1992; Giangreco & Putnam, 1991). Students probably will not involve themselves in another student's life if it necessitates tolerating the presence of an adult. Students at this age typically view an adult's presence as decidedly unnecessary. Once students understand that their own involvement is desired and they are provided with some initial suggestions for becoming acquainted (if necessary), adults probably should maintain as low a profile as possible.

Students at this age can be lab partners in a science class, can be in the same study group for home economics or history, or simply accompany the student from one class to the next. Depending on school district policy, classmates can help in transporting students with severe physical disabilities as well as their positioning equipment (e.g., standers, gurneys) to various classes. In addition to the social benefits for both sets of students, such peer assistance can greatly relieve pressure on paid personnel to be in several different places at the same time.

HELPING STUDENTS UNDERSTAND
SEVERE SENSORY AND MULTIPLE DISABILITIES

Although students with severe sensory and multiple disabilities share many similarities with other children their age in terms of interests and desires, the lack of typical communication skills and the need for certain adaptations may pose initial barriers to development of friendships. Students may need to understand about their classmate's specific strengths and needs in order to feel more comfortable in their interactions (Bowden & Thorburn, 1993; Helmstetter, Peck, & Giangreco, 1994; York & Tundidor, 1995).

Information can be provided informally or formally, depending on the student's age and the given situation. At the preschool and elementary levels, all students at a given school may want and need the information. This information can focus on the fact that the entire class is learning together, even though each individual has slightly different ways to learn that work best for that person. The idea is to share information while building respect and appreciation of differences. A question box can be used by the teacher on a weekly basis. Students can ask specific questions anonymously (if they like), and the responses can be discussed as a class. For instance, a student may want to know why his classmate never looks at him. This child's greater use of peripheral vision needs to be explained so that the lack of eye contact is not misunderstood. During such information sharing sessions, the student with severe disabilities may or may not be present. Family members, with assistance from their child's teachers, will determine what would be most appropriate.

At the secondary level, schoolwide training may be neither feasible nor desirable. Informing just those students who have classes with someone having these multiple disabilities may be the most direct and appropriate course of action. These students, in turn, can educate other students who are interested and want more information. In addition, naturally infusing disability-related information into certain appropriate classes, such as civics or government, English, biology, and drama, may be the most effective and least conspicuous way of bringing attention to issues of disability. Instead of special assemblies or even special lessons, information about disabilities is a natural part of the curriculum and can be studied along with other aspects of the typical curriculum (Hamre-Nietupski et al., 1989). Table 7.2 presents some suggestions for sharing information with students.

Students at any age will need to know how to effectively communicate and what to expect regarding visual, hearing, and physical capabilities. The emphasis on information sharing focuses on the abilities of individuals and provides clear strategies for effective interactions. Students are shown the similarities between themselves, with differences explored matter-of-factly and in a manner that does not diminish the student. The similarities and differences of a group of third graders can be seen in Figure 7.1. Homogeneity is not a requirement for friendship.

Teaching Interaction Skills

Perhaps one of the most important requirements for initiating and maintaining friendships is that of effective interaction skills. When children do not use speech to communicate their thoughts and desires, interactions can become difficult and may be avoided. Students without disabilities will need to learn the modes of communication used by a classmate so that they will feel more comfortable initiating interactions and remaining in these interactions for longer periods of time.

Students who share a class with a student having severe sensory and multiple disabilities and who have an interest in getting to know that person need to learn how to express their thoughts and how to understand the student's expressive communications. Students may need to learn how to use their classmate's augmentative communication system (of pictorial or object symbols), how

Table 7.2.   Sharing information about a student's special condition with classmates

1. A parent or sibling can present information to a class about a student using home videos, slides, photograph albums, and items collected from the student's life.
2. Teachers (general educators and special education support teachers) can hold a formal discussion about a student's abilities and disabilities. The student with disabilities may or may not be present, depending on student and family preference.
3. Teachers can have the class read books about individuals who have similar disabilities to those of a classmate and then discuss it.
4. Teachers can wait for questions to emerge and address them informally as they occur.
5. Information can be infused into a curriculum topic (e.g., civil rights, journalism, discrimination, diversity of the human species).
6. A student's friends can disseminate information informally to other students in other classes and around the school.

to visually or tactually sign or make use of objects and touch cues. If their classmate is slow to respond, peers will need to receive training to wait for this student so as to avoid dominating the interaction (Buzolich & Lunger, 1995). Learning such interaction skills is not necessarily difficult and provides the student with severe sensory and multiple disabilities many different role models and communicative partners throughout the day.

Students without disabilities may need instruction on how to avoid treating their classmate with multiple disabilities in a juvenile manner, especially if that student is very small in stature. There is a tendency to interact with any student having a significant intellectual impairment in a manner considerably younger than that used with a student of the same age with no disabilities. Girls, in

Photograph courtesy of **Pat Danielle Smith**

Figure 7.1.   Friends in third grade.

particular, tend to adopt "mothering" and disciplining roles that may hinder the development of true friendships (Evans, Salisbury, Palombaro, Berryman, & Hollowood, 1992; Kishi & Meyer, 1994). Role playing different scenarios using students without disabilities in the role of a student with a severe disability—taking care not to demean that student—and then exaggerating the interactions allow the class to see ways to improve the situation. It is critical for the classroom teacher, all support personnel, administrators, and any adult who interacts with the student having a severe sensory and multiple impairment to do so in a way that provides a positive model for students without disabilities. When adults model inappropriate behavior, such as using language that is immature, raising their tone of voice when speaking, holding the student's hand when walking (for many upper elementary and older students), and giving students juvenile things to play with and do, they set the stage for the same unequal interactions to occur between students.

Teaching Accommodations for Physical Disabilities

Some students have physical disabilities in addition to their sensory and intellectual impairments. These students use certain devices to accommodate these limitations. Although classmates may not need in-depth information on etiology (if students ask, they should receive information at a level they can understand), they do need to know what the student can do, what the student is expected to do independently, and where assistance may be appreciated. Students need to learn how to assist their classmate when necessary (e.g., safely push someone in a wheelchair, guide someone using a walker). They need to know to present items or choices within the student's range of motion. Some students will feel comfortable stabilizing a classmate's arm to allow maximal use of the other arm when performing certain tasks. Understanding physical limitations can serve as a catalyst for classmates to devise creative adaptations to allow a student greater ability to participate. For example, students in a woodshop class made a slant board with small shelves to hold object choices for a classmate, while other students made a rotary board that allowed a classmate a variety of pictorial choices. In a sewing class, students made an adapted shopping bag to fit alongside a classmate's wheelchair to accommodate her limited range of motion for taking items off of store shelves and carrying them to the counter.

Teaching Adaptations Unique to Sensory Loss

A severe visual or hearing loss (or combination of the two) can alter interactions and require certain adjustments in how peers interact. If a student has usable hearing, but limited or no vision, then classmates need to be aware of the importance of using their voices to help the student anticipate their actions. They should also let the student know who is with them by reminding that student of their names (e.g., "Hey, Jane, it's me, Cindi. Want to go to lunch with me?"). Such use of verbal cueing may also reduce the startle reflex of a student with limited vision and severe physical disabilities. Students need to be given feedback on using certain verbal expressions that are visual in nature and therefore not very helpful (e.g., "put it there," "go over there," "it's by the brown one"). Verbal instructions and comments should be clear and relate to the student's abilities. When giving the student something, a classmate needs to learn to put it into the student's hands or on a table in front of the student and let him or her know where it is, rather than silently holding it in front of the student. Classmates need to understand that it is appropriate to gently touch the student to provide needed information that will increase participation. For example, when a science model is placed before each cooperative learning group, one member of that group should guide the student's hand to the model so that this student will not miss vital information available to the rest of the group visually. When moving with the student around the classroom or from class to class, it may be appropriate for classmates to offer to be a sighted guide for the student with limited or no vision. Serving as a sighted guide does not require much training and helps to develop responsibility on the part of the student.

For the student with limited hearing or no hearing, classmates will need to obtain either visual or tactile attention before trying to exchange information. Yelling at a student across a room or playing field should be discouraged, and alternative visual ways of attracting attention substituted. Using gestures, body language, and other visual cues (objects or pictures) need to be emphasized over an abundance of verbal output.

Understanding Unexpected and Undesired Behavior

Students with severe and multiple disabilities may have learned to engage in certain behaviors that seem unusual and perhaps somewhat frightening. They may sometimes spin in circles with their head back, looking at lights in the ceiling, or rock their head back and forth repeatedly while making a unique sound. Such behaviors initially may be difficult to understand and can have a negative impact on interactions (Ogletree, Wetherby, & Westling, 1992). Students without disabilities can be taught the rationale for these behaviors (e.g., to stimulate or calm oneself) and can see the relationship between these behaviors and the behaviors they themselves commonly engage in for the same purposes (e.g., swinging legs, clicking pens, twirling hair, chewing gum). Students without disabilities can also be asked why such behaviors are different across different people. Recognizing similarities in the reasons why people engage in certain behaviors can greatly reduce the fears and uncertainties that may threaten the development of positive relationships. Once the reasons for the behaviors are better understood by class members, then students without disabilities can brainstorm ways of helping a particular student (with or without a disability) substitute an unacceptable behavior for a more socially acceptable one.

It is also important to know how to respond to unacceptable behavior, particularly when the behavior is aggressive and hurtful. A common reaction to aggression against oneself is to strike back, either physically or verbally. Students must be allowed to reason through the consequences of such reactions to determine for themselves the overall impact. With some guidance from adults, if necessary, students of any age often volunteer that reacting to aggression with aggression will only aggravate the situation. Other means need to be employed. Frequently, aggressive behavior from a student with a significant intellectual impairment is tolerated by classmates, who probably do not understand why it occurred, realize it would be inappropriate to retaliate, and end up trying to avoid the individual. This situation can lead to isolation for the student as classmates avoid interactions. Such isolation is exacerbated by support personnel who may maintain an overly high profile in their efforts to ensure that aggressive behavior is controlled.

As with the stimulatory or self-calming behaviors that all students engage in to a certain degree, students without disabilities must be helped to understand the reasons behind more aggressive behavior, especially when it is usually *not* meant to hurt another. Students of any age are quick to see the frustration that a classmate may feel when the ability to effectively communicate is limited. They can relate the behavior to similar behaviors they express when severely frustrated. Although understanding is critical to avoid the isolation that could result, students also need to know specific things they should and can do when the student engages in the aggressive behavior. Often, students can arrive at specific strategies designed to reduce their avoidance of the individual and simultaneously assist the student gain greater self-control. Knowing exactly what to do will help to alleviate the uncertainty and fear surrounding the situation. For example, the class has decided that, when Danny (age 10) becomes angry and tries to grab someone's hand and bite it, they will tell him "No" quite firmly and then move away from him. When he appears to be calmer, they will return to where they were (next to him). In addition, they will try to be sensitive to what makes Danny angry and try to help him avoid those situations by offering other choices or giving him more assistance.

ROLES STUDENTS WITHOUT DISABILITIES CAN PLAY

The most important role that a peer without disabilities can assume for the student with disabilities is that of a true friend. This is an important role for any student. Although classmates can serve in the official role of peer tutor, being a friend provides invaluable support in numerous ways throughout each school day. (First-grade friends are depicted in Figure 7.2.) A student without disabilities, for example, can play an active role in encouraging a friend with severe and multiple disabilities to engage in social interactions and to clarify communicative attempts. As a friend the student without disabilities is more likely to expect his or her classmate to make his or her needs or desires known and is more apt to give that student enough time when trying to communicate. A friend will also serve as an interpreter to allow interactions to occur with another student who may be less familiar with a unique communicative style. Classmates who are friends also provide valuable information to teachers concerning the types of messages they feel need to be included on augmentative communication systems.

Students without disabilities can furthermore provide natural support for a classmate who has difficulty engaging in expected and desired behavior. Friends can be understanding of their classmate's unique way of expressing himself or herself and provide feedback to the student concerning that behavior. They can also explain the occurrence of undesired behavior to another student who may be annoyed or put off by the behavior. For example, Ian, a second-grader, frequently flaps his hands in front of his face and makes monotonous vocal sounds. His friend, Troy, asks him if he's bored and then provides him with something he likes to manipulate and explore. Jeremy, an eighth-grader, occasionally grabs books or magazines and crinkles them up in his hands and bites them. His friend, Eric, tells him to "cut it out," directs him to put the materials down on the table, and gets him to do something else with different material. Besides specific inci-

Figure 7.2. First-graders enjoying working together on the computer.

dences like those just mentioned, the daily presence of so many students without disabilities in the course of any school day provides the student with severe, sensory, and multiple disabilities with numerous appropriate role models. Of course, the teacher may have to bring such role models to the attention of the student (e.g., "Where is everyone going?"; "Is anyone else screaming?").

When students without disabilities consider themselves friends of students with disabilities, there is a natural inclination to include them in class and school activities. Depending on the student's disabilities, being included in all activities could require a number of adaptations. Classmates can be encouraged to consider different ways to include their friends. For instance, students without disabilities can remind the teacher of the need for a wheelchair-accessible bus and place of destination for field trips. They may determine the need to present material in a different manner (e.g., using objects versus just talking). They can develop ways of working together, making joint presentations and turning in final projects. To encourage such involvement (which can be highly beneficial), teachers need to listen to students and incorporate their ideas when appropriate. Students can make adaptations for a friend (e.g., a book holder in woodshop, photographs for an augmentative communication device in photography), or they can decide upon the level of participation to be expected of their friend. This involvement develops creative thinking skills, problem-solving skills, and respect for everyone's right to be included.

Finally, students without disabilities can help ensure that their classmate moves with the class and gets to the next activity in a timely fashion. Students can push their classmate who uses a wheelchair, provide sighted guidance, and encourage a student who is using a walker to keep up. Sometimes students require that positioning equipment move with them in the classroom and from one class to the next. Classmates can be particularly helpful in this regard, taking responsibility for moving wedges, standers, corner chairs, and so on, so that their friend can have access to necessary equipment when and where needed. Students at the secondary level can be asked to help move equipment that is large and bulky to transport. Table 7.3 lists a number of potential types of peer supports.

STRUCTURING THE DEVELOPMENT OF INTERACTIONS

Sometimes interactions do not occur naturally, for whatever reason. When this happens, teachers may need to implement structured groups. Approaches such as Making Action Plans (MAPs [formerly McGill Action Planning System]) (Forest & Pearpoint, 1992; Vandercook, York, & Forest, 1989), circle of friends (Forest & Lusthaus, 1989), and creative problem solving (Giangreco, 1990; Giangreco, Cloninger, Dennis, & Edelman, 1994) have been used to support interactions between students of vastly different abilities. Each of these approaches is described briefly in the following pages.

MAPs

The purpose of Making Action Plans (MAPs) is to assemble significant people in the child's life to develop an action plan to be implemented in a general education setting. Individuals who are typically involved include the child, the child's parents, sibling(s), other relatives, classmates, teachers, and other friends. Two individuals facilitate the process, one serving as a host and the other serving as a recorder. Forest and Pearpoint (1992) and Vandercook et al. (1989) discussed the seven questions that are asked of each participant. These questions are as follows (Vandercook et al., 1989):

1. What is the individual's history?
2. What is your dream for this individual?
3. What is your nightmare for this individual?
4. Who is the individual?
5. What are the individual's strengths, gifts, and abilities?
6. What are the individual's needs?
7. What would the individual's ideal day at school look like and what must be done to make it happen?

The MAPs process culminates in a graphically represented plan of action, which is then implemented by the involved parties.

Circle of Friends

Circle of friends is a method for developing relationships among students without disabilities and a student included in a general education setting. In this process, an adult asks the students without disabilities to fill in four concentric circles representing their current relationships. The first and innermost circle would include the names of people closest to them; the second, people they like but not enough to go in the first circle; the third, people they like or do things with; and the fourth, people who are paid to be in their life (e.g., doctors, teach-

Table 7.3. Types of peer support

1. Direct student's attention to the teacher or activity.
2. Assist student to take out and ready his or her materials.
3. Assist student with mobility (e.g., sighted guide, pushing wheelchair).
4. Assist student with moving and setting up equipment and materials.
5. Learn and use the student's mode(s) of communication.
6. Plan to be with the student for lunch, recess, and assemblies.
7. Serve as an appropriate role model.
8. Provide corrective feedback when inappropriate behavior occurs.
9. Provide information about what a particular student needs to say via an augmentative communication device.
10. Design and make adaptive equipment or materials as part of a class (e.g., woodshop) or at home.
11. Brainstorm ways to include a classmate in a given activity.

ers). Figure 7.3 provides an example of one child's circle of friends. After all circles are completed, the facilitator shares a circle of a student who has disabilities and highlights the fact that this student's circle contains mostly paid people Figure 7.4 shows an example of a circle of a boy who is labeled deaf-blind. The facilitator generates responses from the students about how this must feel and asks students to think of ways they might become part of the student's circle. Table 7.4 provides one example of how some high school students became more involved in their classmate's life. Figure 7.5 depicts some members of this particular circle of friends.

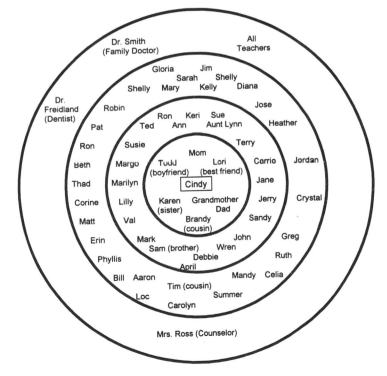

Figure 7.3. A typical seventh-grader's circle of friends.

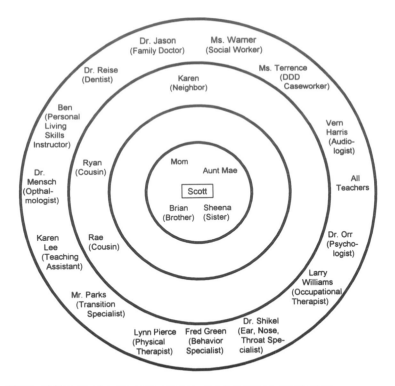

Figure 7.4. Circle of friends of a seventh-grader who is labeled deaf-blind.

Creative Problem Solving

Another suggested approach for including students with severe disabilities in general education settings is the use of the creative problem-solving method developed by Osborn and Parnes (Osborn, 1953; Parnes, 1981). This method has been employed extensively for various applications. It has also been used to help students without disabilities generate ideas for actively engaging a particular student with severe disabilities in general education classroom activities (Giangreco, 1990; Giangreco et al., 1994).

In this six-step process, participants first describe the problem facing them. Next, they compile facts about the problem. This step is followed by restating the problem so that ideas can be generated. For example, it might be stated, "In what ways can Pedro be involved in our unit on consumerism?" The fourth step is to brainstorm ideas, deferring judgment. This is followed by evaluating each idea using set criteria to determine solutions. The final step involves refining targeted solutions and developing and implementing an action plan.

Applying this process in any classroom can provide an opportunity for students at any age level to practice and hone problem-solving skills in a real-life situation. Students are also more likely to use the process in other situations requiring problem-solving abilities. Because students are actively engaged in curricular modification and adaptations, the process also aligns closely with a child-centered approach, as opposed to a model in which the teacher dominates as an authority figure.

Table 7.4. Some results of high school student's circle of friends

Student:	Sierra is a 12th-grader who has developed a number of good friends. Sierra is blind and can move her head only about one-half inch to either side. She does not speak and has a difficult time making her wants and needs known.
Facilitator:	A student teacher from the local university initiated the idea of a circle of friends [see description in the text] in Sierra's life enrichment class. She explained that the hoped-for outcome would be lasting and close friendships in and out of school. She helped the class compare opportunities that most of the students have to develop friendships to Sierra's opportunities and abilities (e.g., sharing classes for several years, hanging out, telephone calls). The student teacher then let the students suggest ways to enhance Sierra's opportunities to make friends.
Ideas:	Sierra's class developed a system of sign-up sheets whereby students signed up to eat lunch with Sierra, to meet and walk to and from classes with her, or to telephone her after school and on weekends. They put these sheets in a folder and passed it around during class. The girls also started a gossip notebook (no adults allowed, except for Sierra's mother who responded for her). The girls learned much about Sierra and began to feel comfortable talking to her about many things. One of the boys recommended that a cassette tape be started the same way as the notebook. This worked well and gave Sierra the opportunity to share her responses with the class independently (via a head switch). The students were pleased with their ideas and at how well they appeared to work.
Results:	After 3 weeks, students stopped signing up and would just come up to Sierra and say "See you for lunch" and "See you after art." They were approaching, speaking, and treating Sierra on the same level as they treated all their other friends. The facilitator had a hard time keeping up with all of Sierra's dates.

VALUE OF FRIENDSHIPS

One of the most highly rated outcomes of the educational process for any student and certainly for the student having severe sensory and multiple disabilities is that he or she will have friends (Bishop & Jubala, 1994). Certainly, the value of friendships cannot be underestimated for anyone. The impact on the student's performance at home and school is obvious. Although friendships cannot be specifically taught, they can and should be encouraged by adult team members who recognize the positive impact of friendships on the academic, behavioral, social, communicative, and motor skill levels of most students. Given the dearth of literature on the development of friendships in inclusive settings, both structured and informal programs may be a good first step when students are included in general education classes. However, Kishi and Meyer (1994) caution readers to recognize that the utilization of structured programs, such as Special Friends, may indeed be reinforcing traditional and stereotypical roles of volunteers or helpers. Several researchers have warned against a tendency for students without disabilities to assume a paternalistic attitude toward a classmate with severe and multiple disabilities (Evans, Salisbury, Palombaro, & Goldberg, 1994; Evans et al., 1992). Although such an attitude may bring students together, over

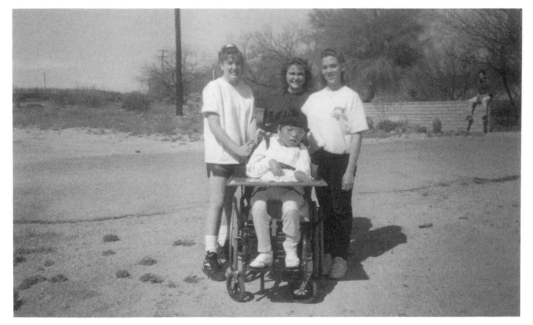

Figure 7.5. Some of Sierra's circle of friends.

time the overall effect can be negative, stressing the "need" of the student to be taken care of versus the need to be like others. With the presence of more longitudinal inclusionary practices, a focus on developing more typical peer relationships and friendships should emerge.

ENHANCING THE ROLE AND IMAGE OF STUDENTS WITH SEVERE AND SENSORY MULTIPLE DISABILITIES

When students with severe disabilities have obvious educational needs, there may be a tendency to perennially cast them in the role of *recipient* of help from classmates. One aspect of facilitating interactions calls for teachers to stress similarities and strengths of different partners. Although students with severe sensory and multiple disabilities may need assistance at times to perform as desired, there are also times when these students can help others. Students can hold doors open for others, pick up dropped items and return them to their owners, pass out homework and other materials, collect homework and turn it in, hold the flag for the pledge of allegiance, sharpen pencils, and obtain necessary materials for a group. With support from home, students can bring in requested items for school or class projects, such as used clothing for the clothing drive, food for a community food bank, and items to be recycled. In cooperative learning groups, students with severe and multiple disabilities can perform the important role of timekeeper with the aid of a kitchen timer or, if need be, a vibrating timer. Teachers need to be aware of the many opportunities that occur daily that would allow a student with severe and multiple disabilities to serve in a helping role. Expecting the student to assist others and assume valued roles in the classroom (e.g., hall leader) helps classmates to perceive this student on a more equal basis.

Photograph courtesy of Kelly Wagner

AFTER-SCHOOL HOURS

A major goal of promoting interactions among students of different abilities during school hours is for these interactions to occur after school as well. As stated, students who have difficulty communicating their thoughts and desires and who have sensory impairments that make interactions more difficult do not usually have an easy time developing friendships (Ferguson, 1994; Haring et al., 1995). By creating daily, ongoing opportunities for these students to interact with and become familiar with a group of students who can be responsive communicative partners, the chance to develop friendships is enhanced.

To facilitate the development of friendships and to provide structured leisure activities for after-school hours, enrolling students with severe sensory and multiple disabilities in typical community activities is one option. Depending on the student's age and interests, the possibility of Boy Scouts or Girl Scouts (and their younger counterparts, Cub Scouts and Brownies, respectively) should be explored. Scout troops offer structured opportunities for students to work together on various projects (many of which do not require substantial adaptation). The most critical consideration is to find a troop leader who is open to new ideas, flexible, eager to learn, and able to recognize the benefit of including all students. Having a student join a scout troop with other familiar students from school should also be a consideration.

In addition, many cities feature Parks and Recreation programs covering a range of leisure and recreation areas. Although these classes may be offered during the school year, they are more typically available during summer months. Classes can include martial arts, crafts, exercise, dance, swimming, basketball, drama, musical instruments, jewelry, photography, yoga, American Sign Language, and other special interest activites. In this connection, during the summer months, extended school-year programs for a student with disabilities may occur in the community, with the student involved in appropriate activities with peers without disabilities (Alper, Parker, Schloss, & Wisniewski, 1993). As part of the student's extended school-year plan, the school district can offer much-needed support to ensure active participation and continued growth. Instead of assembling children with like disabilities at a special site that is unfamiliar to all involved, a district can provide the necessary support on an individual basis to allow students to participate in the local community in summer activities that promote progress according to the individualized education program (IEP).

Besides Parks and Recreation offerings, YMCAs and YWCAs also provide various course offerings for children and youth. These activities do not have to be geared for individuals with special needs, so long as such students have the necessary support from home, the Department of Developmental Disabilities, volunteers, or trained employees at the facility. The objective is to provide organized and structured activities that facilitate interactions among students and enable friendships to develop. Without such structured opportunities that complement efforts made at school, meeting new people and making friends will remain difficult.

Extracurricular activities such as 4-H, pep clubs, and an array of sporting activities and clubs can offer the social structure needed to develop or maintain relationships with other students. Falvey, Coots, and Terry-Gage (1992) provide lists of typical extracurricular activities for preschool, elementary, and secondary students. The interests of individual students with severe sensory and multiple disabilities will determine which extracurricular activities are most suitable and beneficial.

SUMMARY

This chapter has highlighted the crucial role that peers play in the education of students with severe sensory and multiple impairments. Given the opportunity, students of all abilities can and do learn from one another. Bringing students together to learn is an important role that adults in schools can assume, while also providing opportunities for friendships to develop. Although friendships cannot be dictated, they can be encouraged. Social and communication skills can and should be taught so that interactions between students of different abilities can be rewarding and isolation does not occur. As one parent lamented, "They [students with disabilities] know how to interact with their teachers, and they know how to respond to their aides, but they don't know how to respond to each other" (Hanley-Maxwell, Whitney-Thomas, & Pogoloff, 1995, p. 10).

The importance of friendships in everyone's life is indisputable. Allowing (and encouraging) students to learn together is one way to assist students with severe sensory and multiple impairments achieve valued friendships.

REFERENCES

Alper, S., Parker, K., Schloss, P., & Wisniewski, L. (1993). Extended school year programs: A community-driven curriculum model. *Mental Retardation, 31*(3), 163–170.

Bishop, K., & Jubala, K. (1994). By June, given shared experiences, integrated classes, and equal opportunities, Jaime will have a friend. *Teaching Exceptional Children, 21*(1), 36–40.

Bowden, J., & Thorburn, J. (1993). Including a student with multiple disabilities and visual impairments in her neighborhood school. *Journal of Visual Impairments and Blindness, 87*(7), 268–272.

Buzolich, M.J., & Lunger, J. (1995). Empowering system users in peer training. *Augmentative and Alternative Communication, 11,* 37–45.

Erin, J. (1986). Teachers of the visually handicapped: How can they best serve children with severe and profound handicaps? *Education of the Visually Handicapped, 18*(7), 15–25.

Evans, I.M., Salisbury, C., Palombaro, M., & Goldberg, J.S. (1994). Children's perception of fairness in classroom and interpersonal situations involving peers with disabilities. *Journal of The Association for Persons with Severe Handicaps, 19,* 326–332.

Evans, I.M., Salisbury, C.L., Palombaro, M.M., Berryman, J., & Hollowood, T.M. (1992). Peer interactions and social acceptance of elementary-age children with severe disabilities in an inclusive school. *Journal of The Association for Persons with Severe Handicaps, 17,* 205–212.

Falvey, M., Coots, J., & Terry-Gage, S. (1992). Extracurricular activities. In S. Stainback & W. Stainback (Eds.), *Curriculum considerations in inclusive classrooms: Facilitating learning for all students* (pp. 229–237). Baltimore: Paul H. Brookes Publishing Co.

Ferguson, D.L. (1994). Is communication really the point? Some thoughts on interventions and membership. *Mental Retardation, 32*(1), 7–18.

Ferguson, D.L., Jeanchild, L., & Meyer, G. (1992). When inclusion isolates: Dimensions in the creation of "bubble kids." Eugene, OR: University of Oregon, Specialized Training Program.

Forest, M., & Lusthaus, E. (1989). Promoting educational equality for all students: Circles and maps. In S. Stainback, W. Stainback, & M. Forest (Eds.), *Educating all students in the mainstream of regular education* (pp. 45–57). Baltimore: Paul H. Brookes Publishing Co.

Forest, M., & Pearpoint, J.C. (1992). Putting all kids on the map. *Educational Leadership, 50*(2), 26–31.

Giangreco, M.F. (1990). *Using creative problem-solving methods to include students with severe disabilities in general education classroom activities.* Unpublished manuscript, University of Vermont, Center for Developmental Disabilities, Burlington.

Giangreco, M.F., Cloninger, C.J., Dennis, R.E., & Edelman, S.W. (1994). Problem-solving methods to facilitate inclusive education. In J.S. Thousand, R.A. Villa, & A.I. Nevin (Eds.), *Creativity and collaborative learning: A practical guide to empowering students and teachers* (pp. 321–346). Baltimore: Paul H. Brookes Publishing Co.

Giangreco, M., Edelman, S., Cloninger, C., & Dennis, R. (1993). My child has a classmate with severe disabilities: What parents of nondisabled children think about full inclusion. *Developmental Disabilities Bulletin, 21*(1), 77–91.

Giangreco, M.F., & Putnam, J.W. (1991). Supporting the education of students with severe disabilities in regular education environments. In L.H. Meyer, C.A. Peck, & L. Brown (Eds.), *Critical issues in the lives of people with severe disabilities* (pp. 245–270). Baltimore: Paul H. Brookes Publishing Co.

Hamre-Nietupski, S., Ayres, B., Nietupski, J., Savage, M., Mitchell, B., & Bramman, H. (1989). Enhancing integration of students with severe disabilities through curricular infusion: A general/special educator partnership. *Education and Training in Mental Retardation, 24*, 78–88.

Hanley-Maxwell, C., Whitney-Thomas, J., & Pogoloff, S.M. (1995). The second shock: A qualitative study of parents' perspectives and needs during their child's transition from school to adult life. *Journal of The Association for Persons with Severe Handicaps, 20*, 3–15.

Haring, T.G., Breen, C., Lee, N., Pitts-Conway, V., & Gaylord-Ross, R.J. (1987). Adolescent peer tutoring and special friend experiences. *Journal of The Association for Persons with Severe Handicaps, 12*, 280–286.

Haring, T., Haring, N.G., Breen, C., Romer, L.T., & White, J. (1995). Social relationships among students with deaf-blindness and their peers in inclusive settings. In N.G. Haring & L.T. Romer (Eds.), *Welcoming students who are deaf-blind into typical classrooms: Facilitating school participation, learning, and friendships* (pp. 231–247). Baltimore: Paul H. Brookes Publishing Co.

Helmstetter, E., Peck, C.A., & Giangreco, M.F. (1994). Outcomes of interactions with peers with moderate or severe disabilities: A statewide survey of high school students. *Journal of The Association for Persons with Severe Handicaps, 19*, 263–276.

Hunt, P., Staub, D., Alwell, M., & Goetz, L. (1994). Achievement by all students within the context of cooperative learning groups. *Journal of The Association for Persons with Severe Handicaps, 19*, 290–301.

Izen, C.L., & Brown, F. (1991). Education and treatment needs of students with profound, multiply handicapping, and medically fragile conditions: A survey of teachers' perceptions. *Journal of The Association for Persons with Severe Handicaps, 16*, 94–103.

Jorgensen, C.M. (1994). Developing individualized inclusive educational programs. In S.N. Calculator & C.M. Jorgensen (Eds.), *Including students with severe disabilities in schools* (pp. 27–74). San Diego: Singular Publishing.

Kishi, G.S., & Meyer, L.H. (1994). What children report and remember: A six-year follow-up of the effects of social contact between peers with and without severe disabilities. *Journal of The Association for Persons with Severe Handicaps, 19*, 277–289.

Ogletree, B.T., Wetherby, A.M., & Westling, D.L. (1992). Profile of the prelinguistic intentional communicative behaviors of children with profound mental retardation. *American Journal on Mental Retardation, 97*, 186–198.

Osborn, A. (1953). *Applied imagination: Principles and procedures of creative thinking.* New York: Charles Scribner & Sons.

Parnes, S.J. (1981). *The magic of your mind.* Buffalo, NY: Creative Education Foundation in association with Bearly Ltd.

Peck, C.A., Donaldson, J., & Pezzoli, M. (1990). Some benefits nonhandicapped adolescents perceive for themselves from their social relationships with peers who have severe handicaps. *Journal of The Association for Persons with Severe Handicaps, 15,* 241–249.

Ryndak, D.L. (1995). Natural support networks: Collaborating with family and friends for meaningful education programs in inclusive settings. In D.L. Ryndak & S. Alper (Eds.), *Curriculum content for students with moderate and severe disabilities in inclusive settings* (pp. 61–76). Needham Heights, MA: Allyn & Bacon.

Sasso, G., Hughes, G., Swanson, H.L., & Novak, C.G. (1987). A comparison of peer initiation intervention in promoting multiple peer initiators. *Education and Training in Mental Retardation, 22,* 150–155.

Sasso, G.M., & Rude, H.A. (1987). Unprogrammed effects of training high-status peers to interact with severely handicapped children. *Journal of Applied Behavioral Analysis, 20,* 35–44.

Staub, D., & Hunt, P. (1993). The effects of social interaction training on high school peer tutors of schoolmates with severe disabilities. *Exceptional Children, 60,* 41–57.

Staub, D., Schwartz, I.S., Gallucci, C., & Peck, C.A. (1994). Four portraits of friendship at an inclusive school. *Journal of The Association for Persons with Severe Handicaps, 19,* 314–325.

Strully, J., & Strully, C. (1985). Friendship and our children. *Journal of The Association for Persons with Severe Handicaps, 10,* 224–227.

Vacc, N.N., & Cannon, S.J. (1991). Cross-age tutoring in mathematics: Sixth graders helping students who are moderately handicapped. *Education and Training in Mental Retardation, 26*(1), 89–97.

Vandercook, T., York, J. & Forest, M. (1989). The McGill Action Planning System (MAPS): A strategy for building the vision. *Journal of The Association for Persons with Severe Handicaps, 14,* 205–215.

Villa, R.A., & Thousand, J.S. (1992). Student collaboration: An essential for curriculum delivery in the 21st century. In S. Stainback & W. Stainback (Eds.), *Curriculum considerations in inclusive classrooms: Facilitating learning for all students* (pp. 117–142). Baltimore: Paul H. Brookes Publishing Co.

York, J., & Tundidor, M. (1995). Issues raised in the name of inclusion: Perspectives of educators, parents, and students. *Journal of The Association for Persons with Severe Handicaps, 20,* 31–44.

York, J., Vandercook, T., MacDonald, C., Heise-Neff, C., & Caughey, E. (1992). Feedback about integrating middle school students with severe disabilities in general education classes. *Exceptional Children, 58,* 244–257.

Chapter 8

WORKING COOPERATIVELY
The Role of Adults

June E. Downing

Change in educational service delivery can be difficult for all participants. To ease the transition, everyone must be kept informed of the rationale for the change and be allowed to take an active part in its development. Teamwork plays a critical role in a successful inclusion experience. Instead of viewing the situation from the perspective of "my" class and "your" class, and "my" students and "your" students, all teachers share the responsibility for each classroom and for the learning of *all* students. Bringing students together requires bringing adults together. In addition, the value of individual team members is not determined by labels (titles or degrees), but simply by the shared desire to contribute to a student's educational program. Establishing equal parity across all team members is an essential component of true collaboration (Idol, Paolucci-Whitcomb, & Nevin, 1986; Rainforth, York, & Macdonald, 1992). All participants need an equal voice in the decision-making process and time to openly discuss concerns and make suggestions for increased participation of all students.

Resistance to including students may come from a fear of not knowing what to do to make the process successful (Downing, Eichinger, & Williams, 1996; Evans, Bird, Ford, Green, & Bischoff, 1992). Considerable resistance can be avoided when all players feel comfortable with program goals and performance expectations. Sharing information and working as a collaborative team from the time of the program's inception can serve to alleviate concerns and resistance.

WHO'S ON THE EDUCATIONAL TEAM?

In general, anyone who has something to contribute and who wants to be on a student's educational team can be a team member. In the past, the makeup of the team may have been determined by matching the student's disabilities to the professional who had training or expertise in the disability (Rainforth et al.,

1992). Yet training and certification in a given disability area may or may not provide the professional with the motivation or knowledge to contribute to a student's educational program. In other words, being a licensed speech-language pathologist does not mean that that person should be solely responsible for addressing the child's communication difficulties. Such an expectation places considerable stress on a given professional that is both unwarranted and unproductive. A student's communicative needs, like other skill areas, are complex and require the ongoing commitment of several people interested in and knowledgeable about those needs. Depending on training and past experiences, the speech-language pathologist may not have all the necessary information or skills to assist a particular student (at least initially). The most effective support for a given student will probably be a combined effort from a number of people, both professionally trained and not professionally trained who share a common goal for the student's success. The blending of all team members' skills and knowledge leads to a more holistic program for the student.

WHO PROVIDES SUPPORT?

Determining who provides the necessary support for a given student at any given time is a dynamic and ongoing decision. The dynamic nature of this decision rests on the fact that students do acquire skills, learn to recognize and meet expectations, and need more or less support depending on the activity as well as their changing ability to handle the activity. Obviously, students have both "good" and "bad" days depending on a number of physical and emotional factors (e.g., sickness, lack of sleep, hunger). For these reasons, support must be considered in a flexible rather than fixed manner. Those providing support must be alert to when assistance is needed and when it is not.

NATURAL SUPPORTS

The first choice for providing support is the individuals who are typically available in general education classrooms—the teacher and classmates. These supports are the most natural and readily available sources of assistance, as depicted in Figure 8.1. Classroom teachers need to perceive the student with severe and multiple disabilities as a full-time class member, not a visitor or guest (Ferguson, Meyer, Jeanchild, Juniper, & Zingo, 1992). This perception alone can provide considerable support to the student's sense of belonging. Other forms of support by the teacher and classmates can and should be easily provided. Many activities, for example, require no more support than a peer to offer to be a sighted guide or to tactually remind the student to take out needed classroom materials. At times the teacher can intervene to repeat directions, tactually cue a student to go to the appropriate lab group, ask a student to be quiet, or help a student use the desired playground equipment. Salisbury, Gallucci, Palombaro, and Peck (1995) interviewed 10 elementary general educators and found that these teachers felt they could do several simple things to enhance the membership of students having severe and multiple disabilities in their classrooms. Teachers mentioned such strategies as encouraging students to work together, promoting a caring and sharing environment, and modeling acceptance of the student by talking to the student, walking with the student, and encouraging the student to become involved in activities.

Photograph courtesy of Pat Danielle Smith

Figure 8.1. First-grade teacher and students learning from each other.

Other sources of natural supports include other classroom teachers, students in other classes, the school principal, parent volunteers, bus drivers, cafeteria workers, librarian, and any staff member who is at the student's school and has interactions with this student. These people need to feel comfortable interacting and supporting the student when needed and should not rely on someone else to provide all the support. For instance, if a student accidently knocks over some books in the library, the librarian should feel comfortable asking the student to pick up the books via verbal directions, gestures, physical prompts, or modeling. This is much more natural than looking to a special educator or teaching assistant to intervene. Natural support relies on individuals in the natural environment, knowing not only that they can assist when it is logical to do so, but that they *should* assist. In sum, everyone assumes some of the responsibility for everyone else. This policy affords the student greater contact with different people and provides more learning opportunities across different activities, environments, and individuals.

The school principal, as school leader, can facilitate the development of natural supports by setting a tone of shared accountability for all students. The principal can recognize and commend the efforts of teachers and staff when they assume responsibility for students having unique needs. By interacting with each student equally, the principal also can model for faculty, staff, parents, and students the importance and positive aspects of such interactions. Helping everyone to see the value of looking out for one another can provide considerable support throughout the day.

Nevertheless, there will be times when natural supports are insufficient to produce the desired results. A careful analysis of each activity with ongoing feedback from the classroom teacher can help determine when a student may need extra support.

ADDITIONAL SUPPORTS

Special Educator and Teaching Assistant Support

Perhaps the most consistent and expected source of additional support (when natural supports are insufficient) is the special educator or teaching assistant who is designated to ensure appropriate programming for a given student. These individuals are typically trained to meet the unique educational needs of students with severe sensory and multiple disabilities. Their support will be directed toward assessing the compatibility of fit between individual goals and the curriculum and adapting instruction and materials accordingly to best meet learning needs within the typical activities of the class. As emphasized earlier in this volume, care must be taken not to provide excessive support or attention so that the student is isolated from classmates, the classroom teacher, or the activity. The special educator or teaching assistant should be perceived as additional support for the teacher and class, providing one-on-one assistance only when absolutely needed (Ferguson et al., 1992). To reflect this type of role change, special educators may go by the title of inclusion facilitator or inclusion support teacher. The manner in which support is provided also must be given careful thought, so that high expectations for performance are maintained. A study by York and Tundidor (1995) revealed that secondary-age students felt that teaching assistants "babied" the student with disabilities and that these students were not expected to adhere to the same classroom rules. Support does not mean having low expectations or doing *for* the student. Ideally, the right amount of support allows the student to make maximal learning gains while participating in typical and valued activities.

Special educators and teaching assistants usually support several different students across different classes and grades. They therefore move in and out of classrooms, providing support as needed. Their schedules fluctuate according to the changing skill levels and needs of the students they support. They must learn the delicate balance of providing whatever support is needed, but no more.

Related Staff Support

Professionals trained to address specific areas of need are a valuable resource for additional support in inclusive classrooms. These professionals could be vision specialists, hearing specialists, speech-language pathologists or communication specialists, interpreters, occupational therapists, physical therapists, orientation and mobility instructors, adaptive physical education (PE) specialists, and behavioral specialists. Although these individuals (owing to large caseloads) may serve primarily in a collaborative and consultative manner (Rainforth et al., 1992), the direct time they spend with students in classrooms can provide needed support at critical times of the day.

Given some flexibility in their work schedules, related service providers may be able to support students at different times and in varying activities to gain a clearer, more comprehensive picture of a student's program. For instance, the vision specialist may be able to spend time with a student for 30 minutes on a Monday morning 1 week and then 2 weeks later see the same student on a Thursday afternoon. In this way, the support professional can help identify strengths and needs and monitor intervention plans. In addition, the special educator, knowing when specialists will be available to support a given student, can rearrange the schedule of more direct service providers to support other students, collect data, monitor other programs, adapt materials, or plan with another team member (e.g., teaching assistant, general educator).

Professionals who represent different disciplines (e.g., in regard to visual impairments, hearing impairments, communication disorders, motor impairments) need to have access to the student's overall educational program in order to know how best to contribute to the program. By observing the student in as many different situations and activities as possible, these professionals can obtain a better understanding of the student's needs and of how they as professionals can best help the student. Improving skills in isolation that relate to a given specialty area is *not* the goal. For instance, the goal of "seeing better" is too vague and difficult to measure. Rather, the goal should be to support the student in achieving individualized education program (IEP) objectives that are meaningful and activity based and that address desired areas for improvement. For example, one student's objective is to independently move through the lunch line and make food choices. Currently, the student stops, holds up the line, flicks his hand in front of his face, and does not look at the food choices. Observing this activity, the vision specialist can confer with the rest of the team to implement a program that teaches the student to look for the cafeteria workers as natural cues for the appropriate behavior, scan the food options, and respond appropriately when asked to make choices. The student will learn to use his vision during this activity to be more successful and will have opportunities to practice this same visual skill in other activities (e.g., choosing art materials, choosing a library book, choosing a partner for physical education).

Volunteer Support

Developing a volunteer program for a given school can help alleviate some of the need for additional support that certain students have. Volunteers can either provide support to a student with severe disabilities or can provide instructional support to other students so that the classroom teacher can spend more time with students who have special needs. Volunteers can also help make and adapt materials as needed.

Volunteers can be senior citizens; retired individuals; parents or other family members; university or college students in education, psychology, social work, or a related field; or members of various organizations (e.g., Knights of Columbus, Big Brothers/Big Sisters, sororities or fraternities). Volunteers (like everyone else) require training to understand the classroom teacher's expectations and to feel comfortable with the level of support they themselves can provide. They need to know how best to interact with and teach a student. They also need to have a definite schedule and to realize that they are needed and appreciated.

Peer Tutors

The benefits of students supporting students were detailed in Chapter 7 and are not discussed at length again here. However, it is important to mention that adults on the educational team need to keep in mind this valuable resource when planning ways to support students who need extra help. Students who are older, are in different grades or classes, or attend different schools can serve as peer tutors at various times in a student's day. Creative scheduling is needed so that peer tutors do not miss out on other learning opportunities critical for their own success. However, many students finish their work early and need a constructive outlet for their free time and energy. Being a peer tutor (or being given the title of teaching assistant) provides these students the chance to help another student learn. Students can practice skills already acquired, learn creative ways of communicating and teaching, express their creativity by making and adapting materials, and develop strong feelings of self-esteem (McNeil, 1994; Peck, Donaldson, & Pezzoli, 1990). These benefits apply to students labeled gifted and talented as well as to those labeled at risk for academic success.

High school students may be able to acquire credit for serving as teaching assistants while also developing valuable skills that could lead to a related career choice. Secondary age students can leave their own school campus when classes are finished or between classes to assist younger students with severe disabilities at elementary schools. Many schools currently use cross-age tutoring to supplement instructional support by paid professionals (Kamps, Barbetta, Leonard, & Delquadri, 1994; Vacc & Cannon, 1991). These tutors must be trained to communicate effectively with all students, to systematically and positively shape desired behavior versus doing *for* the student, and to accurately and objectively collect data to help measure progress. Training takes time, but the long-term benefits to the teacher and students in the class are obvious.

BRINGING THE TEAM TOGETHER

With respect to the professionals involved, the concept of including all students with diverse learning needs, especially those with severe and complex needs, may not initially be conducive to creating the desired partnership between general and special education. Instead, already overwhelmed teachers with large classes and limited, if any, experience working with such students may express resentment and an unwillingness to participate (Downing et al., 1996). In addition, the new role for special educators and other specialists (vision specialist, hearing specialist, speech-language pathologist) of blending with general education and supporting the classroom teacher may create turf problems and an unwillingness to relinquish control. The benefits for everyone involved must be clearly articulated (Ferguson et al., 1992; Idol, 1993), and the overall educational goals for individual students must guide the process (Rainforth et al., 1992). Professionals will need to relax their unilateral hold on their areas of expertise and work together to develop a unified program for a student within natural settings. Such a change may be more difficult for special educators to accept, as these professionals lose their separate classrooms and locus of control and "move in" with another teacher who is already established in a given room. In addition, those specialists accustomed to removing the child from a given classroom and going to a special place to work will need to adapt to the demands of the classroom, adjusting their intervention techniques accordingly. These specialists also lose total control of how they provide services and instead must consider the dynamics of the typical learning environment (e.g., teacher style, activity in progress, physical layout of classroom, acceptable noise level).

The lack of time experienced by most educational team members is a potential barrier to collaborative teaming (Bardak, 1995). Yet team members must have the time to meet and develop the skills needed to successfully support students in inclusive settings. Once team members feel comfortable working cooperatively together, less meeting time may be needed. Strategies for sharing information with team members in quick and efficient ways are suggested in the following sections.

SHARING INFORMATION

One critical component in facilitating cooperative collaboration among educational team members is the ongoing sharing of information about the student and the overall program. Several research studies have shown that attitudes toward inclusion are more favorable given the appropriate support and training (Gemmel-Crosby & Hanzlik, 1994; Janney, Snell, Beers, & Raynes, 1995). All team members need to be kept informed of program goals and expectations for the student so that they can all see how each person can contribute to the success of the program. Classroom teachers may be reluctant to include a student with severe sensory and multiple disabilities if they do not understand how they can contribute to the student's learning. In general, teachers want to feel that they can have a positive impact upon a student's education (Nevin, Thousand, Paolucci-Whitcomb, & Villa, 1990). Once the student's goals have been clearly stated, as well as ways that the classroom teacher can help the student meet these needs, the initial reluctance will ease. Therefore, it is recommended that the team (or at least the general educator and special educator) complete an activity analysis form (described in Chapter 3) to clarify exactly how each goal and objective will be addressed by subject matter or activity.

Explaining How to Interact

As discussed previously in this volume, the individual characteristics of a given student need to be explained so that everyone will feel as comfortable as possible interacting with this student. Students with severe sensory and multiple disabilities often communicate in unique ways. Everyone involved with such a student needs to know how the student receives information (e.g., speech, sign, pictures, touch cues) and how the student shares information with others (e.g., gestures, pointing, using objects, facial expressions). The entire school community needs to be aware of the importance of interactions, even when they are brief or when the expected or desired response does not occur. Students with severe sensory and multiple disabilities need many opportunities to interact with others to practice their social-communicative skills. They also need to know that all members of the school community are potential communicative partners, not just those trained in special education.

Perhaps the most beneficial aspect of sharing information involves reassuring teachers, administrators, and all other school staff that interactions are encouraged, desirable, and not to be feared. When a student appears to differ markedly from others in communicative and social skills, a hesitancy to even *try* to interact may result from a fear of doing something "wrong." Alleviating these fears and stressing to individuals that the worst mistake is to ignore and avoid this student might help to increase the frequency of interactions for the student. The individual adults in the school also need information about communicating with students with disabilities—not only regarding how to interact but what to do when a student's response is lacking, not understood, or unwelcome. People will react differently according to their unique personalities, confidence, skills working with different students, and time they have to deal with a given situation. Knowing that there is not just one right way to respond to the student, but that there is a range of "best" options, may help reduce the reluctance to become involved.

Explaining How to Respond to Unconventional Behavior

Because many students with multiple disabilities may convey their intent or desires through behaviors that are destructive, disruptive, or harmful to themselves or others (Durand & Kishi, 1987; Jacobson & Janicki, 1985), the reasons behind these behaviors need to be carefully explained to all potential communicative partners so that the behaviors can appear less strange or abnormal. When not understood for their communicative potential, behaviors that are socially unconventional or unacceptable can create a barrier to enhancing interactions, thus highlighting the differences between people rather than bringing them together. For example, adults, as well as student peers, need to know that when a student engages in behaviors such as pulling out his or her hair, destroying papers, scratching others, screaming, or hitting his or her head, the student may be expressing excessive frustration over having to do a given task or not understanding what is expected. Awareness of the student's frustration can make it easier to understand and accept the student. The importance of assisting the individual to communicate desires and feelings in alternative ways also becomes a clearer goal. Durand and Kishi (1987) targeted this need in their study of five students with dual sensory impairments, all of whom used some combination of severely disruptive, aggressive, and self-injurious behaviors to express needs. Functional communication training with these five students to give them alternative and more appropriate ways to express needs reduced the undesired behavior. Sharing this information with teachers, teaching assistants, support staff, and principals is critical to building an understanding network of support for the student.

Sensory impairments also can have an impact on the type of self-stimulatory or self-amusing behaviors that an individual can express. All of us engage in such behavior for a number of reasons (e.g., to relieve boredom, reduce stress). However, given the ability to see clearly, to hear, and to move our bodies fluently, the behaviors exhibited by the majority of us may look different from the same general class of behaviors that someone who cannot see well, hear well, or move well may develop. For example, instead of doodling, twirling hair, fidgeting in a chair, or clicking pens, children with severe sensory and multiple disabilities may make vocalizations they can feel in their throat, flick their fingers in front of their face, or pat their chin repeatedly. Without adequate vision or hearing, these children may not have received the feedback to know that these behaviors are not typically done or acceptable and may not have been able to model more socially acceptable behaviors. In the same way that more customary behaviors of typical students are understood and accepted, the more unique behaviors of students with severe sensory and multiple disabilities need understanding and acceptance. Explanations of stereotypical or self-stimulatory behavior in individuals with sensory impairments, especially with severe and multiple impairments, have been provided by several researchers (Durand & Carr, 1987; Leonhardt, 1990; Repp, Felce, & Barton, 1988). Knowing why individual students engage in certain unique self-stimulatory types of behaviors reduces the perception of strangeness that can develop and allows for greater understanding and acceptance. Sharing this type of information also stresses the similarities among all individuals, rather than concentrating on the differences.

Strategies for Information Sharing

Critical information about how a person communicates and otherwise behaves can be shared in a number of ways. Formal presentations to the entire staff can be given. Information can also be shared in smaller staff meetings (e.g., cafeteria workers, playground monitors, grade-level meetings). Since information shared must be ongoing as the student and situations change, much of the information will probably be exchanged informally when teachers have a few minutes together in class, in the staff lounge, over lunch, walking down a hall together, and while watching children on the playground and through written correspondence in the form of notes and messages. Care must be taken to convey information positively, in a way that shows respect for the individual student and does not impinge upon confidentiality of records; derogatory language can be harmful and isolating. It is never appropriate to refer to any child by an undesirable label (e.g., "runner," "biter," "screamer"). Students need to be referred to by their names and the grade they attend.

The type of information shared and the way it is presented will vary depending on the situation. For instance, some classroom teachers like to share information briefly with a teaching assistant while students are in the midst of changing activities. Other teachers prefer to use this limited time for preparation or checking students' work. Team members need to inform each other regarding how and when they prefer to receive information, and there needs to be a clear procedure for requesting information. Again, demonstrating respect for the student and each team member is critical. Few classroom teachers, for instance, appreciate two or three adults exchanging information at the back of the room while they are trying to conduct class. The temptation to engage in this behavior may be great, especially if one of the adults is a related services provider (e.g., occupational therapist, vision specialist) who has limited time at any one school. In addition, it is sometimes easier to exchange information when the student is involved in an activity and the need for modifications is apparent to everyone. The author recommends that teachers videotape classroom activities and use videotaped segments of the student to discuss problem areas and share ideas with team members, especially parents and related service providers who may not be on campus often. Videotapes can be used before or after school or during planned staff meetings to serve as a focal point for brainstorming ideas and discussions. Videotapes also can be taken home with specific questions attached for a particular service provider or the parent. These questions can be responded to via telephone or written messages if face-to-face meetings cannot occur in a timely fashion. Whatever the option, an alternative must be found to the group huddle of adults in a given classroom. When adults are in the classroom, they are there to support each other as well as the learning of all students.

Initially, greater time may be needed to adequately explain a student's behaviors and how the adult should strive to interact. As individual adults become more comfortable with the student, less assistance in this area will be needed and requests for information will become more sporadic and on an as-needed basis. For example, one second-grade teacher requested weekly meetings for at least 1 hour with the special educator and teaching assistant when she first included a child with severe and multiple disabilities in her room. After 1 month, she reported feeling much more comfortable with this child and decided that the meetings were no longer necessary. The need to meet to exchange information and problem-solve will depend on a range of variables including student performance, transition issues, familiarity, changing needs, and changes in the team. Retaining some degree of flexibility with regard to the number and scheduling of meetings is a necessity.

WORKING COOPERATIVELY AND COLLABORATIVELY

A considerable body of literature exists on parents and professionals working as collaborative teams (e.g., Bailey, 1991; McComas & Bricker, 1994; Salisbury, 1992). Although information abounds on the characteristics of truly cooperative and collaborative teams, achieving the ideals of such a team is difficult. Furthermore, the more individuals on a given team, the more difficult true collaboration may be (Rainforth et al., 1992; Villa & Thousand, 1994). Students with complex educational needs such as those with severe sensory and multiple disabilities typically have many different professionals serving on their teams. Many of these professionals (e.g., occupational therapists, physical therapists, vision specialists, orientation and mobility instructors) have relatively large caseloads and may be assigned multiple schools and even school districts. As a result, their time to work as part of a cohesive team is extremely limited. These professionals also may not have received training in collaborative teaming and may feel more comfortable working independently.

Bringing different professionals and parents together is necessary to integrate their skills and knowledge to help the student achieve valued outcomes. Without a truly collaborative approach, the intervention for students can become fragmented and overly specialized, with related outcomes for students even conflicting. Keeping valued outcomes determined by the entire team (especially family members) firmly in mind will help to focus the team on the child as part of a classroom, school, family, and community, and not on isolated deficit areas. Table 8.1 provides examples of how various team members collaborate to write the IEP objectives. Each student has one unified IEP based on achieving important activities, not multiple IEPs written by individuals acting on their own.

Demystifying Students with
Severe Sensory and Multiple Disabilities

Students with severe sensory and multiple disabilities have obvious impairments and special labels that tend to accompany them. This combination can be over-

Table 8.1. IEP objectives showing shared team input

Student 1:	Sharon—first grade.
Objective:	During mathematics class, Sharon will indicate which is the greater of two amounts by reaching toward the appropriate pile of items with 80% accuracy for 10 trials.
Team Input:	
Parent	Recognizes importance of keeping Sharon with class for all subjects; encourages interest in basic academics.
Teacher	Determines math curriculum and activities and helps establish criteria.
Special Educator	Recommends physical adaptations and limited options.
Speech-Language Pathologist	Suggests method of indicating pile of items.
Vision Specialist	Works with Sharon on looking and shifting gaze from one choice to the next.
Student 2:	Tara—fifth grade.
Objective:	While reading with a peer and using page fluffers on each page, Tara will turn the page within 3 seconds of the peer finishing reading a given page for 70% of each book for 10 reading sessions.
Team Input:	
Parent	Recognizes importance of sharing with a peer, showing respect for property.
Teacher	Stresses importance of reading and criteria for mastery.
Special Educator	Targets responding to classmate, staying on task.
Occupational Therapist	Determines method of turning pages, adaptations.
Speech-Language Pathologist	Encourages positive interactions with peers.
Student 3:	Simon—10th grade
Objective:	While positioned in a standing table, Simon will make at least four choices of materials to use in art class by pointing within 5 seconds of a request for 10 consecutive classes.
Team Input:	
Teacher	Suggests art materials as a choice and presents project.
Special Educator	Determines number of choices and criteria for mastery.
Physical Therapist	Determines best position.
Vision Specialist	Identifies looking as a way to make choices.
Occupational Therapist	Identifies pointing as a way to indicate choice.
Speech-Language Pathologist	Suggests listening to a peer, responding to a peer, helps determine criteria for mastery.

whelming to a teacher with no prior experience interacting with anyone with such seemingly complex challenges. Special educators who use medical and technical jargon with teachers in discussing students with such disabilities do little to relieve fears. Stressing the student's strengths and the similarities among all children will do much to demystify the disability and enhance the possibility of inclusion. Teachers desire and need appropriate information in order to support the child and help him or her feel welcome in the classroom (Janney et al., 1995).

Building Shared Responsibility for Students

As stated at the outset of this chapter, recognizing that all adults can help all students at a given school learn helps to diminish the separation that occurs when teachers refer to "your" and "my" students. Providing classroom teachers with specific information regarding interactions with certain students also helps to clarify roles and responsibilities. These strategies should be easy to perform and to blend into the teacher's natural teaching style (Salisbury et al., 1995). The teacher should be able to recognize that assuming some responsibility for a student will not add to an already challenging role. For example, classroom teachers need to feel comfortable calling on students who are learning to raise their hand, even if the student does not respond when called on. In addition, if this student is working with a peer buddy, the teacher can call on both children for a response to a particular question. This teacher behavior is natural and expected and conveys the message of acceptance and high expectations for behavior to other students. See Table 8.2 for more specific suggestions for teachers.

Working in partnership with the classroom teacher, the special educator or teaching assistant can facilitate interactions among the student having complex needs, students without disabilities, and the teacher. The adult who is trained to work with children with severe challenges can cue the student to respond to a communicative request or statement. Such an adult can ensure that the student has necessary adaptations and materials and then fade back to work with other students. This allows the classroom teacher to work with the student having severe and multiple disabilities as well as with others in the same group, as depicted in Figure 8.2. Table 8.3 lists responsibilities often assumed by the special educator. Whereas the special educator and classroom teacher should work together as equal teachers, some special educators report feeling "like aides" when they teach in typical classrooms. Such feelings should be openly explored and addressed. Each adult needs to be valued and respected for the unique skills and abilities he or she brings to the shared learning environment. The same is true for each student.

Professionals providing related services such as speech-language therapy, physical therapy, hearing and vision instruction, and adaptations for these sensory losses provide some direct assessment and instruction in the general education classroom and other environments such as libraries, computer labs,

Table 8.2.   Suggestions for classroom teacher in assuming responsibility for students with disabilities

1. Role model appropriate behavior toward student with disabilities:
   —Avoid language that is too juvenile.
   —Ignore (if possible) some of the student's inappropriate behavior.
2. Avoid seating student on the periphery of the class.
3. Expect the child to participate:
   —Call on the student to respond.
4. Recognize the need to stand near student when giving instructions.
5. Have student help with demonstrations to maintain interest.
6. Ask student to collect and hand out papers/materials.
7. Assign the student to cooperative learning groups/lab groups.
8. Encourage students to help each other.
9. Praise appropriate behavior/work.
10. Discipline when needed—make expectations clear.
11. Assist with lifts/transfers when needed.
12. Determine some adaptations for lessons.
13. Work directly with student on specific skills, while other adult (teaching assistant, therapist) works with rest of the class.
14. Avoid assigning special education support solely to the student with special needs.

Figure 8.2. First-grade teacher works with student having visual, auditory, and multiple impairments in same group as other classmates.

Photograph courtesy of **Pat Danielle Smith**

cafeterias, and so forth. They also instruct other team members in providing these services, so there is no disruption of a student's program. These professionals infuse their expertise into the student's typical day to facilitate the student's attainment of desired objectives (Ryndak, 1995; York, Giangreco, Vandercook, & Macdonald, 1992). In this way, classroom teachers can see how specialists help them work toward common goals (e.g., how positioning, adaptive switches, augmentative communication devices improve the student's performance in an activity); classroom teachers can thus feel comfortable interacting with the student with disabilities when the specialists are not in the room. In a study by Giangreco, Dennis, Cloninger, Edelman, and Schattman (1993), classroom teachers

Table 8.3. Role of special educator in inclusive classroom

1. Work with general educators and other team members to support *all* students in class.
2. Adapt materials and curriculum as needed.
3. Modify instruction to student's learning styles.
4. Model appropriate ways to interact.
5. Facilitate peer supports and friendships.
6. Coordinate supports (e.g., teaching assistants, related service personnel, volunteers, peer tutors).
7. Share ideas for teaching various subject areas.
8. Teach whole class or, occasionally, small groups.
9. Obtain specific information from various specialists and share with classroom teacher.

expressed the desire for specialists to work with them and to respect the dynamics of the classroom. They did not perceive separate goals and objectives that were taught in separate environments to be particularly helpful.

INTEGRATING THE ADULTS

Keeping children learning together is problematic if the adults involved in teaching are kept separate from one another. Separate rooms lead to isolation as well as difficulty appreciating a student's total program. This means that the adults must feel comfortable sharing the educational environment (e.g., classrooms, playground, gym) instead of "protecting" their own specialized space. Physically sharing the same work environments facilitates information exchange and awareness of each other's interests and skills. Special educators and related services personnel will become much more knowledgeable about typical educational curricula, which will help them be more efficient team players and more mindful of necessary adaptations. By the same token, classroom teachers will become more aware of the different ways children learn and of how various adaptations help students to compensate for missing skills. Kronberg, Jackson, Sheets, and Rogers-Connolly (1995) offered several suggestions for teachers and administrators to integrate themselves into the learning process for all students, including role release, learning strategies to teach diverse learners, and brainstorming ideas to solve problem areas. By working together, all teachers can appreciate the skills and knowledge that comprise teaching a diverse group of learners. As a result, everyone's skill level should improve.

A major advantage of integrating adults in the process of providing truly inclusive and supportive education is that all students benefit from an increased number of teachers in the classroom. Any student can seek assistance from any adult, thus reducing the time students spend waiting for the teacher's attention. In addition, all students can benefit from the ideas generated from more than one person. For example, a special educator may have wonderful ideas for teaching some science units and can share these ideas with the classroom teacher and help present them to the entire class. At the same time, classroom teachers have devised clever adaptations to allow for increased learning and involvement in their classrooms of students with severe sensory and multiple impairments. For example, one first-grade teacher brought in some apples and a mechanical apple corer and had her student with visual, intellectual, and mild physical disabilities be the first one to demonstrate the use of the peeler. This activity helped to clarify the lessons on machines and the benefits of machinery for all of her students.

SUMMARY

Bringing adults together to share teaching responsibilities for all students in schools may be more difficult than bringing children together to learn. The benefits are obvious in terms of more instruction for students, greater learning by adults, and a greater abundance of resources for problem solving and task achievement. However, the type of cooperation and collaboration required of adults in inclusive educational programs will be new to the majority of adults and therefore initially uncomfortable. Working together as a team necessitates an initial desire and commitment on the part of everyone, specific skills to make it happen, and time to provide opportunities for practice. As with any new system, it will take time and effort to work through problem areas. Supporting the adults in the educational system is a critical component of inclusive education (Kronberg et al., 1995). Personnel preparation programs for all professionals involved on the team could support the development of collaborative teams in schools by initiating training programs that are collaborative across disciplines. School principals working toward shared responsibility of all students by all faculty and staff can support this development by providing team members both with sufficient time to meet and with external resources for direction and guidance if needed.

Again, achieving the desired result takes time. Teams are also constantly changing, which affects the team's performance. Meanwhile, students have a right to an appropriate education in the least restrictive environment. They also have a right to feel that they belong. These rights must be kept in mind as a constant guide while adults struggle to achieve their own sense of belonging.

REFERENCES

Bailey, D. (1991). Building positive relationships between professionals and families. In M. McGonigel, R. Kaufmann, & B. Johnson (Eds.), *Guidelines and recommended practices for the individualized family service plan* (pp. 29–38). Bethesda, MD: Association for the Care of Children's Health.

Bardak, J. (1995). Collaboration in schools: Meeting the needs of all students. *Developmental Disabilities Bulletin, 23*(1), 120–138.

Downing, J., Eichinger, J., & Williams, L. (1996). Inclusive education for students with severe disabilities: Comparative views of principals and educators at different levels of implementation. Submitted for publication.

Durand, V.M., & Carr, E.G. (1987). Social influences on "self-stimulatory" behavior: Analysis and treatment application. *Journal of Applied Behavior Analysis, 20,* 119–132.

Durand, V.M., & Kishi, G. (1987). Reducing severe behavior problems among persons with dual sensory impairments: An evaluation of a technical assistance model. *Journal of The Association for Persons with Severe Handicaps, 12*(1), 2–10.

Evans, J., Bird, K., Ford, L., Green, J., & Bischoff, R. (1992). Strategies for overcoming resistances to the integration of students with special needs into neighborhood schools: A case study. *Case in Point: The Journal of the Council of Administrators of Special Education, VII*(1), 1–16.

Ferguson, D.L., Meyer, G., Jeanchild, L., Juniper, L., & Zingo, J. (1992). Figuring out what to do with the grownups: How teachers make inclusion "work" for students with disabilities. *Journal of The Association for Persons with Severe Handicaps, 17,* 218–226.

Gemmell-Crosby, S., & Hanzlik, J.R. (1994). Preschool teachers' perceptions of including children with disabilities. *Education and Training in Mental Retardation and Developmental Disabilities, 29,* 279–290.

Giangreco, M.F., Dennis, R., Cloninger, C., Edelman, S., & Schattman, R. (1993). I've counted Jon: Transformational experiences of teachers educating students with disabilities. *Exceptional Children, 59,* 359–371.

Idol, L. (1993). *Special educator's consultation handbook* (2nd ed.). Austin, TX: PRO-ED.

Idol, L., Paolucci-Whitcomb, P., & Nevin, A. (1986). *Collaborative consultation.* Austin, TX: PRO-ED.

Jacobson, J.W., & Janicki, M.P. (1985). Functional and health status characteristics of persons with severe handicaps in New York State. *Journal of The Association for Persons with Severe Handicaps, 10,* 51–60.

Janney, R.E., Snell, M.E., Beers, M.K., & Raynes, M. (1995). Integrating students with moderate and severe disabilities into general education classes. *Exceptional Children, 62,* 425–439.

Kamps, D.M., Barbetta, P.M., Leonard, B.R., & Delquadri, J. (1994). Classwide peer tutoring: An integration strategy to improve reading skills and promote peer interaction among students with autism and general education peers. *Journal of Applied Behavior Analysis, 27,* 49–62.

Kronberg, R., Jackson, L., Sheets, G., & Rogers-Connolly, T. (1995). A toolbox for supporting integrated education. *Teaching Exceptional Children, 27*(4), 54–58.

Leonhardt, M. (1990). Stereotypes: A preliminary report on mannerisms and blindness, *Journal of Visual Impairments and Blindness, 84,* 216–218.

McComas, N., & Bricker, D. (1994). Using the IFSP to build parent-professional partnerships. *Network, 4*(2), 41–45.

McNeil, M.E. (1994). Creating powerful partnerships through partner learning. In J.S. Thousand, R.A. Villa, & A.I. Nevin (Eds.), *Creativity and collaborative learning: A practical guide to empowering students and teachers* (pp. 243–260). Baltimore: Paul H. Brookes Publishing Co.

Nevin, A., Thousand, J., Paolucci-Whitcomb, P., & Villa, R. (1990). Collaborative consultation: Empowering schooling for all—or, who rang that bell? *Journal of Educational and Psychological Consultation, 1*(1), 41–67.

Peck, C.A., Donaldson, J., & Pezzoli, M. (1990). Some benefits nonhandicapped adolescents perceive for themselves from their social relationships with peers who have severe handicaps. *Journal of The Association for Persons with Severe Handicaps, 15,* 241–249.

Rainforth, B., York, J., & Macdonald, C. (1992). *Collaborative teams for students with severe disabilities: Integrating therapy and educational services.* Baltimore: Paul H. Brookes Publishing Co.

Repp, A., Felce, D., & Barton, L. (1988). Basing the treatment of stereotypic and self-injurious behavior on hypotheses of their causes. *Journal of Applied Behavior Analysis, 21,* 281–290.

Ryndak, D.L. (1995). Education teams and collaborative teamwork in inclusive settings. In D.L. Ryndak & S. Alper (Eds.), *Curriculum content for students with moderate and severe disabilities in inclusive settings* (pp. 77–96). Needham Heights, MA: Allyn & Bacon.

Salisbury, C. (1992). Parents as team members: Inclusive teams, collaborative outcomes. In B. Rainforth, J. York, & C. Macdonald (Eds.), *Collaborative teams for students with severe disabilities: Integrating therapy and educational services* (pp. 43–66). Baltimore: Paul H. Brookes Publishing Co.

Salisbury, C.L., Gallucci, C., Palombaro, M.M., & Peck, C.A. (1995). Strategies that promote social relations among elementary students with and without disabilities in inclusive schools. *Exceptional Children, 62,* 125–138.

Vacc, N.N., & Cannon, S.J. (1991). Cross-age tutoring in mathematics: Sixth graders helping students who are moderately handicapped. *Education and Training in Mental Retardation, 26*(1), 89–97.

Villa, R.A., & Thousand, J.S. (1994). One divided by two or more: Redefining the role of a cooperative education team. In J.S. Thousand, R.A. Villa, & A.I. Nevin (Eds.), *Creativity and collaborative learning: A practical guide to empowering students and teachers* (pp. 79–102). Baltimore: Paul H. Brookes Publishing Co.

York, J., Giangreco, M.F., Vandercook, T., & Macdonald, C. (1992). Integrating support personnel in the inclusive classroom. In S. Stainback & W. Stainback (Eds.), *Curriculum considerations in inclusive classrooms: Facilitating learning for all students* (pp. 101–116). Baltimore: Paul H. Brookes Publishing Co.

York, J., & Tundidor, M. (1995). Issues raised in the name of inclusion: Perspectives of educators, parents, and students. *Journal of The Association for Persons with Severe Handicaps, 20,* 31–44.

Chapter 9

COMMON CONCERNS AND
SOME RESPONSES

June E. Downing

This chapter uses a question-and-answer format to address specific concerns or issues that may remain for readers. The response accompanying each question encompasses one of many possible ideas to consider and should not be perceived as the only possible or even the best response. Each situation is different, and ideas must be considered and applied in context to have optimal value. Suggestions provided here have been employed successfully with specific children in specific situations. It is hoped that some of these strategies, in whole or in part, will prove helpful.

Question 1. How do I deal with the student who is disruptive in class (e.g., screams, hits, runs around, throws items)?

When students display disruptive behavior of this nature, they probably are trying to communicate thoughts and feelings that they cannot otherwise communicate effectively. For instance, they may be having a difficult time attending to a task, receiving the necessary information, or feeling competent to perform what is being asked. They may need more help, a different task, or another way to understand what is expected and why. They may feel sick or may be expressing frustration over an earlier interaction with someone that did not go well. Medications also may compound the problem, making some students more irritable, more easily frustrated, more tired, or less able to attend. Whatever the reason, it is critical not to blame the child or use the undesired behavior as a reason to permanently remove the child from the typical learning environment. Instead, a thorough functional analysis of the behavior (Donnellan, Mirenda, Mesaros, & Fassbender, 1984; Durand & Crimmins, 1988) is needed to determine strategies to help the student gain greater self-control and also reduce the need for this inappropriate mode of communication. Changing the situation (e.g., whole task, aspect of the task, method of instruction, physical position in the room), while also providing the student with alternative communicative modes to express needs, feelings, and so forth, have been documented as successful practices (Carr & Durand, 1985; Carr et al., 1994; Durand, 1993; Durand & Kishi, 1987; Wacker et al., 1990). Offering the student choices (e.g., preferred versus nonpreferred task, where to sit, what materials to use) can have a definitive and positive effect on undesired behavior (Cooper et al., 1992; Foster-Johnson, Ferro, & Dunlap, 1994). The idea behind offering students choices is to allow the student as much control as possible, especially when the student may feel that he or she has little, if any, control. In addition, assisting the student to be as successful as possible at a given task can be another effective strategy to reduce the occurrence of negative behavior. Students feeling incompetent and unable to participate adequately will tend to engage in negative types of behavior to escape the task because it is aversive to them (Cipani, 1995).

When the student is out of control and potentially disruptive to the teacher and other classmates, helping the student to leave the classroom and to go into the hall, outside the building, into a teacher's office, or to the principal's office for a few minutes to regain control and interrupt the inappropriate behavior may be the best course of action. However, this does not mean permanent removal based on negative behavior. By not going to a special self-contained classroom, it remains clear to everyone that returning to the typical classroom as soon as possible is the immediate goal. This also does not reinforce the student who might engage in the disruptive behavior specifically to escape a given situation and go to a less-demanding environment. If a student is always removed from the typical class when there is disruptive behavior and taken to the special education room for hours or for the rest of the day, the student may learn to engage in this undesired behavior for the purpose of escape. Instead, the student is taken to an obviously temporary environment, is shown how to request the need for a change in activity (or whatever the student intended to communicate), and is then returned to the classroom to continue the task with more help or to engage in an alternative activity. In this way, it is made clear to the student that he or she belongs in the classroom, that disruptive behavior does not eliminate all expectations for performance, and that there are other appropriate ways to express frustration, boredom, or anger in a given situation.

Question 2. How do I ensure appropriate language development and social interactions with classmates when the student is deaf?

This book has not focused on the needs of individuals who are deaf with no cognitive impairment and for whom both cultural and language issues are critical, even though such students also benefit from inclusive practices and can be quite successful in such settings (Antia & Kreimeyer, 1992; Kluwin, Moores, & Gausted, 1992; Luchner, 1991; Luetke-Stahlman, 1991). Students targeted in this book may be deaf or have a significant hearing impairment; however, they also have a significant cognitive impairment and possibly additional impairments that further complicate the acquisition of a language. Generally speaking, these students may use minimal signs to communicate (either receptively or expressively) and are not fluent users of American Sign Language (ASL). They do not require teachers and classmates who are fluent in this manual language. Furthermore, they typically are not a part of and do not experience Deaf culture. However, they definitely need the opportunity to interact with classmates and to learn as many communication skills as possible. Teaching the classroom teacher and all students some sign awareness as an ongoing language lesson and using the signed alphabet while practicing spelling in the younger grades will provide everyone with some of the skills needed to facilitate social interactions. Young children and their teachers often express great enthusiasm in learning some vocabulary from ASL, and teachers can see the benefit for all students of learning a second or third language. Zeece and Wolda (1995) reported on the benefits of signing for young children with a variety of disabilities in typical settings. The kinesthetic properties of using one's hands to communicate may contribute to the learning process (Luchner, 1991). At the secondary level, a formal sign language class or club can be developed (possibly with assistance from people in the Deaf community). Students of widely different abilities can be members of this club, with the student having severe sensory and multiple disabilities providing some of the instruction.

In addition to some sign awareness and instruction, students without disabilities, teachers, and other members of the school community need to exploit the many ways the student interacts with others. As described in Chapter 7, communication partners will use facial expressions, natural gestures, body language, objects, pictures, photographs, and any number of other behaviors that allow the student with deafness and other impairments to communicate most effectively. In fact, multimodal approaches to communication are recommended (Downing, 1993; Mirenda, Iacono, & Williams, 1990; Reichle, Feeley, & Johnston, 1993). The intent is to provide a rich social environment in which all students can receive the stimulation they need. Figure 9.1 provides an example of a student using an alternative mode of communication during a class activity.

Question 3. How do I motivate a student to learn?

Some students appear to lack interest in many common activities and refuse to participate. Trying to provide an effective reinforcer for such a student to encourage participation may be difficult, since the student shows little response to any potential reinforcer. A thorough interview with parents and other family members needs to be conducted to determine interests of the student that may possibly be used as reinforcers for less-desired activities. Some unique motivators may be discovered that can aid learning. For example, one 11-year-old would apparently work quite hard if he could play with a pine cone on occasion. Once teachers discovered this bit of information from his parents, they used it not only as a reinforcer but also let him collect pine cones, sort them by size, use them in mathematics as manipulatives, and tear them apart to make artistic designs. These designs then became illustrations for poems and stories co-written with a classmate.

In addition to parental and familial input, providing the student with numerous diverse opportunities to explore new activities and items of potential interest is vital. Owing to sensory, cognitive, or physical limitations, students may not have been exposed to a sufficient array of options to develop interests

Photograph courtesy of Pat Danielle Smith

Figure 9.1. First-grader who has sensory and multiple impairments uses photographs to make a presentation to her class.

and skills. Caregivers and teachers alike may have prejudged the value of certain activities, and the student may have been denied access or exposure to these as a result. Furthermore, simple exposure to activities or items may not be sufficient to foster interest. Repeated opportunities may be needed (as with all of us) before a true interest develops. The novelty of an activity or environment may be too confusing or stimulating to be perceived initially as a positive experience. For example, the author has known several students who initially appeared to hate swimming. They kicked, screamed, cried, and struggled to get out of the water. However, repeated attempts to encourage the enjoyment of swimming and water play resulted in increasingly more positive behaviors until the students perceived the activity as the fun event it was intended to be. A decision on the part of a caregiver that swimming was not a good activity for the students, based on their initial reactions, could have been very limiting for the students.

Part of a community-based program may be to increase exposure, develop interests, and nurture these interests. For example, some students have shown a special interest in birds and guinea pigs after being taken on repeated trips to a pet store. Others have shown interest in clocks, arcade games, and other novelty items (e.g., magnetic doodles, hard rubberized knickknacks, strobe lights, onyx pieces) following excursions into the community with peers who do not have disabilities. To help cultivate a student's interest in activities—especially an older student who may have become comfortable with limited options and expecta- tions for performance—educational staff will need to work closely with parents and significant others to experiment with all available options in the community.

In addition to expanding awareness of what is possible by increasing ex- periences and opportunities to learn, providing students with various choices throughout each activity of the day can have a major impact on increasing a student's motivation to perform as expected. Making choices of preferred activities, parts of activities, materials to use, partner to work with, and so on, not only aids in the development of decision making but also gives the individual a sense of control, which can in turn enhance positive self-esteem. Choice making has been linked to decreasing problem behaviors and increasing desirable behaviors (Johnson, Ferro, & Dunlap, 1994), to motivating the passive learner (Reichle, York, & Eynon, 1989), and to gaining control over the environment (Gothelf, Crimmins, Mercer, & Finocchiaro, 1994).

Question 4. I do not have a one-to-one staffing ratio. How do I provide adequate support for all of the students in typical classes?

Most programs do not have the funding to provide one-to-one teacher–student staffing ratios, nor would that be advisable in all situations. Students with severe sensory and multiple impairments often need considerable support for a variety of reasons. However, for an adult to be present with such a student 100% of the time may seriously interfere with that student's ability to interact with others, make friends, and feel a true part of the class. It may also signal to others that they have little if any responsibility for getting to know the student. Therefore, it is a good idea to early on encourage assistance when needed from classmates so as to fade specialized adult support.

However, since there is a recognized need to adapt materials, use alternative instructional techniques, help the student remain on task, and so forth, added human resources may be necessary. Heterogeneous assignments of students to the special education inclusion teacher can help alleviate the need to provide extensive supports (physical and instructional) to all students at the same time. If a teacher's caseload involves a number of students with different abilities, there is a much greater chance of providing extensive support to a few students as needed. In other words, one teacher's caseload for inclusion might consist of 10 students, one of whom has a severe sensory and multiple impairment and requires considerable assistance throughout the day; the other 9 students have moderate to severe disabilities, but demonstrate varying levels of independence. Although all of these students need support at various times throughout the day, their needs are not constant, and a variety of supports can be used effectively.

If this heterogeneous arrangement is not in evidence, teachers may need to solicit aid from a number of different resources, as described in Chapter 8. Nonpaid and nonprofessional support may come from classmates, older students from either the same school or another school, volunteers, parents, and practicum students from university programs. Scheduling support for all students needs to be creative and flexible and reflect individual needs as they vary throughout the school day. For example, a special educator may have a caseload of 10 students, but not all 10 students will experience the same needs for support at the same time. All of the students may be in different classes depending on their chronological age and their individualized education program (IEP) objectives. That is, at any one time during the day, students could be in mathematics, language arts, science, physical education, music, or study hall, or at recess or lunch. Obviously, supporting students with challenging learning needs will vary depending on the subject being studied and the activities expected of the student. If all students were in different classrooms and all were engaged in mathematics at the same time, the problems for adequate support would be obvious. One of the primary responsibilities of the special education support teacher is to develop (and keep modifying) a schedule of support for himself or herself, teaching assistants, related services providers, volunteers, and others. This will require changing support assignments as needed and continually working to create the best match possible between students' needs for assistance and the expertise of available human support.

Question 5. How do I find time to meet and plan collaboratively with all team members?

This question arises frequently and is perhaps the most challenging aspect of inclusive education for everyone involved in this type of service delivery. In general, educators often feel overwhelmed with work and very short on time. In addition, every educational team supporting a given student operates differently depending on a number of personal and work-related variables. As such, there are no clear guidelines to follow other than the recognized importance of meeting on a regular basis (Rainforth, York, & Macdonald, 1992; Rankin et al., 1994; Wolery, Werts, Caldwell, & Snyder, 1995).

Because time is a critical factor for most educators and related services personnel, meetings should always be held on time and be brief, to the point, and constructive, so that participants can leave feeling that the meeting was worthwhile. Guidelines exist for holding time-efficient meetings (cf. Villa & Thousand, 1993). It is also critical to consider who must actually meet and how often. Obviously, those working directly with the student on a daily basis will need to meet so that daily programming can continue as smoothly as possible. Therefore, the teachers involved (classroom teacher and special educator) and the teaching assistants supporting these teachers need to find time to exchange information and resolve issues on a fairly regular basis. Short meetings can be held during planning periods, at lunch, recess, before or after school, and, in some districts, on early release days. (It is important to note that, in the initial stages of including all students, meetings may be longer or more frequent as the team first learns to work together. As the team becomes comfortable working in this manner, the length and number of meetings should be reduced.) Whatever is not resolved during these face-to-face meetings may be tabled until the next meeting or may require one of the participants to obtain necessary information to share with the other members. Information can be shared through notes, articles put in mailboxes, telephone calls in the evening, or brief exchanges when passing in the hall. Every effort should be made to exchange information as quickly as possible and in the most convenient fashion (which is often *not* another meeting).

Question 6. How can I ensure consistency in programming with so many different staff members?

Consistency in programming is difficult whenever more than one person is responsible for implementation. However, when support staff are working in different classrooms throughout the day, consistency in programming becomes an even greater challenge. As discussed in Question 5, arranging time to meet with critical support personnel is essential to effective inclusive programming. However, meetings alone will not ensure consistency in what and, especially, how a particular student is instructed. Considerable diversity in activities can exist in any classroom, and, as support staff (teachers, teaching assistants, vision specialists, occupational therapists, physical therapists, volunteers, etc.) shift from room to room to meet individual instruction needs, consistency in implementation of IEPs easily could be jeopardized. A system is needed that quickly and clearly describes what the student is to be learning, how instructional support to reach the objective is to be implemented, and how it all fits into the general education curriculum.

Simply and clearly written lesson or participation plans that remain in the typical classroom with the student should serve as written reminders to all staff of the preferred way to support the student. This lesson plan should have the IEP goals or objectives clearly stated on it, so that incidental learning opportunities that address these objectives will not be lost. Data sheets per objective attached to lesson plans also serve as a reminder to collect data of emerging skills. The sample lesson plans provided in Figures 9.2, 9.3, 9.4, and 9.5 may serve as guidelines. Once individual team members become comfortable with the ways the student learns and participates in various activities, these individuals

Student Participation Plan

Student: Carly

Age: 6

Grade: 1st

Outcome for Student: To express herself during school activities.

Objective: Carly will make comments in class when asked by peer or teacher by using a switch-activated message in 75% of all opportunities for five class periods.

Class Activity: Sharing.

What Students in Class Are Expected to Do: Students sit in circle, listen to each other, ask questions after raising their hand. A few students present something they have brought to share—they show it and describe it.

How Carly Participates to Achieve Desired Outcome: Carly sits on floor in adapted chair and looks at classmate presenting. She activates a prerecorded message of "You did a good job" by raising her right arm. When she presents, she holds what she brought with an adapted mitt and raises her hand for peers to see. She activates a prerecorded message about her item by pressing a switch.

Who Provides Support and How: Teacher calls on Carly when appropriate. She helps Carly respond to questions. She cues peers to ask yes/no questions. Peers ask questions, pass items to Carly to see. Teaching assistant sets up switch devices, supports Carly at shoulder and elbow so she can activate switches. She puts the mitt on Carly and massages her arms/hands to relax them.

Sample #1 Data Sheet

Skill sequence	Dates[a,b] 9-20						Prompting strategies
1. Looks at student talking majority of time	| |||						
2. Comments on peer's presentation by activating prerecorded message	| ||||						
3. Responds to yes/no questions.	||						

[a]Dates to be inserted above each column.
[b]Boxes below dates are for recording number of appropriate responses over the number of opportunities given.

Figure 9.2. Sample #1: Student participation plan and data sheet for sharing activity.

Student Participation Plan

Student: Doug	**Outcome for Student:** To gain greater control over social and physical environment.
Age: 11	**Objective:** Doug will make choices during ac-
Grade: 5th	tivities by vocalizing, looking, or reaching toward items within 5 sec. of being asked 80% of the time.

Class Activity: Social Studies—making maps.

What Students in Class Are Expected to Do: Listen to teacher, watch demonstration, get materials, divide into groups, divide up responsibilities, choose colors for different regions, label regions.

How Doug Participates to Achieve Desired Outcome: Doug looks at colors, extends arm to choose color, grasps adapted roll-on applicator filled with paint, places on paper, indicates by vocalizing when finished with color.

Who Provides Support and How: Teacher assigns Doug to a group, monitors group progress, comments on Doug's work. Classmates push Doug in wheelchair to group and to get materials. They ask him questions and provide model. Teaching assistant supports him physically at shoulders to allow greatest movement. She massages his arms and hands in preparation (while teacher gives instruction).

Sample #2 Data Sheet

Skills	Trial 1 Chose to stop/continue	Trial 2 Chose color, materials	Trial 3 Chose peer to work with	Trial 4 Chose where to sit	Prompting strategies
Chose by vocalizing	5 sec				
Chose by reaching		9 sec	—		
Chose by looking			—	—	

Figure 9.3. Sample #2: Student participation plan and data sheet for social studies activity.

should be able to identify similar learning opportunities across many other activities. Therefore, initial training of team members may require considerable time, but subsequent trainings should be less demanding.

Question 7. How do I help the student communicate more effectively within typical classrooms?

Communication is a critical skill for all students and especially for students with severe sensory and multiple disabilities. These students typically do not have effective means of making their needs known, of responding to direct questions, or of expressing their thoughts and feelings about a topic or situation. This limitation affects their ability to be actively involved in most learning situations and to make friends. Every effort, therefore, must be made to ensure that the student has access to and knows how to use as many different communication modes as possible for any given situation. This will take considerable teamwork and creative thinking on the part of team members; it is not the sole responsibility of the speech-language pathologist or any other specially trained person. This effort will also be ongoing and dynamic as the skills of the student evolve and as team members change.

The first step in helping a student communicate more effectively in any environment is to analyze what is needed or expected communicatively (both

Student Participation Plan

Student:	Mark	**Outcome for Student:** To follow directions in or-der to be successful in activities.
Age:	13	**Objective:** Mark will follow 50% of all directions given during 10 class periods.
Grade:	7th	

Class Activity: Science—studying the impact of combining different chemicals.

What Students in Class Are Expected to Do: Students listen to teacher, watch demonstration, divide up into groups of four, get materials, perform experiments, write observations, turn them in to teacher.

How Mark Participates to Achieve Desired Outcome: Mark assists teacher with demonstration by handing him chemicals the teacher points to. Mark goes with peers to get materials. He follows directions of peers and handles items appropriately. He agrees or disagrees with written observations. He signs his name to paper with label and turns it in to teacher.

Who Provides Support and How: Teacher asks Mark to be a partner with him. Teacher monitors all groups, redirects Mark, and gives feedback. Peers provide guidance by modeling and cueing. Special educator cues appropriate behavior, prevents disruptive behavior, blocks Mark's move-ment to other groups. She cues peers to interact.

Sample #3 Data Sheet

Directions followed	Dates[a]							Prompting strategies
	9-20							
Raised hand when name called	+	−						
Approached teacher when requested	−							
Got materials	−							
Went to assigned table	+							

[a]Dates to be inserted above each column.

Figure 9.4. Sample #3: Student participation plan and data sheet for science activity.

receptively and expressively) in that environment. Observing how a teacher in-teracts with his or her students at a given grade level and how students interact with the teacher and each other will help to establish a communicative base (see Chapter 3 for a description of this assessment process). Students may be expected to listen to the teacher for certain time periods, to raise their hand to gain the teacher's attention, to ask questions and respond to peers' questions when work-ing in small groups, or to carry on an informal conversation during recess and lunch. Due to the limitations often imposed by a severe sensory and multiple disability, a student with this disability may not be able to engage in these types of communicative interactions without considerable adaptations. However, it is important to know what typical expectations are for communicative behavior in a given classroom and during a specific activity to determine how the student with this severe disability can participate and what adaptations will be required.

Augmentative communication devices can greatly supplement a given stu-dent's present communicative behaviors (e.g., natural gestures, pointing, vocal-izations). These devices can be small and flexible to accommodate different needs as activities change. One device will probably not suffice. For example Hunt, Alwell, and Goetz (1991) developed "conversation books" for students with mul-tiple and sensory disabilities to use during different classroom and nonclassroom settings. Although these books did not meet all communication needs, they served a distinct purpose—to enhance social interactions. Students will need a means of making the same basic requests as other students (e.g., to use the rest-

Student Participation Plan

Student: _____ Sierra _____	**Outcome for Student:** To enhance her interactions with others.
Age: _____ 18 _____	**Objective:** Sierra will lift her head and turn toward someone talking to her in 70% of all interactions for six class periods.
Grade: _____ 12th _____	

Class Activity: Life Enrichment—discuss life goals, problems; do projects around these issues; class presentations.

What Students in Class Are Expected to Do: Listen to teacher, get materials, join in discussion, interact with each other, work independently and with partners.

How Sierra Participates to Achieve Desired Outcome: Sierra lifts head up and turns toward peer talking to her. She uses a head switch to turn on a radio or cassette if allowed. She chooses materials to be part of projects by looking. She listens to her classmates.

Who Provides Support and How: Teacher greets Sierra, makes sure she has materials and is included in all projects. She responds to Sierra if she vocalizes. Classmates help with all projects, sit close to Sierra, and talk to her. They offer her choices. Special educator sets up switch and provides therapy.

Sample #4 Data Sheet

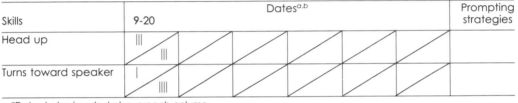

Skills	Dates[a,b] 9-20						Prompting strategies
Head up	III III						
Turns toward speaker	I IIII						

[a]Dates to be inserted above each column.
[b]Boxes below dates are for recording number of appropriate responses over the number of opportunities provided.

Figure 9.5. Sample #4: Student participation plan and data sheet for Life Enrichment activity.

room, to get a drink of water). They will also need a means of sharing what they have learned with their class, as other students do. The creative use of pictures, photographs, or parts of objects that change as topics change, in combination with facial expressions, body language, natural gestures, and manual signs (if known), needs to be explored with each student. Leaving a student in any environment with extremely limited means of communication may well lead to disruptive and negative behavior. Considerable information has been written about the development and use of augmentative communication devices for a variety of individuals. Appendices D and E at the end of this book list resources dealing with this subject.

Question 8. How can I be sure that the child is learning what he or she needs to learn?

This question is often asked by general educators who are concerned that placement of a student with such obvious disabilities in their classroom will not benefit that student. They may see the social benefits for the student, but cannot see other reasons for including that student. Obviously, the question is of consequence to all educators, parents, and administrators who are interested in the education of all students. The best response to this question is to readdress the issue of assessment. Assessment procedures that start with the child and the family and are based on the identification of valued life outcomes (Giangreco,

Cloninger, & Iverson, 1993) help ensure that the student is indeed in the appropriate learning environment and receiving the appropriate instruction. It should be clear that the skills being targeted across the different activities that occur in different classrooms lead to desired outcomes for the student. If these skills cannot be identified in a given activity or class, then changes need to be made. Meaningful participation for each student is the desired goal, with the student being given opportunities to control social and physical events to the maximum extent possible (Brown & Lehr, 1993). To reach this goal, the team should consider whether the activity can be presented in another way (e.g., pictorial information added to verbal, information presented in shorter blocks of time). Perhaps the student's position needs to be changed or membership in a particular learning group changed. Expectations of students' performance (how they work together) may need to be adapted. For example, if a valued outcome for a student is to develop social relationships, social interaction skills need to be targeted across activities. Independent seat work by students does not support the teaching of such skills. However, allowing students to work together to share materials, make joint decisions, and otherwise cooperate on a project or assignment would provide the opportunity to learn valued skills. Giving students adaptive equipment (e.g., switch devices, rotary scanner with pictorial options, voice output communication devices) provides an alternative way to participate.

At the secondary level, it may be possible to change classes altogether if a particular class is taught in a manner not conducive to meeting the learning needs of a given student. However, even in classes that complement a student's learning needs, every effort must be made to ensure that each activity has a sufficient number of opportunities for students to practice critical skills. If these do not naturally occur, it may be possible to alter the situation sufficiently to create the desired opportunity. For instance, a student could be asked to pass out homework assignments or other materials to increase the number of opportunities a student has to appropriately handle materials, gain a classmate's attention, hand materials to a classmate, and respond to any socially interactive behaviors (e.g., "hi," "thanks") that might occur. Although materials might normally be laid out on a table or teacher's desk for students to pick up independently, this modification accomplishes the same objective. Furthermore, it greatly facilitates the opportunity for one student to learn skills that may lead toward the development of friendships and the ability to obtain and handle a job.

Question 9. What do I do when I've planned for one activity and the classroom teacher suddenly changes the lesson?

Unfortunately, the best planning in the world suffers when teachers suddenly make changes without notifying the student's support team. Although the teacher may have a great new lesson in mind, successfully including the student with severe sensory and multiple disabilities (or any severe disability) will take quick and creative thinking. Such spur of the moment adaptations occur in all inclusive classrooms. If a change in plans means movement from the classroom, a note should be left for any related services personnel (e.g., vision specialist, hearing specialist, occupational therapist) who may be planning to provide support services at that time. Flexibility on the part of all support staff is critical.

With but a small delay, the person providing needed related services will likely be able to find the class in time to provide services in the changed environment.

Keeping the student's learning goals and objectives in mind will provide guidance when unexpected changes in lesson plans occur. If these goals and objectives identify truly meaningful skills for the student to learn, addressing these same skills across different activities and settings should not be overly problematic. Knowing how the student acquires information most efficiently also helps teachers to quickly adapt to an unexpected activity.

Many teachers following an inclusive model maintain a collection of easily accessible materials (e.g., "bag of tricks") that allows quick (although not perfect) adaptations to most lessons. These materials might include index cards, felt-tip pens, glue sticks, magazines with different pictures, self-stick notes, easy-to-use scissors, thick paper or file folder sheets to hold textures and parts of objects, and Handitak adhesive to hold the objects to the paper. Larger items that can be practical across different activities are cassette recorders with blank tapes and the necessary switch adaptation for control by the student. Cassette recorders or other simple devices that allow a vocal output for a student and on which small messages can be easily recorded serve a number of purposes. For example, a sudden change in plans found a second-grade classroom in Arizona outside collecting items related to a unit on ecology (e.g., eroded rocks, rain-produced gulleys). For Danielle, a popular student who had very limited movement, used a wheelchair, and had severe photosensitivity (sensitivity to light), running around in the desert was not terribly practical. Instead, she remained in her wheelchair in the shade of the school building and collected the items gathered by her classmates on her wheelchair tray. To involve Danielle in this activity, one of the girls in her class was asked to quickly record the message, "Thanks for bringing me this, can you get more?" and Danielle was given access to her switch, which activated the recorded message. When her classmates brought her various items, they showed her what they had found and waited for the teaching assistant to prompt her to state the prerecorded message. This quick adaptation to an unplanned, yet worthwhile, activity allowed Danielle greater participation with her classmates and also provided opportunities for her to control devices via switch use and respond to her peers. Both of these skills were targeted on her IEP.

Question 10. How can a student with severe medical needs be taught in a typical class?

Students with severe medical complications will have medical personnel as members of their educational team. These professionals will play a significant role in how much time a student can safely spend at school. This decision obviously will be individually determined and will depend on a number of factors, including the student's health, activity level, and expectations of the classroom. Everyone on the team must be well informed so that one factor does not completely override others that are equally important. For example, there may be a misconception about what happens in a self-contained classroom as compared with a typical classroom (especially for medical personnel). Special education classrooms were never meant to be hospital rooms. They were designed to be places where the unique *educational* needs of the student could be met. If education is the primary purpose of schools, then environments geared toward teaching and learning should be considered when determining how much time a student attends school. Therefore, a special education room should not be considered a better environment for a student with severe medical needs because it is quiet and relaxing and the student will be able to sleep. This would represent a major misconception about special education in general.

In this situation, the importance of forming a true partnership among all team members (educational, therapeutic, and medical) is obvious. A study by Izen and Brown (1991) found that teachers felt unprepared to deal with students having profound and multiple disabilities with severe medical problems. If students with these challenging disabilities are to be successful in inclusive classrooms, the fear that can develop from educators feeling uncomfortable with these students must be addressed. Information must be shared so that all of the student's ongoing needs can be addressed and emergencies met efficiently. Several authors have addressed the needs of students with serious medical conditions within typical classrooms (Lynch, Lewis, & Murphy, 1992; Prendergast, 1995; Snell & Eichner, 1989). These authors have stressed the need for shared information, teaming, emergency planning, and individualization to provide the appropriate education in typical classrooms. Like any student, the individual needs of the student with serious medical conditions must be met or the educational services cannot be considered appropriate. Furthermore, services must be provided in a way that respects the student's dignity and need for privacy, if desired. However, a student's medical needs (e.g., gastrostomy feedings, catheterization, suctioning) should not dictate placement in a special education environment. For example, students can and do receive gastrostomy feedings in the cafeteria, where they eat alongside their classmates. For those students who may be learning to ingest some food orally, watching their peers eat can serve as a motivator. What determines where students receive support and educational services are the desired outcomes established for them by those people who know them best and care about their well-being. Therefore, if we want a student to be included in family outings to noisy restaurants, attend birthday parties, and, in general, have friends, then eating in a noisy cafeteria with classmates may be the best place to learn to deal with this type of noisy, yet very social, environment.

Students can and do receive some treatments (e.g., medication, suctioning) in general education classrooms. Obviously, consideration must be given to the potential for distracting other students and the teacher and to respecting the student's needs for privacy. When the student must leave the classroom to receive medical treatments, the nurse's office is a logical option. For example, one second grader left his class every afternoon to go to the nurse's office to receive 10 minutes of respiratory therapy. Given that other students with no disabilities receive their medical assistance from the school nurse, it makes sense that students with disabilites also go to the nurse for this purpose. Catheterization can occur in either the boys' or girls' restrooms, although certain physical adaptations may be needed to accommodate students. One junior high school put in a fold-down single wall "bed" with a curtain running alongside it for privacy. The fold-down bed also hid shelves for diapers, clean clothes, and cleaning items. This system worked well for students needing to be changed or catheterized. When the bed was up against the wall, it was not noticeable and did not take up additional space.

These examples have been provided to help individual teams for students with severe medical needs in addition to other multiple disabilities consider different options before immediately assuming that a student is too medically fragile to benefit from a typical educational environment. Parents interviewed in a study by Lynch et al. (1992) expressed a desire for normalization and enhanced quality of life for their children with chronic illnesses. As with any individual with a special need, we must guard against the tendency to allow one characteristic (usually a limitation) to determine where and how we interact. Creative and collaborative teamwork with clear attention to desired outcomes for children should be the basis for all decisions.

REFERENCES

Antia, S., & Kreimeyer, K. (1992). Project Interact: Final report. Washington, DC: U.S. Department of Education.

Brown, F., & Lehr, D. (1993). Making activities meaningful for students with severe multiple disabilities. *Teaching Exceptional Children, 25*(4), 12–17.

Carr, E.G., & Durand, V.M. (1985). Reducing behavior problems through functional communication training. *Journal of Applied Behavior Analysis, 18,* 111–126.

Carr, E.G., Levin, L., McConnachie, Carlson, J.I., Kemp, D.C., & Smith, C.E. (1994). *Communication-based intervention for problem behavior: A user's guide for producing positive change.* Baltimore: Paul H. Brookes Publishing Co.

Cipani, E.C. (1995). Be aware of negative reinforcement. *Teaching Exceptional Children, 27*(4), 36–40.

Cooper, L.J., Wacker, D.P., Thursby, D., Plagman, L.A., Harding, J., Millard, T., & Derby, M. (1992). Analysis of the effects of task preferences, task demands, and adult attention on child behavior in outpatient and classroom settings. *Journal of Applied Behavior Analysis, 25,* 823–840.

Donnellan, A.M., Mirenda, P.L., Mesaros, R.A., & Fassbender, L.L. (1984). Analyzing the communicative functions of aberrant behavior. *Journal of The Association for Persons with Severe Handicaps, 9,* 201–212.

Downing, J. (1993). Communication intervention for individuals with dual sensory and intellectual impairments. *Clinics in Communication Disorders, 3*(2), 31–42.

Durand, V.M. (1993). Functional communication training using assistive devices: Effects on challenging behavior and affect. *Augmentative and Alternative Communication, 9*(3), 168–176.

Durand, V.M., & Crimmins, D. B. (1988). Identifying the variables maintaining self-injurious behavior. *Journal of Autism and Developmental Disorders, 18,* 99–117.

Durand, V.M., & Kishi, G. (1987). Reducing severe behavior problems among persons with dual sensory impairments: An evaluation of a technical assistance model. *Journal of The Association for Persons with Severe Handicaps, 12,* 2–10.

Foster-Johnson, L., Ferro, J., & Dunlap, G. (1994). Preferred curricular activities and reduced problem behaviors in students with intellectual disabilities. *Journal of Applied Behavior Analysis, 27,* 493–504.

Giangreco, M.F., Cloninger, C.J., & Iverson, V.S. (1993). *Choosing Options and Accommodations for Children (COACH): A guide to planning inclusive education.* Baltimore: Paul H. Brookes Publishing Co.

Gothelf, C.R., Crimmins, D.B., Mercer, C.A., & Finocchiaro, P.A. (1994). Teaching choice-making skills to students who are deaf-blind. *Teaching Exceptional Children, 26*(4), 13–15.

Hunt, P., Alwell, M., & Goetz, L. (1991). Interacting with peers through conversation turn-taking with a communication book adaptation. *Augmentative and Alternative Communication, 7,* 117–126.

Izen, C.L., & Brown, F. (1991). Education and treatment needs of students with profound, multiply handicapping, and medically fragile conditions: A survey of teachers' perceptions. *Journal of The Association for Persons with Severe Handicaps, 16,* 94–103.

Johnson, L., Ferro, J., & Dunlap, G. (1994). Preferred curricular activities and reduced problem behavior in students with intellectual disabilities. *Journal of Applied Behavior Analysis, 27,* 493–504.

Kluwin, T.N., Moores, D.F., & Gausted, M.C. (1992). *Toward effective public school programs for deaf students: Context, process, and outcomes.* New York: Teachers College Press.

Luchner, J. (1991). Mainstreaming hearing-impaired students: Perceptions of regular educators. *Language, Speech, and Hearing Services in the Schools, 22,* 302–307.

Luetke-Stahlman, B. (1991). Hearing impaired students in integrated childcare. *Perspectives, 9*(1), 8–11.

Lynch, E.W., Lewis, R.B., & Murphy, D.S. (1992). Educational services for children with chronic illnesses: Perspectives of educators and families. *Exceptional Children, 59,* 210–220.

Mirenda, P., Iacono, T., & Williams, R. (1990). Communication options for persons with severe and profound disabilities: State of the art and future directions. *Journal of The Association for Persons with Severe Handicaps, 15,* 3–21.

Prendergast, D.E. (1995). Preparing for children who are medically fragile. *Teaching Exceptional Children, 27*(2), 37–41.

Rainforth, B., York, J., & Macdonald, C. (1992). *Collaborative teams for students with severe disabilities: Integrating therapy and educational services.* Baltimore: Paul H. Brookes Publishing Co.

Rankin, D., Hallick, A., Ban, S., Hartley, P., Bost, C., & Uggla, N. (1994). Who's dreaming? A general education perspective on inclusion. *Journal of The Association for Persons with Severe Handicaps, 19,* 325–327.

Reichle, J., Feeley, K., & Johnston, S. (1993). Communication intervention for persons with severe and profound disabilities. *Clinics in Communication Disorders, 3*(2), 7–30.

Reichle, J., York, J., & Eynon, D. (1989). Influence of indicating preferences for initiating, maintaining, and terminating interactions. In F. Brown & D.H. Lehr (Eds.), *Persons with profound disabilities: Issues and practices* (pp. 191–211). Baltimore: Paul H. Brookes Publishing Co.

Snell, M.E., & Eichner, S.J. (1989). Integration for students with profound disabilities. In F. Brown & D.H. Lehr (Eds.), *Persons with profound disabilities: Issues and practices* (pp. 109–138). Baltimore: Paul H. Brookes Publishing Co.

Villa, R.A., & Thousand, J.S. (1993). Redefining the role of the special educator and other support personnel. In J.W. Putnam (Ed.), *Cooperative learning and strategies for inclusion: Celebrating diversity in the classroom* (pp. 57– 91). Baltimore: Paul H. Brookes Publishing Co.

Wacker, D.P., Steege, M.W., Northup, J., Sasso, G., Berg, W., Reimers, T., Cooper, L., Cigrand, K., & Donn, L. (1990). A component analysis of functional communication training across three topographies of severe behavior problems. *Journal of Applied Behavior Analysis, 23,* 417–429.

Wolery, M., Werts, M.G., Caldwell, N.K., & Snyder, E. D. (1995). Experienced teachers' perceptions of resources and supports for inclusion. *Education and Training in Mental Retardation and Developmental Disabilities, 30*(1), 15–26.

Zeece, R.D., & Wolda, M.R. (1995). Let me see what you say: Let me see what you feel! *Teaching Exceptional Children, 27*(2), 4–9.

Appendix A

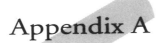

RESOURCES FOR CREATING SYSTEMIC CHANGE

ARTICLES

Hasazi, S.B., Johnston, A.P., Liggett, A.M., & Schattman, R.A. (1994). A qualitative policy study of the least restrictive environment provision of the Individuals with Disabilities Act. *Exceptional Children, 60,* 491–507.

McDonnell, J., & Kiefer-O'Donnell, R. (1992). Educational reform and students with severe disabilities. *Journal of Disability Policy Studies, 3*(2), 53–74.

McLaughlin, M.J., & Warren, S.H. (1994). Restructuring special education programs in local school districts: The tensions and the challenges. *The Special Education Leadership Review, 2*(1), 2–21.

Rigazio-DiGilio, A., & Beninghof, A.M. (1994). Toward inclusionary educational programs: A school-based planning process. *The Special Education Leadership Review, 2*(1), 81–92.

Sailor, W. (1991). Special education in the restructured school. *Remedial and Special Education, 12*(6), 8–22.

Salisbury, C.L., Palombaro, M.M., & Hollowood, T.M. (1993). On the nature and change of an inclusive elementary school. *Journal of the Association for Persons with Severe Handicaps, 18,* 75–84.

Thousand, J.S., & Villa, R.A. (1990). Strategies for educating learners with severe disabilities within their local home school and communities. *Focus on Exceptional Children, 23*(3), 1–24.

Wisniewski, L., & Alper, S. (1994). Including students with severe disabilities in general education settings: Guidelines for change. *Remedial and Special Education, 15,* 4–13.

BOOKS, CHAPTERS, AND MONOGRAPHS

Fox, T.J., & Williams, W. (1991). *Implementing best practices for all students in their local school: Inclusion of all students through family and community involvement, collaboration, and the use of school planning teams and individual student planning teams.* Burlington: University of Vermont, Center for Developmental Disabilities.

Goodlad, J.I., & Lovitt, T.C. (Eds.). (1993). *Integrating general and special education.* New York: Macmillan Publishing Co.

Liberty, K., & Haring, N.G. (1995). Establishing inclusive school communities. In N.G. Haring & L.T. Romer (Eds.), *Welcoming students who are deaf-blind into typical classrooms: Facilitating school participation, learning, and friendships* (pp. 55–86). Baltimore: Paul H. Brookes Publishing Co.

Simon, M., Karasoff, P., & Smith, A. (1992). *Effective practices for inclusive programs: A technical assistance planning guide.* San Francisco: California Research Institute on the Integration of Students with Severe Disabilities.

Skrtic, T. (1991). *Behind special education: A critical analysis of professional culture and school organization.* Denver: Love.

Stainback, S., Stainback, W., & Forest, M. (Eds.). (1989). *Educating all students in the mainstream of regular education.* Baltimore: Paul H. Brookes Publishing Co.

Stainback, W., & Stainback, S. (1992). *Controversial issues confronting special education: Divergent perspectives.* Needham, MA: Allyn & Bacon.

Villa, R.P., Thousand, J.S., Stainback, W., & Stainback, S. (Eds.). (1992). *Restructuring for caring and effective education: An administrative guide to creating heterogeneous schools.* Baltimore: Paul H. Brookes Publishing Co.

Appendix B
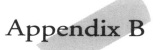

RESOURCES FOR PROVIDING TECHNICAL ASSISTANCE FOR TEACHERS IN INCLUSIVE SETTINGS

Louisiana Systems Change Project for Inclusive Education (Grant No. HO86J30006)
Contact Person: William Sharpton
University of New Orleans
Department of Special Education
New Orleans, LA 70148
(504) 286-5592

New Hampshire's Statewide Systems Change Project: Creating a Permanent Capacity to Implement Quality, Inclusive Educational Programs for Students with Severe Disabilities (Grant No.: HO86J30015)
Contact Person: Jan Nisbet
New Hampshire Department of Education
101 Pleasant Street
Concord, NH 03301
(603) 271-3741

New York Partnership for Statewide Systems Change (Grant No: HO86J00007)
Contact Persons: Luanna Meyer
Syracuse University
150 Huntington Hall
Syracuse, NY 13244-2280
(315) 443-9651

Matt Giugno
New York State Education Department
Office for Special Education Services
Room 1621 EBA
Albany, NY 12234
(518) 486-7462

Together We're Better: Inclusive School Communities in Minnesota—Partnerships for Change (Grant No.: HO86J20010)

    Contact Person: Mary Agnes McDavitt
                      Minnesota Department of Education
                      811 Capitol Square Building
                      550 Cedar Street
                      St. Paul, MN 55101
                      (612) 297-3619

Vermont Statewide Systems of Support Project: Improving the Quality of Education and Support for Students with Severe Disabilities and Their Families in Regular Education Environments in Rural Vermont (Grant No.: HO86J30021)

    Contact Person: Wayne L. Fox
                      The University Affiliated Program of Vermont
                      499C Waterman Building
                      University of Vermont
                      Burlington, VT 05405
                      (802) 656-4031

Wisconsin's School Inclusion Project: Developing Models in Local Schools to Educate Students with Severe Disabilities in an Inclusive Manner (Grant No: HO86J30028)

    Contact Person: Alison Ford
                      Department of Exceptional Education
                      University of Wisconsin–Milwaukee
                      P.O. Box 340
                      Milwaukee, WI 53201
                      (414) 229-6566

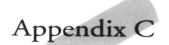

Appendix C

SYSTEMATIC TEACHING RESOURCES

Belfiore, P.J., & Toro-Zambrana, W. (1994). *Innovations: Recognizing choices in community settings by people with significant disabilities.* Washington, DC: American Association on Mental Retardation.

Cipani, E.C., & Spooner, F. (1994). *Curricular and instructional approaches for persons with severe disabilities.* Needham, MA: Allyn & Bacon.

Farlow, L.J., & Snell, M.E. (1994). *Innovations: Making the most of student performance data.* Washington, DC: American Association on Mental Retardation.

Snell, M.E. (1993). *Instruction of students with severe disabilities* (4th ed.). New York: MacMillan.

Sternberg, L. (1994). *Individuals with profound disabilities: Instructional and assistive strategies.* Austin, TX: PRO-ED.

Westling, D.L., & Fox, L. (1995). *Teaching students with severe disabilities.* Columbus, OH: Charles E. Merrill.

Wolery, M., Ault, M.J., & Doyle, P.M. (1992). *Teaching students with moderate to severe disabilities.* New York: Longman.

Appendix D

RESOURCES ON AUGMENTATIVE COMMUNICATION

ARTICLES

Durand, V.M. (1993). Functional communication training using assistive devices: Effects on challenging behavior and affect. *Augmentative and Alternative Communication, 9,* 168–176.

Iacono, T., Mirenda, P., & Beukelman, D.R. (1993). Comparison of unimodal and multimodal AAC techniques for children with intellectual disabilities. *Augmentative and Alternative Communication, 9,* 83–94.

McGregor, G., Young, J., Gerak, J., Thomas, B., & Vogelsberg, R.T. (1992). Increasing functional use of a nonassistive communication device by a student with severe disabilities. *Augmentative and Alternative Communication, 8,* 243–250.

Schepis, M.M., & Reid, D.H. (1995). Effects of a voice output communication aid on interactions between support personnel and an individual with multiple disabilities. *Journal of Applied Behavior Analysis, 28,* 73–77.

Schweigert, P., & Rowland, C. (1992). Early communication and microtechnology: Instructional sequence and case studies of children with severe multiple disabilities. *Augmentative and Alternative Communication, 8,* 273–286.

BOOKS

Baumgart, D., Johnson, J., & Helmstetter, E. (1990). *Augmentative and alternative communication systems for persons with moderate and severe disabilities.* Baltimore: Paul H. Brookes Publishing Co.

Bigge, J. (1991). *Augmentative communication. Teaching individuals with physical and multiple disabilities.* New York: Charles E. Merrill.

Musselwhite, C.R., & St. Louis, K.W., (1988). *Communication programming for persons with severe handicaps: Vocal and augmentative strategies.* Austin, TX: PRO-ED.

Reichle, J., York, J., & Sigafoos, J. (1991). *Implementing augmentative and alternative communication: Strategies for learners with severe diabilities.* Baltimore: Paul H. Brookes Publishing Co.

Van Tatenhove, G.M. (1993). *What is augmentative and alternative communication (AAC)?* Wooster, OH: Prentke Romich Co.

VIDEO TRAINING TAPES

California Deaf-Blind Services. (1990). *Communication: Forms and function*. Sacramento: California Department of Education. [Publisher: California Deaf-Blind Services, 650 Howe Ave., Suite 300, Sacramento, CA 95825; telephone: (916) 641-5855; cost: $20.]

Rowland, C., & Schweigert, P. (1990). *Tangible symbol systems: Symbolic communication for individuals with multisensory impairments*. Tucson, AZ: Communication Skill Builders.

Appendix E

AUGMENTATIVE COMMUNICATION SYSTEM HARDWARE MANUFACTURERS

Ablenet
1081 10th Avenue S.E.
Minneapolis, MN 55414
(800) 322-0956

Adaptive Communication Systems, Inc.
P.O. Box 12440
Pittsburgh, PA 15231

Adamlab
Wayne Co. Intermediate School District
Data Processing
33500 Van Born Road
Wayne, MI 28184
(313) 467-1415

Attainment
P.O. Box 930160
Verona, WI 53593-0160
(800) 327-4269

Baum, USA
17525 Venture Boulevard, Suite 303
Encino, CA 91316-3843
(818) 981-2253

Apple Computer, Inc.
Office of Special Education
20525 Mariani Avenue
Cupertino, CA 95014
(408) 996-1010

Linda Burkhart
8503 Rhode Island Avenue
College Park, MD 20740
(301) 345-9152

Canon USA, Inc.
One Canon Plaza
Lake Success, NY 11042
(516) 488-6700

Computability Corporation
P.O. Box 17882
Milwaukee, WI 53217
(800) 558-0003

Consultants for Communication Technology
508 Bellevue Terrace
Pittsburgh, PA 15202
(412) 761-6062

Creative Switch Industries
P.O. Box 5256
Des Moines, IA 50306
(515) 287-5748

Crestwood Company
6625 N. Sidney Place
Milwaukee, WI 53209-3259
(414) 352-5678

Daedalus Technologies, Inc.
#7-12171 Bridgeport Road
Richmond, BC, V6V 1J4
CANADA
(604) 270-4605

Don Johnston, Inc.
Box 639
1000 N. Rand Road, Bldg. 115
Wauconda, IL 60084
(800) 999-4660

From Tanchak, T.L., & Sawyer, C. (1995). Augmentative communication. In K.F. Flippo, K.J. Inge, & J.M. Barcus (Eds.), *Assistive technology: A resource for school, work, and community* (pp. 80–83). Baltimore: Paul H. Brookes Publishing Co.; reprinted with minor revisions by permission.

Dragon Systems, Inc.
90 Bridge Street
Newton, MA 02158
(617) 965-5200

Du-It Control Systems Group
8767 Township Road 513
Shreve, OH 44676
(216) 567-2906

Dunamis, Inc.
3423 Fowler Boulevard
Lawrenceville, GA 30244
(800) 828-2443

Edmark Corporation
P.O. Box 97021
Redmond, WA 98073-9721
(800) 362-2890

Epson America, Inc.
2780 Lomita Boulevard
Torrance, CA 90505
(800) 922-8911

Flaghouse, Inc.
150 North MacQuesten Parkway
Mount Vernon, NY 10550
(800) 793-7900

Franklin Learning Resources
1 Franklin Plaza
Burlington, NJ 08016-4907
(800) 525-9673

IBM
National Support Center for Persons with
    Disabilities
1000 N.W. 51st Street
Internal Zip 5432
Boca Raton, FL 33432
(800) 426-4832
(800) 426-4833 (TDD)

Innocomp
26210 Emery Road
Suite 302
Warrensville Heights, OH 44128
(800) 382-8622

Innoventions
5921 South Middlefield Road
Suite 102
Littleton, CO 80123
(800) 854-6554

IntelliTools, Inc.
55 Leveroni Ct, Suite 9
Novato, CA 94949
(800) 899-6687

Kurzweil Applied Intelligence, Inc.
411 Waverly Oaks Road
Waltham, MA 02154-8465
(617) 893-5151

Laureate Learning Systems, Inc.
110 E. Spring Street
Winooski, VT 05404-1898
(800) 562-6801

Luminaud, Inc.
8688 Tyler Boulevard
Mentor, OH 44060
(216) 255-9082

Mayer-Johnson Company
P.O. Box 1579
Solano Beach, CA 92075-1579
(619) 550-0084

Microtouch Systems
55 Jonspin Road
Wilmington, MA 01887
(508) 694-9900

Nanopac
4832 S. Sheridan Road
Suite 302
Tulsa, OK 74145-5718
(918) 665-0329

Phonic Ear, Inc.
3880 Cypress Drive
Petaluma, CA 94954-7600
(800) 227-0735

Prentke Romich Company
1022 Heyl Road
Wooster, OH 44691
(800) 262-1984

Sentient Systems Technology, Inc.
2100 Wharton St.
Pittsburgh, PA 15203
(800) 344-1778

Switchworks
P.O. Box 64764
Baton Rouge, LA 70896
(504) 925-8926

Therapeutic Toys, Inc.
P.O. Box 418
Moodus, CT 06469
(800) 638-0676

Tiger Communication System, Inc.
328 Main Street East
Suite 514
Rochester, NY 14604
(716) 454-5134

Toshiba America Information Systems, Inc.
9740 Irvine Boulevard
P.O. Box 19724
Irvine, CA 92713-9724
(800) 999-4273
(714) 583-3000

Toys for Special Children
385 Warburton Avenue
Hastings-on-Hudson, NY 10706
(914) 478-0960

Words+, Inc.
40015 Sierra Highway B-145
Palmdale, CA 93550
(800) 869-8521

Zygo Industries, Inc.
P.O. Box 1008
Portland, OR 97207-1008
(800) 234-6006

Index

Page numbers followed by "f" or "t" indicate figures or tables, respectively.